Nature, Environment and Society

SOCIOLOGY FOR A CHANGING WORLD
Series Editors: Graham Allan and Mary Maynard
Consultant Editor: Janet Finch

This series, published in conjunction with the British Sociology Association, evaluates and reflects major developments in contemporary sociology. The books focus on key changes in social and economic life in recent years and on the ways in which the discipline of sociology has analysed those changes. The books reflect the state of the art in contemporary British sociology, while at the same time drawing upon comparative material to set debates in an international perspective.

Published

Graham Allan and Graham Crow, *Families, Households and Society*
Rosamund Billington, Annette Fitzsimons, Lenore Greensides and Sheelagh Strawbridge, *Culture and Society*
Lois Bryson, *Welfare and the State*
Frances Heidensohn, *Crime and Society*
Stephen J. Hunt, *Religion in Western Society*
Mike Savage and Alan Warde, *Urban Sociology, Capitalism and Modernity*
John Solomos and Les Back, *Racism and Society*
Philip W. Sutton, *Nature, Environment and Society*
Andrew Webster, *Science, Technology and Society*

Forthcoming

Kevin Brehony and Rosemary Deem, *Rethinking Sociologies of Education*
Gordon Causer and Ray Norman, *Work and Employment in Contemporary Society*
Jörg Dürrschmidt and Graham Taylor, *Globalisation, Modernity and Social Change*
David Morgan, *Men, Masculinities and Society*
Julie Seymour, *Social Research Methodology*

NATURE, ENVIRONMENT AND SOCIETY

Philip W. Sutton

palgrave
macmillan

First published 2004 by
PALGRAVE MACMILLAN
Houndmills, Basingstoke, Hampshire RG21 6XS and
175 Fifth Avenue, New York, N.Y. 10010
Companies and representatives throughout the world

PALGRAVE MACMILLAN is the global academic imprint of the Palgrave Macmillan division of St. Martin's Press, LLC and of Palgrave Macmillan Ltd. Macmillan® is a registered trademark in the United States, United Kingdom and other countries. Palgrave is a registered trademark in the European Union and other countries.

ISBN 0–333–99567–8 hardback
ISBN 0–333–99568–6 paperback

This book is printed on paper suitable for recycling and made from fully managed and sustained forest sources.

A catalogue record for this book is available from the British Library.

A catalog record for this book is available from the Library of Congress.

10   9   8   7   6   5   4   3   2   1
13   12   11   10   09   08   07   06   05   04

Printed in China

For Derrick Sutton
A crazy, mother's son who loved his life

Contents

List of Tables

Acknowledgements

First thanks must go to the editorial team at Palgrave Macmillan. In particular, I would like to thank the Series Editors, Graham Allan and Mary Maynard, for initiating and supporting this project. Sincere thanks to Catherine Gray, who recognised the need for the book in the first place and could not have been a more congenial and effective editor. Thanks also to Beverley Tarquini for seeing the book smoothly through the review and production process and suggesting the final, more accurate, title. An anonymous reviewer at Palgrave Macmillan made some extremely constructive comments on the original proposal for which I am grateful and the anonymous referee who read the completed manuscript also made some astute suggestions. Both have, hopefully, contributed towards a more cohesive and readable text.

The various attempts to bridge the divide between environmental issues and sociology take up a large part of the book. In this regard, special thanks are due to Geert de Vries for a stimulating discussion paper given at the ISA World Congress of Sociology, Brisbane, in 2002, which strengthened my growing conviction that a process sociological perspective might offer advantages over others in bringing environmental issues closer to sociology and vice versa. Richard Kilminster was also kind enough to read and comment on an earlier version of Chapter 9 at a significant point in the process of writing.

At Robert Gordon University, I am indebted to Julian Bell for his creative manipulation of teaching timetables, without which the book may never have seen the light of day. Who said Departmental administration had to be dull?! I would also like to mention the students on my *Environment and Society* course who listened to my ramblings with forbearance and good humour, tackled a diverse range of materials and, worst of all, endured the visual pollution of my collection of jumpers. I like to think they enjoyed it really.

Last but certainly not least, heartfelt thanks to Pat for checking the manuscript (again) in her usual thorough way and pointing out my mistakes and inconsistencies.

Introduction

For any student of sociology born after the decade of the 1970s, it may seem obvious that studying the impact of human societies on the natural environment – one side of what we can call the society–nature relationship – should be a subject for inclusion among the discipline's core concerns. They have grown up with highly visible campaigning environmental groups and organisations, Green political parties, environmental education programmes, United Nations 'Earth Summits' and an awareness of the existence of global ecological problems such as ozone depletion, biodiversity loss and global warming. They may therefore be all too aware of the need for sociologists to take an interest in the natural environment and today, of course, many sociologists are. Some of them would perhaps even describe what they do as 'environmental sociology' rather than simply 'sociology' (Catton 1978; Bell 1998; Dunlap 2002). However, it was not always thus. In fact many standard introductory sociology texts still have no distinct chapter on environmental issues and very little, if anything, to say about them in other contexts, concentrating instead on traditional sociological staples such as crime and deviance, health and illness, mass media and social stratification. Even very recently this was the case in two of the best-selling introductory textbooks. Haralambos and Holborn's (1995) text has no chapter dedicated to environmental issues and no indexed reference at all to 'ecology' or 'environment', whilst Giddens's (2000: 529–33) more recent book deals with environmental issues in just four pages from a total of 625. Clearly, environmental issues have still to become fully established within mainstream sociology. And yet, internationalist environmental organisations and Green political parties came into being in the early 1970s, European Green parties had electoral success in the 1980s, the United Nations had already held summits on the environment and the scientific research on environmental issues had already begun to influence the policy-making of national governments. Why then are environmental issues taking so long to make their way to the sociological mainstream?

Irwin (2001) suggests that the underlying reason for this negligence is an assumption that 'the social' and 'the natural', society and nature, are separable. Sociologists focus on society and *its* problems and leave all natural things to the natural sciences. What this means in relation to environmental issues is that:

- issues of pollution and ecology have been seen as outside the remit and competence of sociologists;
- nature and social life have been seen as separable;
- it has not been easy to connect core sociological themes such as power, class and inequality to environmental issues;
- there has been a suspicion that environmental concerns may be a fashion or fad that will not last, and finally that;
- attempts to uncover the social roots of environmental issues might undermine environmental campaigns by suggesting that they are, in some way, less real or urgent (Irwin 2001: 4).

The final point (which really concerns environmental activists) notwithstanding, Irwin's suggestions are well founded. For many sociologists, the defence of ground gained over the twentieth century has militated against an enthusiastic embracing of environmental issues. Given the recurring attempts to explain social phenomena using theories and concepts from the biological sciences though, it has to be acknowledged that this defensive strategy has served the discipline pretty well. Biological reductionism, whether of the kind proposed by sociobiologists in the 1970s or that currently propounded by some evolutionary psychologists, has led to an institutionalised suspicion of the 'non-social' in sociology, which has served a useful function in avoiding overly simplistic explanations. Understandably then, sociologists have tended to adopt a cautious, 'wait-and-see' approach towards environmentalism. It was by no means obvious or perceived as necessary that they should attempt to tackle environmental issues at all, and when eventually some sociologists did, many found existing sociological resources, particularly classical sociological theory, to be less than helpful. The standard response of using existing sociological theories to explore new issues in the form of another, '*sociology of...*', appeared less likely to work in relation to the environment. The classical trinity of Marx, Durkheim and Weber seemed to have little to offer the study of environmental issues. What had they to say about the environment, natural processes or ecosystems?

Classical sociology and environmental issues

For Marx, understanding and explaining the capitalist dynamic was the most urgent priority, not protecting and defending non-human nature. Marx's Enlightenment-inspired ideas looked forward to the rational collective control of society's interchange with nature as well as its social organisation. For many Greens, such an optimistic 'modern' view is part of the problem not the solution, propagating the notion that there are no real limits to human achievement in terms of their ability to exercise control over their natural environment. For their part, Marxist and socialist theorists' early responses to late twentieth-century environmental issues were not exactly enthusiastic (Enzensberger 1974; Pepper 1986; Weston 1986). Environmentalism and Green politics were seen as the populist response of middle-class groups who were likely to see the defence of animals and natural areas as of equal importance to the well-being of humans. Such a view was seen as misguided and misanthropic, the product of woolly thinking and lacking a class-based analysis.

Nevertheless, others looked for common ground between socialism and environmentalism in the form of an 'eco-socialism' that sees capitalism as the source of environmental destruction, thus bridging the divide between their respective positions (Bahro 1982; Wolf 1986; Gorz 1994; O'Connor 1996, 1998). In more recent years, Marxists have also been at the forefront of 'critical realist' attempts to theorise society–nature relations, drawing on Marx's early work, particularly the *Economic and Philosophic Manuscripts* (1844) and the theory of alienation. Critical realism has become one of the most influential recent approaches to environmental issues and now has its own peer-reviewed journal, the *Journal of Critical Realism*, through which theory and empirical research can be extended. So, after a distinctly unpromising start, there is now an ongoing realist research programme inspired by the ideas of Marx in relation to environmental issues.

However, the integration of environmental issues is less advanced in relation to the Durkheimian tradition. As is well known, for Durkheim the imperative was to establish sociology as a new science of human societies and this meant demonstrating that 'the social' was a level of reality in its own right that could not be reduced to either the psychological or the biological. Arguably this led Durkheim and the later 'Durkheimians' away from exploring the interrelationships between the biological and the social (Catton 2002), in spite of his concept of *homo duplex*, which saw human nature as comprising a 'double centre of gravity' in the tension between individualistic desires (rooted in human biology) and the moral restraints of society (Durkheim 1973 [1914]: 152). So far, Durkheim's work has not attracted the same attempts at reassessment as that of Marx, but perhaps the most significant recent attempt to use Durkheim's ideas has been that of Turner (1996, 1999). Turner has argued for a combination of Darwinian evolutionary theory and Durkheim's ideas on changing forms of social solidarity in the study of human emotions. Whilst evolutionary theory helps to explain 'selection pressures for group organisation', Durkheim's ideas could be productive in showing how these pressures are channelled in the creation of social solidarity (Williams 2001: 53). Such a synthesis of biological and sociological theory remains rare, but if others are inspired to follow, then a 'Durkheimian' approach to environmental issues may well be possible.

Finally, Max Weber's productive insights into capitalism, bureaucracy and rationalisation seem to be concentrated on human beings and the institutions they create, having little directly to say about the relationship between society and nature. Again though, as with Marx and Durkheim, in recent years a few sociologists have begun to reassess the Weberian legacy in the light of environmental issues (West 1985; Albrow 1992; Murphy 1994a,b, 1997, 2002). This reassessment or re-reading of Weber points out that an over-concentration on the theme of social action has kept a more balanced appreciation of Weber's work from surfacing. The latter would need to take into account Weber's own recognition that, 'Understanding the distinctive element of intentions among humans does not require the neglect of nature and the effect of its ecosystems on social action' (Murphy 2002: 75). Therefore it is not correct to view Weber simply as an 'interpretivist' sociologist, at least if this implies that he neglected the material bases of social life. Recent

Weberian scholarship has challenged such an interpretation, with Murphy (2002) arguing that a more rounded understanding of Weber requires an acknowledgement of his 'ecological materialism'. That is, Weber's identification of the role of non-social factors such as, 'geography, climate, natural resources and the material aspects of technology in the structure and change in historical social structures' (West 1985: 216). With this much broader interpretation of his sociology, it becomes more realistic to visualise a specifically Weberian approach to the study of environmental issues.

What we can conclude from the above is that the rise to prominence of global environmental problems via new environmentalist organisations and Green political parties has been an important factor in encouraging re-readings and reinterpretations of the sociological classics to test their ability to deal with society–environment relations. This should, on balance, be seen as a very positive development and something which has happened regularly throughout the discipline's history in relation to feminism, black civil rights movements, disability issues, and lesbian and gay movements. It remains to be seen just how successful the sociological traditions will be in the exploration of environmental issues, as not all or perhaps even a majority of sociologists see the need to revisit the classics in this way. This book discusses some of the more significant contemporary social theories and evaluates their efficacy for understanding and explaining environmental issues.

It is important to note that there is a tension running through the various attempts to analyse environmental issues sociologically. For some, it is worthwhile pursing a *sociology of the environment* that draws on existing sociological theories and concepts to understand and explain how and why environmental issues are generated or 'socially constructed'. A sociology of the environment is also able to demonstrate the continuing relevance of mainstream sociological issues such as social class, gender divisions and poverty. Environmental problems have been shown to have markedly different impacts across social classes, men and women, and rich and poor, and this means there is mileage in pursuing mainstream sociological agendas. For others however, what is required is a thoroughgoing *environmental sociology* which, as well as considering standard sociological issues, also introduces theories and concepts from biological and environmental sciences. This is necessary, they claim, if sociologists are to avoid the misleading conclusion that environmental problems are *only* social constructions and are therefore not pressing or urgent. Environmental sociologists tend to accept that there really are serious environmental problems and that these demand action soon if an environmental 'crisis' is to be avoided and this leads many of them to activism and/or a political commitment to environmentalism (Bell 1998: 4–6).

The tension between these two alternatives runs throughout this book and the arguments from both sides are introduced in relation to a variety of issues and problems. However, the book tries hard to avoid coming down in favour of either of these positions, which would entail the creation of yet another sociological specialism. This is because the conclusion reached after surveying the current situation in this field is that what is now required are ways of working towards a sociology that is able to encompass environmental questions and issues, so that the relationship between society and the natural environment would be a constitutive feature of sociology as such. Chapter 9 discusses this conclusion in more detail, but for now it is enough to note that such a sociology is still some way into the future.

Overview and structure of the book

This book provides an introduction to the way that the central ideas of environmentalism, particularly the foregrounding of the nature–society relationship, have been received, evaluated and assimilated into the enterprise of sociology. It attempts to arrive at a sober understanding of the challenges posed to sociology by the mainstreaming of environmentalism and in so doing, it should be borne in mind that the primary focus of the book is how sociologists have responded to the environmental challenge. Therefore, those looking for environmental advocacy and the promotion of environmental political positions will be disappointed. The book does not aim to convert readers to the cause of environmentalism, though it does accept that environmental issues and problems are leading to a reassessment of some cherished sociological ideas and theories. Similarly, those looking for a simple debunking of environmentalist arguments will also find the book wanting. It is not my intention to denigrate or undermine the claims of environmental campaigners, though, of course, the views of those who *are* critical of such claims are discussed here.

Because this is a book about the way that sociology is dealing with, or is capable of dealing with, environmentalism and environmental issues, the chapters cover some important recent sociological concerns including the role of social movements, ideas of risk and risk perception, social identities and self formation, modernity and the development of postmodernity, as well as 'critical realism' and 'social constructionism' as ways of 'doing' sociology. Therefore, the terrain on which environmental issues and arguments are presented should be familiar to anyone with a knowledge of introductory sociology. A further point worth making here is that this contemporary sociological terrain has itself been shaped, to varying degrees, in and through debates around environmental issues.

Charting a route through the current state of sociological knowledge in relation to environmental issues is no easy task today, because interest in this area has expanded enormously in the last 15–20 years. I have tried to select the main theoretical perspectives, environmental issues and arguments that currently shape this field, though it is probably true to say that others would have made different choices. Sacrifices have had to be made in order to provide a more comprehensive and coherent overview, and the treatment of some areas is therefore necessarily rather brief and would have benefited from a more wide-ranging assessment. Two particular examples of this are ecofeminism and the forms which environmentalism is taking in the developing world. Ecofeminist arguments and ideas are included in the book, primarily in Chapters 4 and 5, but the sheer diversity of ecofeminist theories has already been the subject of entire books (Mies and Shiva 1993; Plumwood 1993; Salleh 1997; Sandilands 1999) and cannot be dealt with here. Environmentalism in the developing world is also covered in the book, though again it has not been possible to cover in detail all of the different positions adopted by environmentalists in developing countries, many of whom have an intimate knowledge of their local natural environments and the threats posed to them and the people who depend on them. The necessarily brief treatment of these two areas, and some others too, should not be seen as an indication of their irrelevance, but as simply the consequence of an attempt to provide as broad a coverage of the field as possible. Nonetheless, I hope that readers will still find enough here to guide them into the wider literature in these areas and if so, then the book will have fulfilled one of its objectives.

The material is structured around three central and connected themes, namely those of the book's title: nature (including human nature), environment and society. Environmental ideas and environmental movements are dealt with in Chapters 1–4, environmental identities and theories of natural or ecological selves are discussed in Chapters 4, 5 and 8, whilst theories of the transformation of societies are handled in Chapters 6, 7 and 8. It is therefore possible to read about each theme relatively separately from the rest of the book. However, such a partition is somewhat artificial for two reasons. First, there is a substantial amount of overlapping of themes within each chapter, so that material on each theme is not hermetically sealed within the chapters identified above. Secondly, and more importantly, one of the book's main aims is to present the case for working towards a sociological perspective that is capable of incorporating all three themes in a coherent way, and it is only by reading the whole book that this will become evident.

Breakdown of chapters

So far, the idea that the environmental agenda is relatively recent has remained unchallenged. However, environmental concern has a much longer history and modern ideas promoting the conservation and preservation of nature and wilderness can be traced back at least to the early part of the nineteenth century. Chapter 1 locates environmental ideas and interests in their proper historical context and this effectively sets the scene and the tone for the rest of the book, which takes a longer-term view throughout. A long-term perspective helps us to avoid leaping to unwarranted conclusions about the novelty of contemporary environmentalism and Green ideas, but also allows us to see lines of development over time.

From here, Chapter 2 then describes and explains the emergence and growth of environmental movements from relatively small, local organisations through to today's international or global environmental networks. Although this transformation was clearly not inevitable or part of a unilinear progression, it has been much more of a continuous developmental process than some sociological theories have argued. Environmental movements have been extremely influential in problematising the society–nature relationship and as a result, in partly shaping the field of environmental sociology.

Having established the way that environmental issues have been brought to a wider audience, which includes sociologists, Chapter 3 begins to review the ways that sociologists have responded to the challenge of theorising environmental issues. The theme which recurs throughout is whether we need an 'environmental sociology' that integrates natural scientific knowledge, or whether a 'sociology of the environment' is more productive. For environmental sociologists, the discipline of sociology has to change if it is to say anything significant about the looming 'ecological crisis', whilst for sociologists of the environment, it is precisely the relatively detached and critical character of sociology that is potentially able to bring something new to the study of environmental issues. It may be that these are not strictly polarised alternatives as there are many areas of overlapping concern. However, currently they do seem to be producing different research programmes with alternative approaches to the study of the environment and society.

Recent debates have tended to divide into social constructionist and critical realist perspectives and these form the spine of Chapter 3. The often rather polarised debate between constructionists and realists has been widely seen as an obstacle in the way of environmental sociology and has prompted some sociologists to attempt to move beyond it. Two such examples are discussed here, namely Macnaghten and Urry's *Contested Natures* (1998) and Irwin's (2001) idea of environmental issues as 'hybrids' that expose the artificiality of division between the social and the natural.

The substantive ideas of environmentalists and radical ecologists are outlined in Chapter 4 and their significance for sociology is assessed. In particular, the chapter contrasts 'ecocentrism' or 'nature-centred' thinking with modern 'anthropocentrism' or 'human-centred' thinking. For the discipline of sociology, arguably the most anthropocentric of the social sciences, ecocentrism throws down a kind of challenge different from those presented by other humanistic social movements such as labour, feminist and disabled people's movements. Whilst the latter demand social inclusion and equality, longstanding sociological issues in themselves, ecocentrics demand a recognition of the significance of natural processes and natural limits in theories of society, not factors with which sociologists have generally been overly concerned, until now. The question for sociologists then is how to respond to the challenge of ecocentrism?

One interesting aspect of the ecocentric challenge is the attempt to encourage people to experience their connectedness with nature at a personal level. This is an important issue for deep ecologists and many ecofeminists, who believe that civilised, modern societies cut off people from their 'natural' roots. Their antidote is to encourage people to realise their 'ecological selves' in a project to re-connect alienated moderns with both 'external' nature and their own 'internal' human nature. If they are to do so, then it may require simpler lifestyles which use up fewer natural resources, are less energy intensive and encourage local self-sufficiency. Chapter 5 outlines this combination of ideas and practices in the light of existing socio-logical theories concerned with the formation of the self and the construction of identities. Just how realistic are the ideas of deep ecologists and some ecofeminists?

Chapter 6 begins to connect environmental issues to sociological theories of society by exploring the most influential recent social theory that puts environmental issues at its centre, namely Beck's (1992, 1999, 2002) theory of the emergence of the 'risk society'. Beck's ideas are important because, unusually, they have environ-mental issues right at their core and as such, could be a source of support for environmental and Green movements, which have, after all, been central to producing a greater popular awareness of environmental risks. Things are rather more complex than this however, and the chapter discusses Beck's theory alongside potential alternatives in order to arrive at an overall assessment of the risk society theory.

Chapters 7 and 8 examine a range of alternative 'solutions' to environmental problems in the context of sociological debates around 'modernity' and 'postmodernity'. A key question in these two chapters is whether environmentalism and Green politics can be understood as modern or postmodern phenomena, a debate that may enable a deeper understanding of the character of the various elements of modern environmentalism and Green politics. Chapter 7 focuses on 'modernist' solutions to environmental problems based on three broad platforms: the discourse of sustainable development, ecological modernisation and green consumerism (or 'green capi-talism'). These are considered 'modernist', as they take an optimistic view regarding the prospects for solving environmental problems and make some concrete proposals for doing so. The concept of sustainable development, in particular, has been influential in informing the environmental policies of governments, and in doing so has brought environmental concern into the mainstream of political life.

It is also possible though, to build a case for seeing Green politics as a specifically 'postmodern' phenomenon. That is, as one element of the wide-ranging attack on modern society and its rational, scientific ordering of social life. A 'postmodern environmentalism' would concentrate instead on the diversity, unpredictability and indeterminacy of natural processes. Chapter 8 introduces this argument, but also deals with postmodernist and poststructuralist *critics* of modern environmentalism, who argue that there is ample reason to be suspicious of those who propound modernist solutions, including most environmentalists themselves. Drawing on the ideas of French philosopher, Michel Foucault, poststructuralist writers see an intimate connection between scientific knowledge about the environment and the creation of a new environmental morality and discipline that may prove to be more controlling than the preceding forms. Because 'nature' needs people to speak for it, the danger of experts promulgating authoritarian solutions to environmental problems is always a possibility and this means that the apparently 'progressive' credentials of Green politics can never be taken at face value.

Finally, in Chapter 9, the main themes of the book – nature, environment and society – are brought together. In this chapter, a more explicit case is made for pursuing theoretical perspectives that are able to take account of all three themes and one potentially fruitful avenue, inspired by the work of the twentieth-century sociologist, Norbert Elias, is outlined.

By the time they reach the end of the book, students should have a good grasp of the kinds of challenges that environmental issues pose for sociology as well as the way that sociologists have responded. As environmental issues are slowly beginning to make their way into the mainstream of sociology it is an interesting time to take part in this process. Therefore, I hope that some will be encouraged to pursue further some of the issues discussed here, and will find in the main chapters a useful series of starting points from which to approach the wider literature. They should also have a better understanding of the way that environmental issues and movements have developed over time and thus be able to avoid the seductions of radical theories of social transformation which lack solid empirical support. In this way I hope that the book goes some way towards fostering and preserving that sociological imagination which encourages us all to face social (and environmental) problems 'with sober senses' and with a degree of detachment from our own normative biases.

A note on terminology

The field of environmental sociology or sociology of the environment is characterised not only by a diversity of theoretical perspectives but also by the diversity of its terminology, which can be somewhat confusing for anyone new to the field. In particular, there is no general agreement of the meaning of such fundamental terms as 'Green', 'green', 'environmentalism', 'radical ecology', 'political ecology' and 'ecologism'. The same term is often used to describe radically different positions and different terms are used to describe the same position. For instance, the meaning of the central term, 'environmentalism', even differs across texts in this field. In some, environmentalism refers to the whole range of organisations and arguments that try to bring about radical social change, whilst in others 'environmentalism' is used to describe a specific type of reformist politics, which *fails* to take account of the need for radical social change. Similarly, the distinction between radical and reformist environmental politics is sometimes made by contrasting 'Green' with 'green', 'ecological' with 'environmental' or 'deep' ecology with 'shallow' ecology. In this field therefore, context is everything.

Throughout this book, 'environmentalism' is used to describe a form of nature protection based on practical reform measures, whilst 'radical ecology' and 'Green' are both used to refer to a perspective which sees nature protection of this kind as ultimately ineffective, arguing instead for radical social and political change in order to ensure the survival of both human societies and nature. As will become evident, though not all organisations working for nature protection are 'environmentalist' in character, Green political parties tend to attract more 'radical ecologists'. Because of the latter, but also for grammatical reasons, I will use 'Green' and 'radical ecology' interchangeably.

1 Modern Ideas of Nature and Environment

For many contemporary environmentalists 'nature' or 'the natural' has something of a sacred character and should be treated, like all sacred things, with reverence and respect. An understanding of nature's processes provokes feelings of humility and puts human plans and achievements into a wider and higher context. What one philosopher has called the 'arrogance of humanism' (Ehrenfield 1981), giving priority to the needs of people over the rest of nature, is dissolved when faced with the timelessness, grandeur and beauty of nature's own 'plans' and 'achievements'. Such a view of the natural world is not uncommon in the industrialised world today; in fact such views may even be those of the majority. However, such a perspective is a relatively recent development that would have seemed quite alien to most people in the eighteenth and most of the nineteenth century. For these people nature was wild, disordered, uncivilised and even cruel. The animal world offered a model of precisely that 'war of all against all' that the seventeenth-century philosopher Thomas Hobbes had warned could be the fate of human societies without some overarching power to keep self-interested people in check. How could such a nature be treated with reverence?

Instead, nature had to be subdued and dominated if humanity was to make progress. Wilderness had to be tamed, land had to be cultivated and swamps had to be drained. In short, nature had to be worked on, cultured and transformed, not left wild or intact. Such a view supported the practices of capitalist industrialisation in the extraction of raw materials, the use of scientific knowledge to produce new sources of energy and of course, the transformation of 'uncivilised' people themselves into a disciplined and trained new workforce. Culture and civilisation were demonstrably better than nature in the raw. In the same year as Britain's revolutionary industrial achievements went on show to the world at the Great Exhibition at Crystal Palace in London (1851), the nineteenth-century philosopher, John Stuart Mill asked, 'If the artificial is not better than the natural, to what end are all the arts of life?' He noted that,

> Everybody professes to approve and admire many great triumphs of Art over Nature: the junction by bridges of shores which Nature had made separate, the draining of Nature's marshes, the excavation of her wells, the dragging to light of what she has buried at immense depths in the earth; the turning away of her thunderbolts by lightning rods, of her ocean by breakwaters. But to commend these and similar feats, is to acknowledge that the ways of Nature are to be conquered not obeyed: that her powers are often towards man in the position of enemies, from whom he must wrest, by force or ingenuity, what little he can for his own use, and deserves to be applauded when that little is rather more than might be expected from his physical weakness in comparison to those gigantic powers (Mill [1851] cited in Clayre 1979: 307).

Today many environmentalists agitate and campaign *against* continuing with those admirable 'triumphs of Art over Nature' that Mill's contemporaries once celebrated. Nature 'in the raw' is no longer 'the enemy' of human society, to be conquered and dominated. Instead it is modern society itself that is in the dock, charged with threatening to destroy the natural ecosystems on which all human beings depend. Similarly, rather than admiring high culture and sophisticated manners, some have suggested that human beings should get back in touch with their 'animal' nature, which has been hidden beneath the unnecessary layers of social convention and urbane living. Clearly, the transformation of attitudes and sensibilities since Mill's time has been quite dramatic. This chapter, then, describes the way that recent historians and historical sociologists have understood such social and attitudinal changes, in the belief that a long-term perspective is a necessary prerequisite to understanding the currently constituted field of environmental sociology.

The environmental revolution

The period we are living in, and through, has been described as a 'new environmental age' (Nicholson 1987), an 'age of ecology' (Worster 1985) and an 'age of risk' (Beck 2002), in which the main threats to human societies stem from their relationship with the natural world. In so far as human beings cannot exist apart from the rest of nature, this relationship constitutes a permanent feature. However, the social awareness of nature and society or of 'environmental' problems differs widely across different societies and over time. So, whilst it may seem possible to evaluate objectively the relative seriousness of environmental problems, with global issues such as climate change and ozone depletion appearing to pose much more *serious* problems for *more* societies than say an isolated local problem such as the London city smogs of the 1950s (though these could be deadly, as one particularly bad smog in 1952 reportedly led to the deaths of around 4000 people), in practice it is very hard to distinguish between the objective problems and the societal awareness of them. In addition, Harvey (1993: 1–2) has argued that,

> the 'environmental issue' necessarily means such different things to different people, that in aggregate it encompasses quite literally everything there is...words like 'nature' and 'environment' convey a commonality and universality of concern that is, precisely because of their ambiguity, open to a great diversity of interpretation.

In general terms Harvey is right, but concretely, 'environmental problems' have come to mean those that involve the society–nature relationship and its institutional management rather than problems of the urban environment or inner cities.

If this is so, then it is important to recognise that environmental problems have a long history (Pepper 1984; Guha 2000). The historian Gould (1988: viii) notes that 'The history of green politics or social ecology can be made to stretch from pre-industrial societies', though this would indeed be stretching the argument too far and threatens to underplay the originality of contemporary Green politics. A more realistic and better evidenced case is that the latter decades of the nineteenth century in Britain, Europe and the USA mark an extremely active period for nature conservation and early 'environmentalism' during which concerns about society–nature relations became established. Placing environmentalism in quotation marks here is an acknowledgement of the use of a certain linguistic licence, in the light of Coates's (1998: 14) critical comment that, 'To attach the terms "environmental" and "environmental protection" to the pre-1945 era is, strictly speaking, anachronistic.' This is strictly correct because the term was not widely used by self-styled conservationists and preservationists before that time. However, there are good reasons to connect preservationist, conservationist and environmentalist ideas as phases in a gradual process during which nature protection has continued, albeit in a changed form. I hope that Chapter 2 will serve to justify the use of 'environmental' in relation to the long-term development of contemporary environmental social movements, which developed from the earlier conservationism and preservationism.

The late twentieth-century 'greening' of academic disciplines has led to the possibility of reinterpreting social development in the light of ideas and evidence from ecology and the environmental sciences. One example of this is the retrospective study of historical 'ecological revolutions' as an addition to established scholarship on major social revolutions. The former being, '...major transformations in human relations with non-human nature. They arise from changes, tensions, and contradictions that develop between a society's mode of production and its ecology, and between its modes of production and reproduction' (Merchant 1989: 3). An emerging sub-discipline of 'environmental history' has also produced some interesting comparative studies of the relationship between human history and the transformation of natural systems (Worster 1989; Simmons 1993; Grove 1994; Beinart and Coates 1995). The greening process has even prompted some to consider the ambitious task of writing a 'Green history of the world' (Ponting 1993) that examines the part played by overuse of natural resources in the collapse of the world's historical civilisations. Such a range of specialisms has opened up new, ecologically informed ways of approaching world history that explore the interaction between human societies and the natural environment on which they depend.

Historians have also found recognisably 'ecological' ideas and sentiments in previous periods, albeit amongst relatively smaller numbers of people than today. Gould's study of late nineteenth-century Britain details a variety of ideas, initiatives and activities that would fall within an ecological or Green perspective today. Those who hated industrialisation, urbanisation and Victorian 'over-civilization' (Carpenter 1917; Tsuzuki 1980) turned to nature as a reference point from which to mount their attacks. Critics argued that people had lost touch with nature and needed to get back-to-nature and back-to-the-land in order to re-connect with their natural environment as well as their own natural selves. Nineteenth-century urbanisation and industrialisation, the spread of towns and cities, rapid expansion of population and evidence of a seemingly irreversible shift from rural to urban lifestyles prompted much concern. Reformers argued that fresh air, country life and access to nature are the keys to a healthier population, and as Williams (1973: 1) has observed,

> On the country has gathered the idea of a natural way of life: of peace, innocence and simple virtue. On the city has gathered the idea of an achieved centre: of learning, communication, light. Powerful hostile associations have also developed: on the city as a place of noise, worldliness and ambition: on the country as a place of backwardness, ignorance, limitation.

The early environmentalists played up the positive virtues of the country and the negative aspects of urban living, and this contrast is an important motivation for contemporary environmentalists too, evident for example in the anarchistic 'social ecology' strand of radical ecology. Its foremost advocate in the USA, Bookchin (1982: 366), argues that,

> Civilization as we know it today is more mute than the nature for which it professes to speak, and more blind than the elemental forces it professes to control. Indeed, "civilization" lives in hatred of the world around it and in grim hatred of itself. Its gutted cities, wasted lands, poisoned air and water, and mean-spirited greed constitute a daily indictment of its odious morality. A world so demeaned may well be beyond redemption ...

Sentiments of this kind would not have been out of place amongst nineteenth-century environmental campaigners, demonstrating a significant line of continuity connecting industrial critics over the last 150 years.

The idea of re-connecting with nature can also be found today in Kirkpatrick Sale's (1984, 1985) advocacy of 'bioregionalism', which promotes new ways of getting to know and living in the land, but for many nineteenth-century reformers, industrialisation disfigured both the landscape and human values (Evans 1893). Also in the late nineteenth century, G.P. Marsh's influential *Man and Nature* (1864) set out an early case for nature conservation in America (Lowenthal 2000), on the grounds that '... wanton destruction and profligate waste were making the earth unfit for human habitation and ultimately threatened the extinction of man...' (McCormick 1992: 11). Such an assessment retains its force for many environmentalists, though for radical ecologists Marsh's statement still focuses on the extinction of 'man' rather than the rest of nature. In a similar vein, Schmitt (1969) and Marx (1964) have convincingly demonstrated the historical roots of contemporary 'arcadian' and pastoral ideals in the USA too, where people could live close to the land and in harmony with nature.

What is perhaps more surprising than these early origins of conservationist ideas is that the early social movements based on such ideas have tended not to be included as particularly important in mainstream histories of that period. In a study of the 'back-to-the-land' movement in Britain, the historian Marsh (1982: 245) says that,

> When I first became intrigued by the subject I searched the general histories dealing with the period for accounts and references to the movement, which was everywhere visible in the literature of the time. I found virtually none, no doubt because history records only the dominant events and ideas, those that influence and determine what happens next.

Recognisably 'Green' ideas and activities were not considered significant enough to be included until quite recently, probably because they failed to change the course of continuing industrial and urban development. Instead, the state became increasingly active in many areas of social life, industrialisation and urbanisation continued apace and the disparate elements of the labour movement began to crystallise into an effective, organised force capable of bringing 'the social question' to the attention of all classes in society, working through as well as outside existing political institutions (Przeworski 1986). It may be that when characterising the most significant events and movements of a particular period, just as in a painting, some elements are open to view in the foreground, whilst others are partially hidden in the background. The success of organised labour effectively pushed environmental initiatives into the background, out of direct view and attention.

Nonetheless, an increasingly organised environmentalism emerged in the second half of the nineteenth century producing a series of interlinked conservationist and preservationist societies and organisations. This early environmentalism had some success in promoting the regulation and control of human activities that impact on the natural world and the development of organised environmentalism, and its influence is taken up in the next chapter. If, as many have suggested, there really has been an 'environmental revolution', then it may be more accurate to say that it began in the middle of the *nineteenth* century rather than the late *twentieth* century. The latter period certainly marks the extension and expansion of environmental concern and its assimilation into mainstream politics, but it was in the earlier period that the very modern idea of protecting and defending nature against human interference really came into its own (Ranlett 1983).

Changing sensibilities and attitudes towards nature

'Nature', says Williams (1987: 219–21), 'is perhaps the most complex word in the language' and he notes that '. . . any full history of the uses of nature would be a history of a large part of human thought'. Williams identifies three main areas of meaning, which have gradually developed over time and which co-exist today (see also Collingwood 1945). Chronologically these are:

1. Nature as the essential quality and character of something (from the thirteenth century);
2. Nature as the inherent force which directs either the world or human beings or both (from the fourteenth century);
3. Nature as the material world itself, taken as either including or not including human beings (from the seventeenth century).

John Stuart Mill (cited in Clayre 1979: 306) argued that the principal meanings in the mid-nineteenth century were the second and the third of these. Today, although all the three meanings can be found, Williams notes that from the seventeenth century, a change in the use of the word 'nature' is discernible, from the description of a process to that of a thing-like entity – nature as a series of landscapes or simply as 'scenery' (Cornish 1937) – and this shift in meaning is important because the early environmentalism was based in part on the defence of 'thing-like' natural objects that could be clearly identified and protected in ways similar to that of old buildings. Conwentz (1909) accurately describes these thing-like objects as 'natural monuments'. In this sense the idea is rooted in one of modern culture's most basic dualisms (Kelsen 1944; Moscovici 1976), that of culture–nature and since the eighteenth century the countryside, 'unspoiled places', and 'plants and creatures other than man' have increasingly come to be seen as natural compared with the less natural world of human beings (Purdue 1987). Even today it is not unusual for Green campaigners and writers (and some sociologists) to refer to cities and urban environments as 'artificial' in comparison to the 'reality' of nature (Goldsmith 1988).

The emergence of this new dominant meaning of 'nature' can be seen as the outcome of a gradual, long-term change in the sensibilities and attitudes of modern people. However, it should be remembered that early environmentalist arguments in defence of nature usually related this defence to the continuing well-being of human beings, and in this sense its orientation would best be described as 'human-centred' or 'anthropocentric', rather than 'nature-centred' or 'ecocentric'. Arguments in favour of protecting nature were couched in terms of the benefits of nature protection for human beings. Such arguments continue to form the mainstream of environmentalism today, though the attempt to develop a coherent ecocentric orientation in recent years (Naess 1973, 1984; Fox 1984; Eckersley 1989, 1992; Goodin 1992) is one important difference between the two periods. The ecocentric project has, however, been severely criticised in some quarters as unrealistic and even dangerous (Neuhaus 1971; Manes 1990; Mellos 1990; Harvey 1993; O'Neil 1994) as it refuses to accept that human welfare should take priority over that of other animals or nature as a whole. Ecocentric philosophies often argue that nature has 'intrinsic value' which therefore exceeds the scope of possible human valuations of it. This kind of argument is not wholly new as there are some similarities with the ideas of William Morris, the socialist and inspirational figure in the British Arts and Crafts movement, for example (Glasier 1921; Thompson 1976). However, although concerned with nature and the environment, as a committed socialist, Morris's primary concern was with the quality of life for people, and to attribute a contemporary ecocentric orientation to his motivation would be misleading.

Closer to modern nature-centred thinking are the mid-nineteenth-century American transcendentalists who claimed that 'Nature... enjoyed its own morality which, when understood, could lead the sympathetic and responsive human being to a new spiritual awareness of his own potential, his obligations to others, and his responsibilities to the life-supporting processes of his natural surroundings' (O'Riordan 1981: 3). Henry David Thoreau (cited in Worster 1985: 79) was quite clear that nature was not a lifeless world, the mere background to human life: 'The earth I tread on is not a dead, inert mass, it is a body, has a spirit, is organic, and fluid to the influence of its spirit, and to whatever particle of that spirit is in me.' This meant that, '... all nature is alive, and that whatever is alive has a claim on man's moral affections'. From here it is a short step to the ideas of more contemporary ecophilosophy, as in Naess's (1988: 4–7) ideal of 'biocentric egalitarianism in principle', which recognises human beings as just one species in the wider 'web of life', having no legitimate claim to special rights or to be able to treat other life forms as inferior to themselves. Thoreau also felt this equalitarian attitude whilst on his forays into American woods, 'I believed that the woods were not tenantless, but choke-full of honest spirits as good as myself any day, – not an empty chamber in which chemistry was left to work alone, but an inhabited house, – and for a few moments I enjoyed fellowship with them' (Thoreau cited in Worster 1985: 93–4).

The history of recognisably ecological ideas is also conflictual, containing both 'imperialist' and 'arcadian' strands, extending back beyond the emergence of the discipline of scientific ecology. Worster (1985: xi) argues that, '... one might very well cast the history of ecology as a struggle between rival views of the relationship between humans and nature: one view devoted to the discovery of intrinsic value and its preservation, the other to the creation of an instrumentalized world and its exploitation'. In this way, scientific ecology is bound up with modern culture itself, which is Janus-faced, alternating between modernism and romanticism (Eder 1990, 1993; Szerszynski 1996). With some modifications, these rival views underpin many current debates between reformist environmentalists and radical ecological groups.

Despite attempts to demonstrate the originality of contemporary ecocentrism then, most of its main tenets can be found in earlier periods. Its focus on a holistic perspective, intrinsic value residing in nature and the primary importance of the needs of nature (recently described as the 'nature-knows-best' principle), can all be uncovered in earlier periods. In the midst of the 1960s and early 1970s counter-culture and political protests in the USA and Europe, Musgrove (1974: 65) observed that 'Nineteenth-century Romanticism was strikingly like the contemporary counter-culture in its explicit attack on technology, work, pollution, boundaries, authority, the unauthentic, rationality and the family.' In the USA, Roszak's (1969) *The Making of a Counter Culture* was introduced with a quotation from the Romantic poet, William Blake, 'Rouse up, O Young Men of the New Age!.' Modern 'new age' ideas have also been seen as one part of contemporary ecological movements (Bloch 1998), though the extent to which they are connected to formal environmental organisations is less clear.

Similarly, philosophies which see in the organisation of nature a 'vital principle' or a 'natural spirit' can be traced back at least to the seventeenth century. It has been noted that the revival of vitalist philosophies in the 1880s fed support for nature conservation and nature protection sentiments. Allen (1978: 202) goes so far as to say that the influence of vitalism was 'immense and crucial' in this respect, 'even though few of those who then rushed in can have been conscious of owing their inspiration to it specifically'. The relationship between cultural trends, radical ideas and organised environmentalism in the 1880s lends support to the thesis that counter-cultural waves such as those of the 1890s and the 1960s tend to revive or reinvigorate social movements (Brand 1990), particularly those that argue for a return to more natural ways of life. This can be clearly seen in the enormous rise in memberships of all conservation and environmental organisations over the last 30 years, riding the wave of the 1960s' counter-cultural critique (Conley 1997).

A further distinction has been identified by Szerszynski (1996: 120) between two main strands within romantic forms of ecology, the 'expressive' and the 'traditionalist'. Expressivist ecology is characterised by attempts to re-connect individuals with nature and with an authentic or pre-social state of being, and can be found in the writings of the French philosopher Jean-Jacques Rousseau, the

English poet William Wordsworth and as we saw earlier, in that of
the American transcendentalists such as Thoreau and Ralph
Waldo Emerson, as well as in the organic 'bio-dynamic' agriculture
of Rudolf Steiner in the 1920s and 1930s (Pepper 1996). This
Expressivist form is also apparent in today's ecocentric attempts to
experience and explore an 'ecological self'(Chapter 5; Griffin
1978; Naess 1988, 1989; Devall 1990: Chapter 2; Mathews 1994;
Fox 1995). 'Traditionalist' ecology instead promotes collectivist
solutions that re-embed people, 'in a concrete community and substantive tradition' (Szerszynski 1996: 120), and is to be found in the
ideas of Thomas Carlyle, John Ruskin and William Morris (Briggs
1986) as well as in the anarchism of Kropotkin (1899). This tradition
lives on today in Bookchin's 'social ecology' or eco-anarchism
(1980, 1982, 1986, 1987). Bookchin advocates small-scale, self-
sufficient communities as more ecologically benign than large-scale
modern social organisations. Even if existing or historical examples
of the former are not intentional or self-conscious attempts to be
'Green', the 'small is beautiful' notion (Schumacher 1973) suggests
that such forms of social organisation should produce more sustainable
ways of living. Szerszynski's argument is that modern environmentalism and Green politics contain both of these romantic strands
in varying degrees.

To understand why such parallels exist between late nineteenth-
and late twentieth-century environmental philosophies and ideas,
it is necessary to return to the emergence of changing sensibilities
in relation to the natural world. A growing interest in and concern
for the non-human natural world amongst some social groups
predates the formation of the first environmental organisations in
the mid-1860s by at least two centuries. These shifting sensibilities
form part of the necessary cultural background to the formation of
those specialised organisations, whose aims were to intervene in
the management of society's relationship with non-human nature.
Such gradual changes in cultural values and emotional sensibilities
provided a base of support for the aims of early environmentalists.

The historian, Thomas (1984), demonstrates that attitudes in
England underwent a gradual change, over a very long period,
between 1500 and 1800. The overall direction of this change could
be described as moving towards a non-utilitarian attitude towards
non-human nature, which can also be observed in other parts of
Europe and North America. White (1967) traces exploitative

attitudes towards nature to the Judaeo-Christian tradition with its injunction to subdue the natural world to human purposes. What Thomas shows is that rather than continuing to see nature as God's creation *for* humans, which they could therefore legitimately use at will, a concern for the well-being of non-human animals gradually came to be expressed, along with growing interest in the effects of human actions on the integrity of Nature 'writ large'. Thomas (1984: 301) provides some fascinating insights into this process, explaining the changes thus:

> The growth of towns had led to a new longing for the country-side. The progress of cultivation had fostered a taste for weeds, mountains and un-subdued nature. The new-found security from wild animals has generated an increasing concern to protect birds and preserve wild creatures in their natural state. Economic independence of animal power and urban isolation from animal farming had nourished emotional attitudes which were hard, if not impossible, to reconcile with the exploitation of animals by which most people lived.

A non-utilitarian attitude towards the natural world can therefore be seen to have its origins in the urban distancing of everyday life and social production from nature, together with a gradual reduction in the level of fears in relation to natural events and forces (Dyos and Wolff 1973).

In sociological terms, Thomas describes the psychological and emotional effects of a steady alteration in people's orientation to the natural world brought about by changes in social organisation and the rise of a scientific worldview. Elias (1987b) argues that the possibility of increasing control over, and hence the reduction of fears in relation to natural events is also connected to growing chains of interdependence among larger numbers of people across more distant geographical areas of the world. Elias argues that '. . . as humans have gradually come to understand natural forces more, fear them less and use them more effectively for human ends, this has gone hand in hand with specific changes in human relationships. More and more people have tended to become more and more interdependent with each other in longer chains and denser webs' (cited in Mennell 1992: 169–70). In this way, more sympathetic attitudes towards the non-human natural world have been generated.

The reduction of fears in relation to the natural world does not arise wholly because of the ability of humans to protect themselves from the unpredictability of natural forces or threats from wild animals, though of course these probably played the most important part. Fears of this kind were also generated by the threats posed by the activities of humans, for example robbers and bandits for whom wild woods and forests provided opportunities for attacks. In this respect the non-utilitarian attitudes to nature which gathered pace from the sixteenth century are related to the 'pacification' of larger areas of social life, which has been described as part of a 'civilising process'. As Elias (2000: 419) points out,

> The manner in which "nature" is experienced is fundamentally affected, slowly at the end of the Middle Ages and then more quickly from the sixteenth century onwards, by the pacification of larger and larger populated areas. Only now do forests, meadows and mountains gradually cease to be danger zones of the first order, from which anxiety and fear constantly intrude into individual life....[P]eople – more precisely the town-people for whom forest and field are no longer their everyday background but a place of relaxation – grow more sensitive and begin to see the open country in a more differentiated way...They take pleasure in the harmony of colour and lines, become open to what is called the beauty of nature...

Changes in this direction led to an aesthetic appreciation of nature which formed one part of the complex shifts in sensibility which provided the cultural context for later nineteenth-century environmental campaigns for nature protection. However, the development of a scientific interest in nature study from the seventeenth century onwards also helped to give conservationist arguments credibility and make them politically respectable, whilst preservationist arguments emphasising the need to 'save man from himself' also played a part (Gilig 1981: 97–8). It is also worth remembering that although cultural shifts of this kind provide the necessary backdrop for the formation of environmental movements and organisations, they do not in themselves account for the specific character of those organisations. American 'resource mobilization' theorists are right to point out that the actual formation and maintenance of such organisations forms an area of study in its own right (Zald and McCarthy 1987; Rucht 1990; Kitschelt 1991;

Klandermans 1991). Nonetheless, the combination of emotional sympathies and scientific studies was a powerful one in the
longer term.

Both Thomas and Elias take a long-term or gradualist view of
the changing sensibilities with which we are familiar today. We
should add, though, that not only did these new sensibilities develop
over a long period of time, they also spread gradually across different
social groups. For many, the perception and experience of living in
an industrial society came relatively late, and the movement of people
from rural to urban locations was a transformation whose implications did not really become widespread until well into the twentieth
century. The extension of non-utilitarian attitudes towards nature
has been drawn out into the late twentieth century and beyond.
In the context of the gradual transformation of attitudes and sensibilities outlined above, the formation of organisations dedicated
to the preservation of the natural world and access to it is not
unusual. Rather, such organisations are one consequence of the
intensifying spread of industrialisation and urbanisation.

In tracing the emergence and development of discourses on
nature, it is important to bear in mind that such discourses are
never totally dominant, nor are they identical. In the USA the idea
of 'wilderness preservation' has been much more effective in raising
awareness of environmental issues than in most of Europe, where
ideas of conservation have proved to be enormously popular. This
difference can be explained with reference to the differing national
histories, with the USA's development involving pioneer settle-
ment where wilderness came to be seen as part of the new nation's
heritage. For example, Nash's (1982) survey of changing attitudes
traces the shift from an attitude which saw wild nature as in need
of cultivation to one which saw wilderness as 'a precious national
resource' (Hannigan 1995: 110). In many developing countries,
environmental concerns have been couched in yet different ways
as protecting national interests or those of indigenous peoples. The
different environmentalisms in the north and the south have presented some of the most difficult problems for those seeking
a truly global form of environmentalism. This suggests that the
meaning of 'environmentalism' is not consistent or fixed and is
to some degree dependent on context. This has not been an
insurmountable obstacle to international co-operation and joint
action however, as, 'Within the First, Second and Third World

radical ecology movements, theory and practice are linked, each informing and inseparable from the other' (Merchant 1992: 239).

Conclusion

Today, the attitudes of the early modern period, which viewed natural scenery as barren, unappealing and in need of cultivation, seem distant indeed. Tourists now travel the world seeking out just such natural scenery, whilst environmentalists campaign against industrial and commercial developments that threaten to 'cultivate' the natural landscape. Such a transformation of social attitudes has taken many generations and is bound up with industrial and urban development. 'Civilization' seems now to be measured by its ability to avoid damaging the natural environment rather than by its capacity for intervening and shaping it to human ends.

It seems that the less danger natural processes pose for people and the more their basic material needs are met, the more likely it is that they will take pleasure in nature. The trend of modern sensibilities has been described as towards idealistic preferences for country life over that of towns and cities, a love of wilderness rather than cultivation, conservation over the conquest of nature, and an increasing concern for the welfare of animals (Thomas 1984). However, the extent to which such cultural trends lead to institutional change depends not just on ideas and attitudes but also on intentional political activity. In recent years sociologists have become much more interested in the role played by social movements in mobilising support for non-established political issues, with environmentalism and Green politics being particularly good examples. Environmental movements have grown into mass social movements, Green political parties have had successes in elections across the world and mainstream political parties have had to develop their own 'green' policies. The story of how environmental movements moved from outsider status into the political mainstream is a complex one which has provoked much disagreement and this is the subject of the next chapter.

2 The Development of Environmental Movements

The gradual changes in attitudes and sensibilities towards the natural world discussed in the previous chapter underpin modern environmentalism, providing a continuing source of support for conservationist and environmentalist initiatives. However, this is a necessary but not sufficient condition for the 'mainstreaming' of environmentalism. One of the main explanations for the rise to prominence of environmental issues lies in the emergence and growth of active, campaigning environmentalist networks and organisations and their attempts to alert the non-committed public to the damage caused to natural ecosystems by human population growth, mass consumerism, industrial pollution and urbanisation. Collectively, these networks and organisations can be described as 'the environmental movement', the subject of this chapter. Nevertheless, the emergence of environmental movements cannot simply be read off from the social awareness of the existence of environmental problems. As Beck (2002: 159) puts it, 'Dying forests and songbirds do not metamorphose, in accordance with the laws of reincarnation, into protesting humans.' As we saw in Chapter 1, from the vantage point of the present it is possible for environmental historians to identify ecological problems across a wide sweep of time, without the corresponding rise of environmental movements. In common with other social movements, modern environmentalism is a product of industrialisation, democratisation and the creation of nation states and 'civil society' (Held *et al.* 1994). Modern social movements are bound up with, and active in attempting to regulate, the dominant social processes of capital accumulation, militarisation and industrialisation. These dominant processes provide the framework for the creation of a range of social movements as people collectively strive to shape and direct the overall process of modernisation (Giddens 1990). So for example, organised labour movements intervene to shape capitalism; peace (and anti-nuclear) movements resist militarisation; feminist movements challenge the structures of patriarchy; and environmental movements resist unchecked industrialisation. We could easily add more movements to this selective list, such as disabled people's movements, gay and lesbian movements, black civil rights movements and other equal rights campaigns. In this chapter though, the focus will be on environmentalism, referring to other movements where comparison adds something to the discussion or provides new insights.

The chapter examines the emergence and development of organised conservationism, preservationism, grassroots environmental networks and distinctively Green political parties, considering all of these as constitutive elements of that nebulous thing, the environmental movement. In so doing, it will take a longer-term view of the development of a broadly conceived environmentalism, even though the European literature, at least, has been dominated by the theory of 'New Social Movements' (NSM), which interprets contemporary or 'new' environmentalism as qualitatively different from earlier manifestations (Olofsson 1987). Although the NSM thesis has produced some provocative work and illuminating insights, it is now clear that the timescale adopted in such theories is too short to tell us the whole story of the rise of environmentalism and a longer-term perspective deepens our understanding. Without this we risk misunderstanding the character of contemporary environmentalism, its chances of success and its relationship to industrialisation and modernisation. Emphasising the discontinuities between old and new forms of environmentalism has tended to produce a partial understanding of both.

Environmental movements as new social movements

European sociology has come to understand the emergence of modern environmentalism largely through New Social Movement theories (Touraine 1969, 1971, 1981, 1983; Melucci 1980, 1985, 1988, 1989, 1996; Habermas 1981, 1987). These theories have been produced to account for a wide range of social movements, political protests and forms of collective action in the post-World War II period that appear to differ in significant ways from the social movement activity of the older established labour, socialist and communist movements. New social movements originated in the late 1960s and early 1970s and include student movements, peace and anti-nuclear movements, disabled peoples movements, gay and lesbian movements, animal rights movements as well as environmental movements. Sociological interest in environmental movements can be traced to the late 1960s counter-culture in America and Western Europe (Musgrove 1974; Conley 1997), which attacked industrial culture, bureaucratic domination and Cold War militarisation. The recourse to 'back-to-nature' arguments as a critique of human-centred concerns and of urban, human environments gave existing conservation and environmental organisations a political edge, attracting many new supporters and activists. The main dimensions of difference between the new movements and the earlier forms can be illustrated along several related dimensions.

Organisational form

NSMs are said to be much more loosely structured and organised than earlier social movements. Rather than developing a formal structure based on hierarchical and bureaucratic principles, NSMs seem to deliberately avoid this kind of organisational style. Instead, NSMs adopt a polycephalous ('many headed') design that allows for the creation of small autonomous groups. This protects the movement as a whole against damaging legal action, though it also serves the emotional needs of the community of members and supporters rather than being a simple rational calculation of what might be most efficient (Hetherington 1993). In the UK, the Animal Liberation Front is an exemplar of this structure (Tester 1991), which is similar in form to terroristic guerrilla groups, though it has to be recorded that NSMs overwhelmingly adopt non-violent methods. However, the cellular form also reflects the desire to challenge conventional politics and prevent the accretion of power in the hands of an elite few. In doing so, NSMs throw down a symbolic challenge to the rest of society (Melucci 1985, 1995, 1996). In the tradition of 'bearing witness', the new forms of networking act as a constant reminder that things might be different. Because this unconventional approach does not look to take state power, it has been described as a form of 'self-limiting radicalism' (Papadakis 1988).

Social constituency

NSMs have been described either as 'non-class based' or as attracting support from across a wide spectrum of social groups. This is seen as in stark contrast to the self-interested actions of labour movements concerned with wealth redistribution. Many large-scale protests and non-violent direct actions are noteworthy for the social constituency of support they gather together, including students, retired people, first-time protestors and traditional conservatives, trade unionists as well as 'professional' socialist agitators. Such coalitions are seen as relatively unusual. Nonetheless, other research has shown that many NSM activists tend to be drawn from a specific fraction of the middle classes, namely the 'new middle class', those involved in the welfare, creative, artistic and education fields (Cotgrove and Duff 1980, 1981; Mattausch 1989). This means that large demonstrations tend to look diverse whilst core activist groups share similar social-class backgrounds. There is no contradiction in these observations and it has been argued that environmental activism is perhaps best seen as the activities *of* a specific social constituency rather than as the self-interested actions *on behalf of* that constituency (Bagguley 1992: 40). In Eckersley's (1989) terms, environmentalism is a 'virtuous' movement rather than simply a 'self interested' one.

New issues

A further consideration is that NSMs bring into the foreground a set of postmaterial political issues that have not traditionally been part of formal organised politics. Environmentalism is obviously the best example of this, but we could also mention gay and lesbian issues, disability politics, animal rights and so on. Since the 1970s such areas have become increasingly salient in national and international politics, arguably at the expense of conventional class-based political divisions. This shift could be interpreted as the beginnings of a post-industrial political realignment (Chandler and Siaroff 1986; Frankel 1987) with 'Nature' or 'Life' becoming the central political cleavage rather than class, inequality and wealth distribution. Amongst those who place environmentalism at the centre of the new politics is Eder (1993: 118) who argues that, '... instead of continuing to talk of 'new' social movements, the time has come to give these new social movements a name. Any term from environmentalism, ecological movement, life politics movement might serve as a possible candidate for name-giving. They all denote the same problem: the nature–society relationship or 'the question of nature'. This broad problematic therefore constitutes an emerging 'politics of nature' (Dobson and Lucardie 1995; Sutton 1999).

It is also argued that much environmental campaigning constitutes an expressive form of politics focused on the creation and maintenance of social identities (Cohen 1985). This post-1960s expressivism is perhaps connected to the post-scarcity socialisation (Inglehart 1977, 1990) emergent in the relatively rich nations after the Second World War, allowing 'higher level needs' to find expression (Maslow 1954). Once basic material needs for food and shelter have been largely satisfied, people are able to pay more attention to quality of life issues, with the quality of urban and natural environments being at the forefront of these. Identity politics shifts the emphasis towards the integration of self and the social world, and in this sense the quest for new types of social identity is also the quest for a new type of society. Clearly the lack of formal authority structures in the relatively loosely structured NSMs would support this argument.

Action repertoires

The most striking feature of NSMs is simply the range of activities they engage in, what social movements scholars call their 'action repertoires' (Rucht 1990). Organisations such as Greenpeace International have become experts in the production of spectacular media events or 'eco-dramas' (Harries-Jones 1995) designed to bring environmental issues before the public. However, more recently the loose networks organising under umbrella names such as 'Critical Mass', 'Reclaim the Streets' and 'Earth First!' have attracted media attention through their unconventional forms of protest. Nonetheless, environmental movements do also engage in conventional political lobbying alongside the alternative festivals, sit-ins, tree occupations and all the other varied, creative actions for which they are known.

Provided they are non-violent, NSM activists use whichever methods seem most likely to achieve success. Rather than any specific activity being definitive of environmentalism, it is the sheer diversity of their action repertoire that is thought to mark them out as unique and different from previous social movements, particularly that of labour movements focusing on workplace actions.

This fourfold characterisation makes NSMs significant as a reflection or representation of a rapidly changing society (Hall and Jacques 1989). Underlying NSM theory lies a set of assumptions about the social and economic transformations of the industrialised societies, which amounts to a thesis of fundamental change. This can clearly be seen in the widespread use of the prefix 'post' in such terms as post-industrialism, postmodernisation, post-Fordism, postmaterialism, and so on. In the social sciences, this prefix is also used to denote various attempts to move beyond older theoretical perspectives, as in poststructuralism, postmodernism, post-marxism, post-feminism and post-humanism. Despite many critical rejoinders to such theories, which have led to reformulations of the original arguments, such a wide range of theorists beginning to use 'post' in these ways does suggest a broad feeling that industrial societies are being transcended, perhaps requiring new forms of analysis and explanation. NSM theory is just one more example of this perception. Because environmental movements have been used as an influential support for NSM theories and by implication, as support for a post-industrial characterisation of contemporary societies, criticisms of environmental movements as NSMs also amounts to a critique of some forms of post-industrial theorising (Calhoun 1993). This interpretation marks out environmentalism as *the* central new social movement that offers the potential for alliance building and thus a more effective challenge to newly established authorities and sources of power (Touraine 1981; Eder 1990, 1993). This is because the environmental movement's focus on nature informs a 'life politics' (Melucci 1989) that includes disability issues, anti-nuclear movements, feminism's challenging of women's natural role, and gay and lesbian arguments around 'natural' sexualities.

On the face of it, environmentalism *is* a relatively new political perspective, some commentators describing 'ecologism' as a political ideology dating only from the 1970s (Heywood 1992: Chapter 9; Dobson [1990] 2001: Chapter 1). In Dobson's view, the main reason for the emergence of this new ideology is the identification of environmental problems or risks of greater magnitude or 'higher consequence', together with genuinely post-industrial alternatives to continuing economic growth. These alternatives began to coalesce in the early 1970s, culminating in major reports such as *The Limits to Growth* (1974) and The World Commission on Environment and Development's *Our Common Future* (1987), alongside the UK journal *The Ecologist*'s call for the formation of a 'movement for survival' (1972). A significant precursor of these important reports was the publication of Carson's *Silent Spring* (1962), now considered one of the foundational texts of the 'new environmentalism' (Nicholson 1972; Atkinson 1991: 15). Carson was concerned with the consequences of the widespread use of agricultural pesticides on wildlife, especially birds, hence the provocative title. The introduction of nature into political life has therefore transformed the older conservationism into a political force. Ecologism thus constitutes a novel ideological position, which now sits alongside longstanding ones such as socialism, liberalism, conservatism and feminism, all of which trace their origins to post-Enlightenment Europe. If this interpretation is correct then it marks out environmental politics as a genuinely postmodern or post-industrial phenomenon.

Clearly, NSM theory and disjunctive interpretations of environmentalism have important things to say about environmental movements and their role in raising awareness of environmental damage, but the lack of a systematic, historically oriented perspective is serious because by downplaying earlier forms of conservation, preservation and environmental concern we are denied the opportunity to trace lines of development, risking having to reinvent the wheel every time there is an eruption of social protest and collective action. For this reason, criticism of NSM theories has grown significantly since the theory was advanced, with Steinmetz (1994: 179) describing historical critiques as a 'small cottage industry' in their own right. Perhaps a better way of expressing this point is to suggest that 'bold conjectures' often attract a variety of attempts at refutation, in this case resulting in a more historically adequate view of the 'new' movements. The more significant criticisms have tended to question the historical validity of NSM theory's claims to novelty, albeit in different ways (Bagguley 1992; Calhoun 1995b; D'Anieri *et al.* 1990; Sutton 2000). All of the features identified as 'new' have been found to exist previously and across a range of social movements and collective actions. Neither loose forms of networking, environmental concern, a middle-class constituency nor a varied repertoire of actions marks out contemporary movements as unique. However, notwithstanding the detail of such criticisms, the main problem with NSM theory is that it shortens the time span of modern environmentalism. In doing so, it makes the whole environmental problematic appear to be relatively recent when there is now good evidence to the contrary. Many of the critical interventions which challenge NSM theories, have baulked at their 'present-centred' argument and once we examine some of the historically oriented critiques, a subtly different perspective emerges that potentially changes our view of what the environmentalist challenge actually amounts to. The next section therefore describes the sociogenesis of environmental movements in the industrialised 'north', drawing on evidence from the developing 'south' where necessary.

The sociogenesis of environmentalism

During the latter half of the nineteenth century a series of informal networks and formal organisations came into being in Western Europe and North America, which can be seen as the legitimate organisational origin of modern environmental concern (Lowe and Goyder 1983; McCormick 1992; Brulle 2000; Sutton 2000). The French Society for the Protection of Nature was founded in 1854; the Commons Preservation Society (CPS) was founded in Britain in 1865 and in the USA, John Muir helped to found the Sierra Club in 1892. These landmarks are only a few of the most well-known organisations concerned with the conservation and preservation of the natural world, but it is important to remember that before this time there were no organisations dedicated to environmental conservation and therefore no recognisable environmental movements. Following these pioneers came a flurry of organisational activity with the end of the nineteenth century marking the close of a very active initial phase of organisation-building in the emerging environmental movements (Table 2.1).

In Britain, the CPS, with its origins in London, spread across the country with the aim of saving common land from commercial

Table 2.1 Formation of selected nineteenth-century environmental organisations and groups

Organisation	Date of formation
Society for the Protection of Nature (France)	1854
Commons Preservation Society (UK)	1865
The Kyrle Society (UK)	1876
Metropolitan Public Gardens Association (UK)	1882
Lake District Defence Society (UK)	1883
Natal Game Protection Association (South Africa)	1883
National Footpaths Preservation Society (UK)	1884
The Selbourne League (UK)	1885
The Audubon Society (USA)	1886
Society for the Protection of Birds (UK)	1889
Sierra Club (USA)	1892
The National Trust for Places of Historic Interest or Natural Beauty (UK)	1895
Coal Smoke Abatement Society (UK)	1898
Society for the Preservation of the Wild Fauna of the Empire (UK)	1903
Smoke Prevention Association of America	1907
Wildlife Preservation Society (Australia)	1909
Swedish Society for the Protection of Nature	1909
Swiss League for the Protection of Nature	1909

and industrial developments. Green spaces were coming to be seen in organismic terms as 'lungs for the Metropolis' (Brabazon 1881), and a necessity for a healthy life (Hill 1888, 1899). Despite some setbacks, the Society succeeded in preventing the destruction of many commons, with its founder claiming that 95,000 acres had been preserved in the Society's first 20 years. CPS historian and first chairman, George Shaw-Lefevre, saw the fight for public access as a step towards the restoration of the land to the people, if only 'at weekends and holidays' (Marsh 1982: 47). This argument was important for future developments as conservationist ideas of preserving wild areas and wildlife habitats, a central feature of environmentalist activity, developed from arguments for public access to nature. In the UK, the formation of local natural history field clubs reached 100,000 members by the 1880s (Enloe 1975: 25), producing documented evidence of the destruction of flora and fauna and strengthening the arguments of conservationists. Amenity organisations were formed using such public access arguments (Gregory 1976; Hill 1980), committed to the defence of areas of outstanding natural beauty such as the English Lake District, and the acquisition of land and property for preservation. As Wiener (1981) points out, to some extent the early conservationism reflected the adoption of aristocratic values by the urban bourgeoisie, which adopted a value system that 'disdained trade and industry [and] stressed the civilised enjoyment, rather than the accumulation, of wealth, and which preferred social stability to enterprise' (Lowe and Goyder 1983: 19). The defence of wild nature was necessary, it was argued, for the material and spiritual health of the people, and as a source of fresh air and physical health. Seen in longer-term perspective, the championing of the beneficial effects of wild nature and the desire to preserve open spaces was indicative of the profound changes in attitudes and sensibilities outlined by Thomas (1984), discussed in the previous chapter.

Similar sentiments can be detected in the USA where urban and industrial development came to be seen by many as inferior to 'arcadian' living (Schmitt 1969). It may be that secular industrialism produces such reactions wherever it becomes established or dominant. The difference in the late nineteenth century was that these sensibilities had begun to crystallise into organisations capable of achieving legislative change, influencing public opinion and making an impact on the regulation of industrial and urban expansion. The early environmental organisations were not democratic, but were based on small groups of enthusiasts who managed to garner wider support. This pattern can still be seen in many newer environmental organisations including the likes of Greenpeace. In the USA, environmentalism developed over a similar period, from the final decades of the nineteenth century, through an extremely active initial period between 1890–1915 (Brulle 2000: 238). The movement went through a major split in 1913 when disagreement over the building of a dam in Hetch Hetchy Valley brought out the different attitudes of 'conservationists' and 'preservationists'. Preservationists, following John Muir and the Sierra Club, were opposed to such an intervention whilst conservationists, such as Gifford Pinchot, saw it as an appropriate use or 'wise use' of natural resources for human needs (ibid.). Brulle argues that this division still exists in the USA, as the Sierra Club remains committed to the removal of the dam, whilst in recent years America has seen the emergence of a new 'Wise Use' movement that draws on Pinchot's arguments, describing itself as seeking to '"destroy environmentalism" and promote the "wise use" of natural resources...' (McCarthy 1998: 126). In the post-World War II period both American preservationism and conservationism gave way to a more widespread environmentalist orientation concerned with wider definitions of nature and expanding concern about human influence on natural environments (Hays 1985, 1987). Again however, it is important to recognise that such active periods are neither discrete nor unconnected to the longer-term process of development. Taken as a whole, the development of environmentalism is best seen as relatively continuous from the late nineteenth century, as evidenced by Brulle's description of the 'historical evolution' of the movement.

The campaigning styles of the early organisations included lobbying through established political channels, though direct actions were not uncommon even in the late nineteenth century. Shaw-Lefevre's history of the early years of the CPS details several campaigns to save London Commons. The successful campaign to save Berkamsted Common in the Chiltern Hills in 1866 involved both direct and legal actions. The CPS was asked for assistance by local people and planned a symbolic demolition of the fences, which would be 'not less conspicuous than their erection' (Shaw-Lefevre 1894: 62–8). Today we would probably describe such actions as 'symbolic direct actions'. Enclosure fences were removed covertly under the cover of darkness in order to buy time for the preparation of the Society's legal case against enclosure, which was later won on behalf of the commoners, but also as a visible demonstration of the implacable resistance of the emerging movement. Similarly, the formation of the Lake District Defence Society (LDDS) in 1883 provided a focus for opposition to private landowners' enclosure attempts. In 1885, Canon Hardwicke Rawnsley organised a mass action to remove all physical barriers erected by a local landowner and was assisted by the CPS to defend this action when writs for trespass were issued against the activists (Dwyer and Hodge

1996: 72), an example of the interconnected networks amongst separate organisations. Another organisation which made use of direct action campaigns was the Society for the Protection of Birds, which arose to stop the importation of the plumage of rare birds for the fashion trade. The Society carried on the ideas of the Plumage League, which demanded that all members sign a pledge not to wear the feathers of any bird in their hats (Doughty 1975). In 1868, Professor Alfred Newton (cited in Sheail 1976: 5) argued that '... fair and innocent as the snowy plumes may appear on a lady's hat, I must tell the wearer the truth – she bears the murderer's brand on her forehead', another example of the changing sensibilities and extension of moral concerns outlined by Thomas (1984). In 1911 a demonstration was organised in London to publicise the cause which involved the distribution of leaflets describing the 'barbaric slaughter' and the carrying of placards, whilst throughout the country large posters were pasted on walls and hoardings (Sheail 1976: 11–15). In the 1920s the Royal Society for the Protection of Birds (RSPB) and International Council for Bird Preservation (ICBP) campaigned against the effects of oil pollution on seabird numbers and helped to draw up the International Convention on Oil Pollution at Sea (Evans 1992: 54) and the RSPB raised the issue of the damaging usage of pesticides. Both of these issues are often seen as new areas of concern today, marking the shift to a more radical ecological analysis. Demonstrations of this kind, though not definitive of the early environmentalists' strategic methods, do show that symbolic direct action campaigns are not entirely novel inventions of radical ecological movements, and again there are some direct parallels with the activities of today's environmental and Green activism and with the protests of social movements more generally.

The original aim of early environmental organisations was to protect the countryside, nature and wilderness against the inroads made by industrialism. However, In Europe, countryside conservation and the rational ordering of the society–nature relationship were central issues, whereas in the USA, John Muir's idea of the preservation of wilderness came into conflict with rational 'conservationists' who sought to conserve in order that the exploitation of natural resources could continue. Nonetheless, Muir's preservationist arguments were broadly similar to those propounded by British conservationists of the time. The establishment of very active and campaigning environmental organisations gave the impression, at least, of widespread concern and encouraged governments to take conservation more seriously than previously. The regular creation of new organisations and groups has served to gradually expand the range of environmental concerns over the twentieth century and taken as a whole, the history of environmentalism is one of continuous developments. National cultural and political differences give environmental movements somewhat different characters (Kvistad 1987), and in addition the reasons for environmental concern do vary considerably, between scientific, aesthetic and public access motivations with conflict sometimes arising between these groups (Gilig 1981). For instance, groups pursuing free public access to common land have found opposition from others seeking to control such access to prevent mass access destroying areas of countryside and wilderness. Such conflicts have their theoretical basis in Hardin's (1968) idea of the 'tragedy of the commons', the paradoxical degradation of natural areas by people seeking to get closer to nature. For these reasons, when we speak of an 'environmental movement' we are describing organisations, groups and social networks who share similar goals (the protection of nature) but whose motivations often differ, thus leading to room for disagreements and therefore a certain lack of unity. It is now widely accepted amongst social movement scholars that social movements of all kinds more closely resemble networks of relationships than heroic 'personages' (Scott 1990; Diani 1992; Melucci 1996; Doyle 2000). Nevertheless, the concept of an environmental movement is a useful one in so far as it allows us to see the connections amongst environmental organisations, between these organisations and states and between environmental organisations and mass publics, thereby laying open the social dynamic created by all of these relationships. If we take the early environmentalism seriously, and I think we should, then it seems clear that environmentalism is not simply a product of post-industrial development but is rather, a response to processes of modern industrialisation. Goldblatt (1996: 136) rightly argues that '...the British and American conservation movements of the late nineteenth century as much as the green parties, for all their differences, can be considered elements of different historical phases of the environmental movement'. This is a conclusion that is consonant with the historical evidence.

Twentieth-century environmentalism

During the inter-war years environmental organisations continued to be formed (Table 2.2) and the state began to be involved in the conservation of natural resources (Walker 1989). Lowe and Goyder (1983) mark this period out as the second 'episodic' phase in the development of environmentalism though, given the inevitable disruption caused by war, it may be better to see this period as part of the long-term growth and expansion of environmental concern rather than as a discrete episode. One interesting development at this time was the first attempt at international co-operation for conservation. The International Council for Bird Preservation sought to prevent the annual shooting of migrating birds, which required international collaboration, but was unsuccessful in its efforts due to the lack of an international political framework or set of institutions, which could be lobbied for legislative change. After the Second World War, the International Union for the Protection of Nature (IUPN), a mixture of governmental and

Table 2.2 Formation of selected early twentieth-century environmental organisations and groups

The Federation of Rambling Clubs (UK)	1905
Society for the Promotion of Nature Reserves (UK)	1912
International Council for Bird Preservation	1922
The Izaac Walton League (USA)	1922
Council for the Preservation of Rural England	1926
Association for the Preservation of Rural Scotland	1931
Council for the Preservation of Rural Wales	1935
Ramblers Association (UK)	1935
The Wilderness Society (USA)	1935
Ulster Society for the Preservation of the Countryside	1937
International Union for the Protection of Nature	1948
The Nature Conservancy Council (UK)	1948
The Council for Nature (UK)	1958
World Wildlife Fund (now Worldwide Fund for Nature)	1961
The Conservation Society (UK)	1966
Committee for Environmental Conservation (CoEnCo)	1969
The Countryside Commission (UK)	1969

non-governmental bodies, was created as part of the growing United Nations interest in resource conservation for human needs. Its founders managed to fight their corner, finally changing the Union's name and orientation to IUCN ('Conservation' replacing 'Protection') in 1956 (McCormick 1992: 35–7). With the creation of international institutions, conservation organisations began to move beyond national definitions of nature towards a more biospherical definition taking in the entire planet.

Since the 1970s, the industrialised north and the developing south have witnessed the emergence of a range of new environmental organisations and Green political parties (Table 2.3), from

Table 2.3 Formation of selected late twentieth-century environmental organisations and groups

Australian Conservation Foundation	1966
Friends of the Earth (USA)	1969
Greenpeace (USA/Canada)	1971
UK Green Party ('People Party' in 1973, 'Green Party' from 1985)	1973
Values Party (New Zealand Green Party)	1972
Chipko Andalan Movement (India)	1973
European Environmental Bureau	1974
Tasmanian Wilderness Society	1974
Green Belt Movement (Kenya)	1977
Ecolo (Ecologist Party, Belgium, Walloon)	1978
Agalev ('Live Differently' [Greens], Belgium, Flemish)	1978
Earth First! (USA)	1979
Die Grünen (West German [*sic*] Green Party)	1979
Bündnis 90/Die Grünen (United German Green Party)	1993
Vihreät (The Greens, Finland)	1980
Miljöpartiet (Ecology Party, Sweden)	1981
De Groenen (The Greens, Netherlands)	1983
Reclaim the Streets (UK)	1980s
Citizens' Clearinghouse for Hazardous Wastes (USA)	late 1980s
Black Environmental Network (UK)	1988
Critical Mass (UK)	1992

Greenpeace and Friends of the Earth in the 1970s, through to the 1990s loose networks of Earth First!, Reclaim the Streets, Critical Mass and the anti-Genetic Modification (anti-GM) and anti-capitalist/globalisation networks (Wall 1999; Purdue 2000). The 'new' environmentalism has increasingly global concerns and is organised and campaigns internationally. The forms, action repertoires, aims and social constituencies of these new organisations have often been cited as evidence of a radical shift towards post-industrial social movements. It should be clear by now that whilst there are some genuinely novel features in the new environmentalism, these are best explained by locating them within the context of the development of the environmental movement as a whole. The failure to take a longer-term perspective has led to a distorted image of the new environmentalism as well as raising unrealistic expectations of what it might achieve. To an extent this reflects what Elias (1987a) once called the 'retreat of sociologists into the present' and has led to a reliance on theories which portray static pictures of 'industrial' and 'post-industrial' societies, modern and postmodern cultures, Fordist and post-Fordist regimes of accumulation and so on, rather than focusing on social and economic *processes* and the changing forms of resistance to those dominant processes.

For many commentators, the earlier phase of nature politics has little relevance to our understanding of contemporary environmentalism. The early conservationist and preservationist organisations were unrepresentative of the wider population, were confined to an upper-class elite with no intention to challenge the dominant mode of modernisation and despite some early stirrings of concern, failed to make any impact on industrialism. However, what these arguments do not take seriously enough is the possibility that contemporary organisations are part of a longer-term development with the new environmentalism drawing on and reacting to the earlier forms, starting from a position left to them by their predecessors. It also raises key issues about the relationship between disparate social movements and between social movements and the state. Evans's (1992: 93) cautious conclusion is perhaps closer to the evidence than disjunctive NSM theories: 'The war years had interrupted the momentum of the voluntary conservation movement.... But, with the return to peace, the time was right to renew the thrust. Conservation fitted into the ideal of a brave new world very comfortably.'

During the course of the twentieth century, membership of environmental organisations steadily increased until the 1980s, when there was a pronounced phase of growth, reflected in the enormous expansion of memberships. It is this transformation of environmentalism into a mass movement, which influenced NSM theories. Dalton and Kuechler (1990: 284) argue that 'In the past, local solutions were sought. It was (or at least it seemed) possible to geographically restrict the impact of environmental hazards.... Obviously such local strategies are insufficient today.... The fundamental goal of the movement today is not particularistic. It serves the very survival of the human species.'

This is of course correct, but the point is that the current global orientation of contemporary environmentalism is inconceivable without the gradual development of an environmental perspective and environmental initiatives of the past century. By the early 1990s it became possible to speak of a global, mass membership environmental movement covering almost every society on Earth. It has been estimated that the UK movement can count around four and a half million formal members constituting 8 per cent of the total population (McCormick 1991: 34), whilst in the mid-1980s, 17 million people, around 7 per cent of the population, belonged to an environmental group in the USA (McCormick 1991: 137). The mass character of the movement is credited to the expansionary phase from the 1970s, which was linked to student countercultural protests across Europe and the USA. Stephen Cotgrove's 1982 study found that students were significantly over-represented amongst members of Friends of the Earth and the Conservation Society in the UK (8 per cent compared to 1.4 per cent in the total population), indicating a possible generational contrast. Membership of all environmental organisations appears to be predominantly middle-class, a conclusion drawn in numerous studies covering a range of organisations and groups (Lowe and Goyder 1983; Worcester 1995). In particular, a specific fraction of the middle class, the so-called 'new middle class' employed in welfare and creative professions, which expanded after 1945, are over-represented in environmental groups. One section of society noticeably absent from environmental politics is the traditional working class, perhaps, as Cotgrove argued, because their employment is tied into industrial manufacturing and structurally reduces their potential for criticising such dominant industries. It is important to remember though that the number of regularly active environmental campaigners is relatively small, and large public demonstrations attract a diverse supportive population, as do most other large demonstrations. This is certainly true of many Greenpeace and Friends of the Earth campaigns and public protests, with the larger demonstrations pulling in anti-nuclear, peace and anti-globalisation protesters as well as anarchists, socialists, feminists and others, rather than being purely middle-class environmental actions. More typical are the symbolic protests (Melucci 1985) in which a few committed campaigners can attract media attention with unconventional media-presented 'eco-dramas'.

In addition, we need to remember that older, established environmental groups have also fared well since the 1970s. The most traditional of all UK organisations, the National Trust, saw its membership grow steadily during the twentieth century, and by 1980 the Trust had 950,000 members, growing to around 3,000,000 at the time of writing. The WWF, RSPB, Ramblers Association, the Royal Society for Nature Conservation and even the Council for the Preservation of Rural England have seen enormous increases in their memberships. Indeed, the majority of new members drawn into the environmental movement joined either more moderate groups and organisations or, more significantly, organisations which pre-date the new environmentalism, hardly solid evidence for an NSM interpretation. Indeed the National Trust itself accounts for around half of all the members of environmental movement organisations in Britain, its rate of increase remaining remarkably constant 'over the whole period [since its formation]' (Dwyer and Hodge 1996: 23). Claims that the mass environmental movement represents a new oppositional force with the potential to replace the old labour movement (Touraine 1981; Olofsson 1987; Eder 1993) are at least premature and currently hard to sustain. The late twentieth-century phase of renewed interest in nature and environmental issues has not occurred in a political or organisational vacuum, and it is precisely because the environmental movement pre-dates the 1970s resurgence that this renewed interest and concern has been channelled as much through existing organisations as newly formed ones.

One further development requires discussion here, namely the emergence in the USA of grassroots 'environmental justice' networks (Szatz 1994; Bell 1998: Chapter 1; Faber 1998). Such groups began to form and campaign during the late 1980s against the siting of toxic waste sites and incinerators in urban areas with high ethnic minority populations. The concept of environmental justice has now spread to other parts of the world and represents a different kind of environmentalism that also begins to take social inequalities into account. Backed by social scientific research findings showing that toxic waste sites tend to be located in black and Hispanic communities, environmental justice movements in the USA grew from grassroots citizens rights campaigns. In the UK, the Black Environmental Network was founded at a 1988 Friends of the Earth and London Wildlife Trust conference and has focused on trying to get environmental organisations to take the concerns of ethnic minority groups on board (Hannigan 1995: 125). Environmental justice groups are an important development for several reasons. First, they have the potential to bring under-represented groups into the wider environmental movement, enabling it to throw off the charge that environmentalism is a middle-class, post-materialist movement that is not capable of forging wider alliances. Environmental justice is precisely about peoples' material conditions of life and social exclusion based on class and 'race'. Secondly, their focus is not 'the environment' as defined by established environmental organisations – the 'Green environment' (Smith 1998) – but also urban and inner city environments. Again, this potentially widens the scope of what 'counts' as environmental politics, thus opening up the possibility of alliances with other social movements. Finally, environmental justice networks provide inspiration for those seeking to connect environmentalism in the relatively wealthy north with the environmentalism practiced in the relatively poorer, developing south. The polluting impact of Shell's Nigerian operations on the environment of the Ogoni people and their resistance campaign is one example of the potentially unifying concept of environmental justice. Attempts by the Nigerian government to put down the resistance movement involved torture, ransacking villages and, in 1995, the eventual execution of the movement's leadership, including the writer Ken Saro-Wiwa, in the face of international protest. Such events reinforce the argument that the relatively powerless are made to bear the brunt of environmental pollution. To a degree, the tendency for unified environmental justice campaigns can be seen in the form of recent anti-capitalist and anti-globalisation protests campaigning for the writing off of debt and fairer trade, though the extent to which northern environmental organisations are involved in these protests is not yet clear. Although currently a minority orientation in northern environmentalism, environmental justice campaigns demonstrate the potential for linking social class, ethnicity and the environment, which promises to make environmentalism more than a nature defence movement. As such they may have some potential to perform a synthesising function in relation to many issues formerly seen as outside the strictly environmental concern. Environmental justice movements are clearly an interesting recent occurrence, but perhaps the most surprising development lies in the formation of Green political parties across the world, a genuinely novel development (Poguntke 1987).

Green political parties

Charlene Spretnak and Fritjof Capra's influential *Green Politics* (1984) saw the emergence of Green parties as one element of a new vision of reality, which they argued, was becoming widespread in the industrialised north. The new paradigm was inspired by an ecological perception of the unsustainable practices of industrialism, which was destroying natural systems and therefore the basis of all life on Earth. Once again, though, understandable as these claims were at the time, we have to be cautious about arguments for the cultural shift to a 'new paradigm'. Green parties seem to be largely a European phenomenon and have not been electorally successful in the USA or Canada (Parkin 1989; McCormick 1992: 142). This would seem to support the contention that other factors are influential in determining Green party formation and success including national cultures, political systems and electoral opportunities and the character of democratic institutions.

Nonetheless, the first recognisably Green political party was New Zealand's Values Party, formed from local citizens groups in 1972. The party gained 5 per cent of the vote in the 1975 national election before disappearing as an electoral force amid squabbles over its direction (Spretnak and Capra 1984: 163–4). The British Green Party was the first European Green party, beginning life as 'People' in 1973, having adopted *The Ecologist* magazine's 'Blueprint for Survival' (1972) as its manifesto in the two 1974 General Elections. A more appropriate name change occurred in

1975, when 'Ecology Party' was adopted and a final change occurred in 1985, when the Ecology Party became the 'Green Party'. The most famous and electorally successful Green Party is *Die Grünen* (*Bündnis 90/Die Grünen* after German re-unification), formed in West Germany [*sic*] in 1979 (Papadakis 1984). In the context of the German political system of proportional representation, which favours the representation of smaller parties, *Die Grünen* won 27 seats in the Bundestag in 1983, a huge incentive for Greens across Europe and elsewhere. Again, the German Greens grew out of local citizen's associations and promoted an anti-economic growth agenda (Hulsberg 1987; Müller-Rommel 1989a). The Green slogan, 'act locally, think globally', is therefore an accurate reflection of the roots of Green parties and their concern to promote a participatory democratic approach that encourages active rather than passive citizenship (Princen and Finger 1994).

Green parties now exist right across Europe, though their electoral fortunes have differed widely as has their commitment to a new kind of 'anti-political politics' (Müller-Rommel 1982, 1989b; Havel 1988) and a steady state economy. Once Green parties enter political systems there are new pressures on them to conform to existing organisational models and to compromise on their radical policies. In West Germany, *Die Grünen* and, since re-unification, Bündnis 90/Die Grünen, have been part of coalitions with the Social Democrats (Sozialdemokratische Partei Deutschland [SPD]) in order to gain influence, and this has forced them to drop some of their demands. Dropping opposition to animal experimentation led to the resignation of Rudolf Bahro, an influential East German activist, who saw this as symbolising the incorporation of the party into the political establishment.

In the UK, the European Election of 1989 seemed to have marked a turning point as the party fought all 79 seats, gaining an unprecedented 14.93 per cent of the vote with a highest constituency vote of 24.5 per cent. However, under British 'first-past-the-post' electoral rules, not a single Member of the European Parliament (MEP) from Green Party was elected. Under a system of proportional representation the party could have expected to gain 12 of the 79 seats. This result pushed the other parties to develop their own 'ecological' policies, which to some extent began to undermine the Greens' originality (Young 1993: 37–8). The Green Party was apparently unable to deal with their overnight success and membership fell back rapidly after 1990. In the same year, Greens in Scotland separated from England and Wales, becoming established as an autonomous party. The Scottish Greens won seven seats in the 2002 Scottish Parliamentary elections under a system of proportional representation, thus demonstrating the restrictions of the 'first-past-the-post' system for smaller parties. However, in the UK-wide General Elections of the 1990s, the England and Wales Green Party averaged just 1.4 per cent before doubling its vote to 2.85 per cent in the 2001 election. Given that membership of the voluntary environmental movement stands at approximately 4.5 million, even allowing for the possibility of overlapping memberships, the Green Party does not seem to attract the regular support of environmentalists in national elections. One recent survey of the party (Bennie *et al.* 1995), carried out after an acrimonious split between 'realists' and 'fundamentalists' suggests that in comparison with environmental organisations, the British Green Party seems to attract a higher proportion of radical ecocentrics, who share a belief in the value of nature in itself. Some 95 per cent agreed with the statement that 'Plants, animals, streams and mountains, the earth as a whole, have intrinsic value independent of their appreciation by humans' (ibid.: 223). Complaints that the party fails in national elections miss the point because many party members do not see this as its main role.

One of the main reasons for the small number of UK Green Party members (around 6500) in relation to that of many environmental organisations, and the poor performance of the Greens in elections is that a radical ecological perspective is just not widespread in the wider environmental movement. Most environmental activists are reformists, working within the institutional framework of modern industrial societies in order to regulate and reform them. Rather than being mutually supportive, Green politics and environmentalism are in a state of tension, with environmentalists proposing practical measures for nature conservation whilst Greens promote significant social change. As McCormick (1991: 123) notes, 'There is much evidence that many environmentalists have shunned the Greens, and certainly there have been few formal or informal links between the party and the environmental lobby.' More research into the levels of support for radical positions and Green Party policy proposals within the membership of environmental organisations across the world would enable us to draw firmer conclusions, but on the basis of the present evidence we cannot conclude that there has been a mass 'Green' radicalisation of the wider environmental movement. Given this assessment, there is little basis for the conclusions reached by NSM theorists of the 'transition to a new age' in the development of the 'new' environmental movement. These radical conclusions are only possible because NSM theories concentrate on the minority who propound radical ecological ideas, taking them as constitutive of the mass environmental movement; however, this is presently poorly supported by empirical studies.

The British case shows that because of the very success of Green parties, existing mainstream parties have been forced to develop a platform of environmental policies of their own. McCormick (1991: 143) argues that 'Perhaps the most basic explanation of the rise of the Greens is the failure of older established parties simply to respond adequately to the needs and demands of the environmental movement.' However, if this assessment is correct then we might expect Green parties to lose support when established parties *do* begin to adopt such concerns and perhaps this is one reason (amongst several) for the failure of most Green parties to make a significant electoral breakthrough. The consequence of the assimilation of certain 'Green' policy ideas by mainstream parties has had the effect of either making Green parties themselves appear less novel to voters, or pushing the Greens towards more radical policies in order to maintain their distinctiveness. Depending on which of these roads national Green parties have taken, this has either hindered their initial originality or served to maintain the tension between reformist environmental organisations and Green parties. Green Party programmes tried to show that an ecological analysis embraced all political issues and that they could not be reduced to a 'single issue party', but once mainstream parties adopted Green policies, it seemed an ecological analysis could be compatible with existing ideological positions. Of course, many analysts might see the eventual establishment of environmental issues within the political system as a clear success, a sign that environmentalism has finally come of age. But this conclusion will not be shared by Green Party members or those pursuing de-industrialisation, as this very 'success' could well mark the demise of Green parties together with the incorporation of formerly radical environmental ideas into mainstream political life.

Globalising the environmental movement

Whilst all of the nineteenth-century organisations operated with a concept of nature seen in local or national terms, over the course of the twentieth century what we see is a gradual reinterpretation of what constitutes 'nature' to take in first the international dimension and later a much more global orientation. One index of this is simply the use of words such as 'International', 'World' and 'Earth' in newly formed organisations such as the Worldwide Fund for Nature, Earthwatch, Friends of the Earth and Earth First!, which shows an increasing recognition that environmental problems are potentially damaging to large regions of the planet (Jamison 1996). Nonetheless, these groups did not simply emerge from nothing, but were able to distance their perspective and analysis from earlier ones, which came to be seen as restricted and constrained by the national cultures in which they developed. As Young (1993: 53) has argued, '...environmentalism is not possible in one country'. In relation to the kinds of issues with which the newer groups are concerned, it is evident that there are also continuities with those of the developing environmental movement. Such new groups and networks are part of a globalising phase in the development of the environmental movement, which mirrors the current heightened or intensified period of globalisation (Wallerstein 1974, 1979, 1983; Featherstone 1990; Robertson 1992; Sklair 1991, 1994; Albrow 1992; Kilminster 1997, 1998; Waters 1998). A number of developments have contributed to the generation of a global framework. First, continuing industrial developments such as nuclear power, the production and distribution of oil, factory-ship whaling and worldwide transportation systems. Secondly, the scientific discovery of global environmental problems such as ozone depletion, acid rain, marine pollution, climate change and the rapid extinction of species. Finally, the emergence of international political institutions such as the United Nations (including UNESCO and the United Nations Environment Programme) and the European Union (including the European Parliament) has generated an increasingly regional and international political opportunity structure for environmental lobbying. The formation of 'global' environmental organisations such as Birdlife International, Earthwatch, Friends of the Earth International, Greenpeace International, the International Union for the Conservation of Nature and Natural Resources,

Wetlands International and the Worldwide Fund for Nature provides clear evidence of this globalising process. However, despite all of this, the general tenor of environmental concern remains reformist, and can thus be seen as consonant with the values of the majority of local and national groups. The evidence also strongly suggests that the post–1970s wave of environmental concern represents a generational contrast, with younger environmentalists establishing their own organisations embodying the relatively new internationalist or global outlook.

Given the wide range of environmental organisations and the different levels on which they operate (local, national, international), generalisations about them are difficult. Some organisations are insider groups in contact with, and in some cases dependency on, government and ministerial offices. Others are outsider groups, which shun formal links to government, jealously guard their independence and often campaign openly against government policies. Some organisations are closed with effectively self-perpetuating hierarchies, others are relatively open, allowing members to rise to the top levels of the organisation, and a few mix these 'monologic' and 'dialogic' forms across local, national and international levels (Offe and Wiesenthal 1980; Bagguley 1992). Earth First! is a good example of the informal networks, preferring a radical individualistic approach which emphasises the individual's responsibility for ecological protest (Foreman and Haywood 1989). In addition, there are widely differing ideological allegiances and motivations amongst environmental groups. Some are amenity groups campaigning for public access to nature, others seek to restrict such access; some are conservationist, others preservationist; some are more concerned specifically with animal welfare or individual animal rights, others with 'nature writ large'; some take a human welfarist position, others see this as part of the problem, which legitimises the destruction of nature. Despite all of this however, a few tentative general conclusions can be drawn.

Conclusion

Although there have been some innovative ways of organising and campaigning, the basic structural forms of most voluntary environmental organisations bear the stamp of their place within the long-term development of the movement as a whole, and this applies to many more recent groups as much as to older ones. The symbolic direct actions with which Greenpeace, Friends of the Earth (FoE) and Earth First! (EF!) made their names are best seen as the creative use of the potential offered by new forms of visual media such as television, video and latterly the internet and not as symptomatic of qualitatively different types of 'new' social movement. As one of the founder members of Greenpeace has remarked in relation to the Rainbow Warrior's first voyages to disrupt nuclear testing in the Pacific, '... nothing had yet happened to convince me that the boat was not, after all, a mind bomb sailing across an electronic sea into the minds of the masses' (Hunter 1980: 67). Direct actions have also been one part of the initial attempts of new organisations to carve out a place within the existing structure of the environmental movement, rather than constitutive features of the organisations themselves. Direct actions in defence of nature (though clearly of a limited kind) can be traced all the way back to the first environmental organisations in the late nineteenth century and to some extent the move away from simple direct actions, towards professionalism and strengthening of internal organisational structures reflects the success of FoE and Greenpeace in marking out their own space, or becoming an established part of the movement as a whole. This process of professionalisation or 'institutional self-transformation' (Offe 1990) has opened up a gap within the movement for more loosely organised direct action groups, which EF!, Critical Mass, Reclaim the Streets and others currently fill, drawing some members away from the formerly 'radical' groups. This means that there exists an ongoing relationship between environmentalism and radical ecology, and as Dobson ([1990] 2001: 213) argues, 'The point is that the reformists need the radicals just as the radicals need the reformists.'

In briefly reconstructing and reinterpreting the long-term development of the global environmental movement it has been possible to bring out some of the less well-known or debated aspects of earlier environmental campaigns. In doing so we can see that there are some fairly direct similarities between 'old' environmentalism and 'new' radical ecology, which leads us to reject the idea that any single element is definitive of either the former or the latter. With this in mind, what social movement theory needs and some researchers are now producing are theories of movement development over time, which explore the interrelationship between non-established and established organisations and the way these operate in differing political systems generating different political opportunities (Offe 1985; Kitschelt 1986, 1989, 1990; Klandermans 1990; Tarrow 1991, 1998). Probably more than any other movement, the environmental movement has provided fertile ground for sociologists seeking a 'diagnosis of our time', partly due to its obvious successes but perhaps also because unlike the subjects of other social movements, 'nature' cannot speak for itself and is therefore particularly amenable to interpretation or 'construction'. And though disagreements abound on this important issue, what all might agree on is that environmental movements raise issues which challenge the discipline of sociology to reconsider the society–nature relationship. What can existing sociological traditions contribute to the analysis of global environmental issues and to what extent do we need new forms of theorising to be able to tackle them? These questions are the subject of the next chapter.

3 Theorising the Social and the Natural

Generations of sociology graduates have learned that Durkheim's attempt to establish the discipline in the late nineteenth century involved arguing that there exists a social level of reality that cannot be reduced to the biological. Indeed, the ability to espouse such an argument is a basic prerequisite for developing the 'sociological imagination' (Mills 1959). For most of the twentieth century this suspicion of biological reductionist arguments in relation to the study of social life served sociology well, enabling the institutionalisation of the discipline and a certain respectability in the hierarchy of University establishments. However, just as feminist, black civil rights and disabled people's movements challenged the apparently biological or physiological location of fixed gender roles, stereo-typical racial characteristics and bodily normality respectively, so now are biological facts being reconsidered in response to the discourse of environmentalism and radical ecology. This process can be seen as allowing biology back into sociological discourse through such sub-disciplines as the sociology of the body, the study of human emotions and, of course, environmental sociology.

We are concerned here with the latter and the question provocatively posed by Catton (2002), namely, has the Durkheim legacy misled sociology? This question can also be asked of Weberian sociology, Marxism and the various interactionist and phenomenological alternatives. What do such theoretical perspectives offer the analysis of environmental problems? Why were environmental issues not part of their respective analyses of society? Does this mean that we need new theoretical perspectives? These are serious questions that will be with us for some time and certainly cannot adequately be answered in a book of this kind. What this chapter aims to do is to explore the terms of the current, often heated debates between 'social constructionists' and 'critical realists' in the study of environmental issues. As Dickens (1996: 72) points out, this dispute is about as close as academics can get to having a stand up row, though some have argued that these positions share more common ground than they would care to admit (Burningham and Cooper 1999). In addition, there have been some interesting and potentially attractive attempts to move beyond the constructionist or realist alternatives and a discussion of these concludes the chapter.

The social construction of environmental problems

Although the origin of social constructionism in sociology can be traced back to the 'social problems' perspective of the early 1970s (Hannigan 1995: 32), it can also be seen to draw from work on the sociology of scientific knowledge (Yearley 1991; Irwin 2001: Chapter 3). From the former comes the idea that those social problems considered in most need of urgent action may not be the ones that are most socially harmful. Instead, the way that such problem-claims are made is itself a subject for sociological research. From the latter comes a reminder that all of our knowledge of nature, including modern science, is still human knowledge, which has been produced in social situations and is open to the influence of similar social factors that influence other forms of knowledge production.

A social constructionist perspective has been used to analyse a bewildering variety of social and natural phenomena including the social construction of Europe (Christiansen, Jorgensen and Wiener 2001), serial homicide (Jenkins 1994), dementia (Palfrey and Harding 1997), anorexia nervosa (Hepworth 1999), sexuality (Fausto-Sterling 2000), the ocean (Steinberg 2001) and of course, environmental issues of various kinds. If there is a common theme in these studies it is the attempt to raise questions about the natural or objective status of their objects of inquiry. In doing so, social constructionist arguments insist on the (at least partial) social creation of the phenomena being studied. If this is correct, then it is evident that the initial premise of social constructionism is an essential moment in all sociological research, in so far as this requires definitional questions and a demonstration that our taken-for-granted concepts and ideas have a history or social development that can be traced historically. Constructionism amounts to much more than this however.

In relation to environmental issues, a social constructionist perspective can show how and why some environmental issues rise to prominence, rather than simply accepting that those currently identified environmental problems have arisen through self-evident necessity. In this way, constructionism raises questions of a quite fundamental kind. It can also ask important questions about who makes claims for the existence of environmental problems and who opposes them, thus allowing us to locate environmental issues within social and political contexts. Some social groups are in more advantageous positions than others to make environmental problem-claims and to make those claims stick. Some social groups are similarly better placed to deny or oppose the claims of less powerful groups, preventing issues they consider significant from ever rising to prominence. In addition, social constructionism insists on the inexorably *social* nature of all knowledge about natural phenomena, thus placing human societies at the centre of the analysis. The claims to valid knowledge of the natural sciences need to be subjected to the same critical approach that may be applied to knowledge production within environmental movements (Braun and Castree 1998). Perhaps this focus on societal knowledge production goes some way to explaining why this perspective has become most widespread in sociology, the discipline that has done most to advance the arguments for the social level of reality. However, it is also this insistence on the social that makes constructionism suspect to those who view the environmental crisis as *the* most pressing of issues, demanding immediate action. For many environmentalists, radical ecologists and environmental sociologists, social construction-ism can appear as something of an irritation. At a time when urgent action is required, the detailed deconstruction of, say, arguments for and against global warming may appear irrelevant or even politically naïve, lending tacit support to those who would deny the need for urgency in tackling environmental problems.

Social constructionism is not a unified perspective however, and can take a variety of forms. A well-established distinction taken from the sociology of scientific knowledge can be made between 'strong' and 'weak' forms of constructionism, though some constructionists object to the terms 'strong' and 'weak', preferring 'strict' and 'contextual' instead (Irwin 2001), and I will adopt the latter terms in the rest of the chapter. There are some central points that emerge from the varied social constructionist accounts. Strict constructionism begins from the premise that nature does not present itself in unmediated form and has always to be interpreted. All natural objects and systems are accessible only to analysis through human concepts and theories and these of course are open to change, meaning that any claim about nature is also a claim about how it can be known. Some constructionists go so far as to suggest that natural objects only exist in so far as they are either amenable to investigation and/or useful in some way to human beings (Douglas and Wildavsky 1982). In a now (in)famous passage from his book on the animal rights discourse and movement, Tester (1991: 46) states that, 'A fish is only a fish if it is socially classified as one, and that classification is only concerned with fish to the extent that scaly things living in the sea help society define itself. . . . Animals are indeed a blank paper which can be inscribed with any message, and symbolic meaning that the social wishes.' Here, Tester effectively eliminates the reality of fish, reducing them to the changeable categories created by human societies. If societies were to perceive and categorise fish differently, then their reality for people changes. By extension of course, this argument suggests that the entire natural world relies for its reality on socially constructed categories. At one level, Tester is correct in that there already *do* exist different social constructions of fish. Fish can be a foodstuff; valued and loved pets living with humans; part of decorative fish tanks used as ornamental features in hospital waiting rooms; or entities with natural rights that should be respected in the same way that human rights are. And, all of these constructions can and do co-exist within one national society, let alone across cultures or at different times. In a very real sense then, fish already are what humans say they are. However, critics might argue that none of these 'constructions' alters the reality of fish. They can all be said to be *uses* of fish *for* human beings, rather than saying anything at all about the reality of fish, their natural powers, potentials or necessary capacities. We can only know fish through socially created categories, but even without such human categories, the entities we call 'fish' would still exist and behave in the world. In short, fish are real in a way that strict constructionism seems reluctant to accept. Nonetheless, others who would still consider their position to be social constructionist would probably accept the above account. Burningham and Cooper (1999) rightly point out that there are in reality very few strict constructionist studies of environmental problems that go so far as Tester does. The majority of constructionist studies do accept that there is a reality external to discourse, but insist that environmental problems cannot be simply reduced to that reality.

Contextual constructionism accepts that environmental problems *may* be real, but argues that the way such problems are discovered and the claims about them put together can tell us much about them. As Hannigan (1995: 30) puts this, 'social constructionism . . . does not deny the independent causal powers of nature but rather asserts that the rank ordering of these [environmental] problems by social actors does not always directly correspond to actual need'. For contextual constructionists, sociology can perform a useful role in the investigation of the making and denying of environmental claims; that is, the way that claims about environmental issues are put together to make a case for action, or the way that arguments are constructed, which deny the claims of environmental claims makers. In order to explore the potential utility of this form of social constructionism for environmental sociology we can examine a recent attempt to do just this in relation to specific environmental issues. Hannigan (1995) provides several case studies of the social constructionist approach to environmental issues including the development of biotechnologies, acid rain and biodiversity loss. A reconstruction of his account of the latter will show what the benefits of adopting a constructionist approach are, before considering its possible limitations.

Concern about the loss of plant and animal species through extinction became a key environmental problem of the late twentieth century and continues to exercise environmentalists. The reduction of planetary biodiversity can take place at three levels: the ecosystemic level, through loss of habitat; the species level, through extinction of particular life forms; and the genetic level, through elimination of genetic information coded in species (Hannigan 1995: 146–7). Clearly these levels are interconnected, so that the loss of a particular habitat can also bring about species extinction, which eliminates genetic information. Hence when journalists and commentators speak of 'the loss of biodiversity' they could be referring to one or more of the above levels. The issue of biodiversity loss began to be seen as a serious global environmental problem during the 1980s, reaching a high point at the United Nations 'Earth Summit' in Rio de Janeiro in 1992. It may be thought that the issue of biodiversity has arisen at precisely the moment that scientists have become increasingly aware of the dangers posed by the spread of industrialisation to developing countries and their formerly 'intact' ecosystems, such as those found in tropical rain-forests. This may then lead to the optimistic conclusion that, strange though it may seem, as Karl Marx (cited in Bottomore and Rubel 1990: 68) famously argued, '...mankind always sets itself only such problems as it can solve; since, on closer examination, it will always be found that the problem itself arises only when the material conditions necessary for its solution already exist or are at least in the process of formation'. Hannigan argues that the situation is much more complex than this conclusion would suggest.

The issue of biodiversity loss had been raised in relation to species loss as early as the 1911 Convention for the Protection and Preservation of Fur Seals, but was also evident in other legislative attempts to protect birds and animals. However, as we saw in the previous chapter, in the early twentieth century no stable inter-national institutions existed that could have provided a focus for political lobbying and the issue remained restricted to concerns over individual species. Similarly, biodiversity loss did not become an important problem during the deforestation of the industrialised nations, thus questioning any simple notion of an objectively urgent environmental issue forcing its way into the consciousness of society. This raises the question of why biodiversity loss did become such a major international problem only in the 1980s. Hannigan's argu-ment takes a social constructionist position, identifying three factors that provided the background for the emergence of a discourse on biodiversity. First is the involvement of corporations with an interest in the exploitation of genetic resources and claims to intellectual property rights and patents over these. The intentions of Western companies to take ownership of natural resources in developing countries has led to the formation of movements of resistance and governmental concern. Secondly, in the 1970s came the creation of a new academic specialism, the so-called 'crisis' sub-discipline of conservation biology, which was officially recognised in 1985 with the formation of the Society for Conservation Biology. Thirdly, the establishment of 'a legal and organisational infrastructure' within the United Nations provided a lobbying focus for environmental organisations. This produced a series of conservation conventions covering Wetlands and Waterfowl Habitat (1971), World Cultural and Natural Heritage (1972), Endangered Species of Wild Fauna and Flora (the Convention on International Trade in Endangered Species or 'CITES') (1973), and Migratory Species of Wild Animals (1979). These international conventions served to significantly raise the profile of biodiversity loss at the international level and provided a new locus for environmental campaigners.

It was against this background that research data on species extinction, deforestation and tropical biology came to be interpreted and a new meaningful discourse generated. The climate of 'crisis' allowed the voices of particular scientists and research programmes to play an influential role in assembling the claim for biodiversity loss. Paul and Anne Ehrlich were already well-known figures in American environmentalism after their 'catastrophist' (Cotgrove 1982) writings on the perils of global human overpopulation (Ehrlich 1968; Ehrlich and Ehrlich 1970), and in 1986 they founded a new Centre for Conservation Biology at Stanford University. Hannigan (1995: 153) notes that the 'active engagement' of E.O. Wilson, one of the founders of sociobiology, in environmentalism led to his edited collection, *Biodiversity* (1988), becoming 'one of the best-selling books in the history of the National Academy Press'. In summary, a network of influential scientists, which Wilson later jokingly described as 'the rainforest mafia' (cited in Hannigan 1995: 154) working in different sub-disciplines of biology helped to construct an environmental claim about the apparently 'new' issue of bio-diversity and its endangered status at the hands of human activity. At this time, the 'knowledge interests' (Cramer *et al.* 1987; Eyerman and Jamison 1991) of this group of scientists and environmental writers came together to produce an influential claim on behalf of biodiversity loss.

Once the claim was made it then had to be presented effectively if it was to be raised to the level of other international problems such as marine pollution or nuclear waste dumping. This was not as simple as it may seem. Biodiversity loss has many causes, which cannot be pinned down to a single identifiable target or enemy. People in the relatively wealthy countries do not feel any immediate impact from this loss and it is therefore difficult to argue that there would be recognisable benefits from taking action to prevent it, especially when the economic costs of doing so are obvious.

Hannigan (ibid.: 155) argues that biodiversity campaigners overcame this problem by adopting a 'rhetoric of loss' drawn from the 1970s catastrophist discourse of overpopulation combined with more recent research on the extinction of dinosaurs on Earth. The former acts to make inaction an active step on the road to catastrophe, whilst the latter gives the long-term process of species extinction a direct contemporary reference through television and film reconstructions. In a secondary argument, biodiversity is also seen as a positive financial benefit to human societies as it preserves biological resources, which might produce cures through 'bioprospecting' thus creating a wider constituency of support for the preservation of biodiversity as a form of enlightened self-interest. The point of digging into the historical detail here is to demonstrate that biodiversity loss was not a self-evident environmental problem but had to be socially constructed as a significant environmental issue.

Importantly, the discourse of biodiversity loss makes claims about human societies and their impact on the natural world in ways that demand not simply understanding, but action by individuals, organisations, governments and international institutions. Its catastrophist tenor gives the issue a real sense of immediacy, which has enabled biodiversity to take its place among the few key international environmental issues. However, this conclusion ignores the activities of claims-deniers, those who challenge some or all of the biodiversity-loss claims. At the 1992 Rio Summit, many delegates from countries in the developing South contested the ownership of genetic resources identified in their countries against the claims of Western biotechnology companies to have the legal rights to patent genetic material. At issue was the question of national autonomy and sovereignty against the unhindered exploitation of bioresources. The USA delegation refused to sign the Biodiversity Convention, which would have meant US companies had to pay royalties and share their patents on genetic material. In addition, a coalition representing indigenous farmers and ecological activists were opposed to the Convention on the grounds that local people were not consulted. Despite these challenges, biodiversity loss now has an emotional and widespread political resonance, it continues to feed off new data on species extinctions and habitat loss, and both the global environmental movement and the World Development Movement have a strong interest in the issue. For these reasons it is likely that biodiversity will continue to be a major environmental problem.

What conclusions can be drawn from this case study about the utility of social constructionism as a way of analysing environmental issues? First, Hannigan's discussion shows that current concerns over the loss of biodiversity have been socially constructed and that the process of construction can be retraced and analytically reconstructed. Secondly, it is clear that other environmental issues have been similarly constructed, so that those issues which seem to be the most urgent at any particular time may only appear that way because of the success of some environmental claims-makers over others, rather than simply being read off from the substantive content of the claims-making discourse itself. Thirdly, social constructionism can be extremely valuable for sociology in so far as it gives sociologists a clearly defined task in relation to environmental issues, namely examining the way that environmental problems are generated and brought before the public. So far so good. However, what seems to be missing from this account is that it has very little to say on the central question at issue; that is, whether biodiversity loss is in fact an increasingly serious problem in need of our urgent attention. This question is sidestepped via the social constructionist detour into analysing claims-making and claims-denying processes. In one sense this is understandable as very few sociologists can claim to have the kind of expert knowledge required to engage in detailed debates about the science of biodiversity, but also of acid rain and global warming (Buttel and Taylor 1994). For environmental campaigners and others close to policy-making processes this is unhelpful and largely a distraction from the real business of 'saving the planet'. From this perspective, sociology remains on the fringes of real world issues rather than at their core. In short, social constructionism risks reducing sociology to a form of discourse studies in which the only things studied are texts, albeit interpreted in the widest sense, with little actual analysis of an external reality that impinges on human discourse.

I think such a conclusion would be unfair. It assumes that environmental issues *can* 'speak for themselves', a claim that is very difficult to substantiate. All environmental issues have to make their way into political life if any action is to be taken to solve them, and Hannigan's examples simply lay bare that process. In doing so of course, a public debate about the issues becomes possible rather than simply leaving such matters to self-appointed experts and claims-makers. In this way sociology can claim to be fulfilling its role as the organised, systematic reflection of modern societies on their own conditions of existence (Bauman 1992). This function should not be underestimated. Without it, the policy-making process becomes evermore specialised, leaving out the views of ordinary people (Hannigan 1995: 31). What seems most upsetting about constructionist analyses is their intentionally 'agnostic' stance regarding the veracity of environmental problem claims. But this agnosticism may be precisely the way to avoid the kind of politically dubious catastrophist predictions of the 1970s that have signally failed to materialise. A relatively detached perspective is one that sociologists have been constantly striving to achieve, and it would be rather ironic to judge constructionism a failure for having achieved it. By laying bare the claims-making process, social constructionist analyses can also be said to be bringing more 'reality' to the debate rather than less (Irwin 2001: 167) by opening up previously hidden aspects of environmental issues, however messy and indeterminate this eventually proves to be. Nonetheless, social constructionism has drawn much critical fire from the alternative 'realist' or 'critical realist' perspective.

Critical realism and the environment

For some environmental sociologists, social constructionism in its various guises does not provide enough solid ground for studying environmental issues. In particular, a group of British-based socio-logists and philosophers including Benton (1991, 1994), Martell (1994) and Dickens (1992, 1996), using ideas from the critical realist philosophies of science of Bhaskar (1978, 1989) and Sayer (1992), and the early writings of Marx (1844), have formed a centre of gravity for an alternative 'realist' or 'critical realist' approach to the study of society–environment relations. Because this approach has, so far, been less influential than constructionism, there are fewer specific examples of research using this perspective (though this may change, as the *Journal of Critical Realism* becomes peer-reviewed). Therefore, this section will focus more on outlining the theoretical arguments for adopting realism in the study of environmental issues, using examples in an illustrative way.

Bhaskar's version of realism has been attractive to those socio-logists unhappy with what they see as the unnecessary agnosticism of social constructionism about real world problems, and who are seeking an alternative way of 'doing' environmental sociology that gives due weight to the reality of natural forces. Such realist perspectives have tended to build on the work of Marx (Foster 2000; Hughes 2000) and to a lesser degree, Engels, and in the case of Dickens and Benton at least, to the 'early' Marx of the *Economic and Philosophic Manuscripts* (1844), which is interpreted as using a critical realist method to analyse the process of alienation as a distortion of human powers and 'species being' via the capitalist social division of labour. Whether realism is inevitably Marxist is not a question I propose to take up here, but suffice to say that 'critical realism' does tend towards marxism whilst other varieties of 'realism' need not. The main issue for us is how do realist perspectives approach environmental issues?

A fundamental tenet of realism is that knowledge is stratified or connects different levels of reality. For Dickens (1992), a realist perspective works with both abstract and concrete levels of knowledge. Abstract knowledge means high level theories and natural laws of development – the laws of gravity, thermodynamics and so on – which outline the generative mechanisms underlying natural phenomena. This includes the natural powers, potentials and capacities of species, taken to include human beings. On the other hand, concrete knowledge refers to knowledge of the more contingent and historically specific circumstances that shape how these powers, potentials and capacities, established through abstract knowledge, actually work out in practice. The study of specific historical situations or 'conjunctions' is required in order to explore the ways that these are differently expressed. This means that any understanding will require detailed empirical research to sort out how contingent factors interact with necessary relations to produce specific conjunctural outcomes. An example will help to flesh out the explanatory potential of the realist method.

Dickens (1996: Chapter 5) examines the case of the industrialisation of agricultural production. Since the introduction of industrial techniques into the farming of animals and crops, human interventions in food production have enormously expanded the possibilities for extensive and intensive production. It has become possible to alter the natural breeding capacity of dairy cows, which now can be made to produce more calves and milk than would be the case without human intervention. Similarly, industrial and commercial seed production has pushed crop yields beyond anything that could have been achieved 'naturally' in previous times. From a strict social constructionist perspective this may be seen as good evidence of the way that natural objects have become thoroughly socialised, so that to speak of nature and natural capacities as separate from society would make little sense. However, for realists, what such examples do is help us to understand why it is that some of the industrial interventions in nature result in unexpected and unintended outcomes. This sometimes happens because such interventions push the species' natural powers, potential and necessary capacities beyond their natural bounds. In contrast to a constructionist reading therefore, realism is much more forceful in recognising the natural limits to human intervention. Nature is not simply what human beings categorise it as. Attempts to introduce intensive feeding regimes, battery farming or genetic modifications produce unintended outcomes, which then have to be dealt with. This demonstrates that there are limits not simply to human knowledge, but to what can be achieved in the use of what remain natural beings. As Martell (1994) puts it, sociological explanations can sometimes be 'too sociological', if they refuse to accept the intransigent reality of natural forces and powers. Humans are not free to construct nature just as they please.

Similarly, Benton (1994) has argued that the acknowledgement of the natural powers, potentials and capacities of non-human animals provides a critical perspective from which the concept of animal rights could be defended, as it can be argued from this premise that not to allow animals to develop their natural capacities constitutes an unnecessary restriction of their natural and species being. This argument is also made by Noske (1989), who uses Marx's theory of alienation to analyse the capitalist use and exploitation of animals and their alienation from their nature. Dickens (1996: 62–4) sees the typical specialisation of the capitalist division of labour as productive of animal alienation, expressed for example in factory-farmed pigs that bite each other's tails due to boredom and lack of stimulation, or in the thousands of chickens kept in broiler houses which are unable to establish a natural 'pecking order' and wind up pecking each other to death. Once an animal–human continuum is accepted rather than a 'human exemptionalist paradigm' (Catton 1978; Dunlap 1980) then it becomes much more difficult to ignore the moral significance and welfare of other animals than human beings. As Benton (1994: 18) argues, 'Any consistently naturalistic view of human well-being will necessarily have implications for the ability of non-human animals to secure conditions for their well-being.' A realist approach may therefore be able to empirically demonstrate why arguments for animal rights are consistent with current ideas of human rights.

What these examples show is that acknowledging nature's effectivity may necessitate a rethinking of sociological theories and traditions to accommodate natural processes. We can see this as one part of the ecocentric challenge for sociology, which is discussed in more detail in Chapter 4. For now it is enough to bear in mind that realists find in environmental issues a rich seam of empirical material and case studies with which to advance their methodological and theoretical positions. This is because all environmental issues bring together the natural and the social, allowing some of the scientific findings embedded in the presentation of environmental problems to be aired as evidence for the effectivity of natural forces. Significantly, environmental issues are also highly attractive to social constructionists as they offer a chance to demonstrate the constructed character of environmental problem claims which undermines their apparently objective character. Nature is therefore a site of contestation not just for social actors in real world debates, but also for polarised sociological perspectives to make their own claims to dominance within the sub-discipline of environmental sociology. Perhaps strict constructionists are partly right after all in that although nature may not *really* be a blank slate, it does provide a remarkably vacant lot for the polarised arguments between realists and constructionists. Because nature does not simply speak to society, environmental issues remain open to widely diverging interpretations and it is this which marks out the sociology of environmental issues as different from the issues raised by other human-centred social movements.

Roads beyond the dualistic horizon

Given the entrenched positions of the realism vs constructionism debate, some sociologists have attempted to move beyond both positions to develop new ways of thinking about and researching environmental issues. Sismondo (1993) has recently devised a

fourfold scheme, which outlines several subtly different constructionist positions, and Demeritt (1998) argues in favour of one of these,
'artefactual constructivism', as a way of bringing together constructionism and realism. Two recent books have, in different
ways, made the case for bypassing or moving beyond the polarised
choice of either social constructionism or realism. The argument
for doing so is that dualisms of this kind tend to produce one-sided
accounts which give us partial knowledge. What is needed are
ways of connecting the social and the natural within a single framework that would enable a new research programme for sociologists
interested in the environment. Examples from each account follow
with a view to evaluating whether they amount to an improvement
on current debates.

The first example is the work of Macnaghten and Urry (1995,
1998). In a series of publications culminating in the book *Contested
Natures* (1998), Macnaghten and Urry (1998: 2) intervened in the
realism–constructionism debate trying to 'transcend the by now
rather dull debate between "realists" and "constructivists". In order
to do this, they suggest that sociologists should concentrate instead
on 'embedded social practices'. These practices are constituted in
several ways – through *discourse*: in the way that people in social
groups speak of, write about and construct models of nature and
the environment; through *embodiment*: the way that people sense or
experience nature and natural objects; through *space*: via differing
conceptualisations of local, national and global forms of nature;
through *time*: in changing ideas around the immediacy or longevity
of environmental problems; and finally through *models of human
activity*: including theories of human nature and what the specifically human natural capabilities might be. Taken together, these
elements are constitutive of, or generate, particular social practices
that are amenable to analysis. Given the complexity inherent in
such social practices it is not surprising that Macnaghten and Urry
see the social engagement with nature and the environment as
diverse and necessarily unstable. A further feature of social practices is that they require new sociological methodologies capable
of capturing this complexity. The focus on social practices is
intended to open up new questions that realism and social constructionism have not considered and to explore a sociology of the
environment after the society/nature dualism has been dissolved.
An example from *Contested Natures* will demonstrate how such

a project might work and what it might tell us about environmental problems.

Most modern societies have areas of land, countryside or wilderness that are highly valued and protected for scientific, aesthetic or public-access reasons. In Britain, or more specifically England, the area of the Lake District is today seen as just such an area of natural beauty and national heritage. It is also a National Park under the authority of the National Trust. If we think of why the Lake District is valued this way, one notable aspect would be the much wider *social discourse* that sees 'unspoiled' natural areas as inherently beautiful. A host of writers, poets and novelists have spoken of the Lakes in this way, with some of the most internationally famous English writers of the eighteenth and nineteenth centuries, such as William Wordsworth and John Ruskin, expressing the natural beauty of the Lakes and its people in their work. However, at the start of the eighteenth century, Daniel Defoe had seen this same landscape as 'the wildest, most barren and frightful' he had ever seen (Macnaghten and Urry 1998: 114). Thomas (1984) reports that during this period, wild nature was widely seen as unproductive, untamed and containing all manners of hidden dangers that were best avoided. 'Development' was then seen as necessary and beneficial rather than, as today, something to be protested and stopped. The discursive construction of the Lake District has clearly changed and rather than discussing the area as in need of development and cultivation, since the late eighteenth century the Lake District has come to be protected as embodying the English idea of natural beauty. Not only has the discourse on the Lakes changed, but so too has people's *sensual experience* of it. Viewing this landscape is now experienced as pleasant, satisfying and often, even emotionally moving. Other human senses are also involved. Hearing the sound of rivers and waterfalls, smelling the woods and flowers, touching the bark of old trees, all of these activities are involved in the re-configuration of 'the nature experience'. Of course it is not being suggested here that people did not hear, smell or touch natural objects in previous times. What has changed is the *meaning* of such experiences for modern people. Instead of interpreting these things as dirty, obnoxious and uncivilised, many natural objects are now routinely experienced as positive and life-affirming (Elias 2000 [1939]). Such practices suggest that rather than experiencing themselves as separate from and superior to the rest of nature, people are experiencing themselves and other humans as bound up with, and part of, nature. The concept of *space* also enters Macnaghten and Urry's analysis in the form of a discussion of 'walking practices' such as dog-walking around lakes and through forests and woods, which allows people to experience and perhaps discuss the natural sights and sounds in such environments. However, in the Lake District the practice of hill- or fell-walking has also become popular with tourists. Fell-walking makes a statement about the capacities of humans and their connection to the rest of nature and rather than seeing such activities as the exclusive preserve of experts and risk-takers, Macnaghten and Urry note that not only is fell-walking more common, but even climbing mountains such as Mount Everest, once thought only accessible to experienced mountaineers, is now on the itinerary of many Western tourists. Such spatial practices help to shape the experiences of people in such environments. One reason for this new appreciation is that people now see nature as an eternal and continuous feature that can be compared favourably with the transient, continually changing modern society. To climb the Lake District fells is to commune with traditional and timeless natural forces, and in this way the concept of *time* is brought into people's experience of nature. Hunter (1995) contends that the arguments of some conservationists in the Western Highlands of Scotland, which draw on the emotional pull of the beautiful barren mountainous scenery to make their conservationist case, fail to appreciate that for many indigenous Highlanders, such a landscape represents a depopulated and 'devastated countryside' in the wake of the elimination of the practice of crofting during the Highland clearances. The relatively new social practices of the mass tourist industry have helped to change the way that such landscapes are now appreciated and experienced.

What such an analysis shows is that all of the elements in Macnaghten and Urry's model come together, not simply through discourse or textual meanings, but via changing *social practices* that serve to alter dominant meanings and sensual experience, together with understandings and experiences of time, space and human nature. This means that environmental sociology needs to find ways of examining and getting at the sensual experiences of people as well as exploring what they say and do. Existing research methods such as attitude surveys can of course play a part, but clearly other methods will need to be developed to tap into the significant experiential dimension, perhaps drawing from methods more commonplace in other disciplines. The benefit of focusing on the constituent elements of social practices is that this effectively bypasses both realism and constructionism as distinct approaches to the study of environmental issues. We do not simply have to accept that nature speaks directly to society, nor is it necessary to claim that nature has no causal powers of its own, apart from those that humans give to it. Rather, the natural and the social are closely bound together within the same embodied social practices.

The second example of attempts to go beyond constructionism and realism comes from Alan Irwin's *Sociology and the Environment* (2001). This takes a somewhat different line, but nevertheless one that still takes us in a direction away from polarised alternatives. Irwin uses a sociology of scientific knowledge perspective as a guide to approaching environmental problems, arguing that most environmental problems are neither self evidently problems, environmental or otherwise, nor are they entirely social constructions. Rather, environmental issues have a hybrid or 'co-constructed' character that becomes clear during empirical research and challenges the social–natural dichotomy: 'Whilst it may be possible to maintain such a dichotomised approach at an abstracted level, such a dichotomy crumbles when confronted with the hybrid co-constructed character of social and environmental processes and practices' (Irwin 2001: 26). This is because unlike many other social problems, environmental issues involve understandings of non-human nature and these understandings are to a large extent dependent on scientific research and knowledge. Hence, sociologists need to explore these scientific understandings and their relationship to 'lay' understandings, which gives the sociology of scientific knowledge a more central role than other approaches allow for. Rather than focusing wholly on social practices, as do Macnaghten and Urry, Irwin's method involves looking at the way that hybrid environmental issues are co-constructed. Again, a specific instance of this will help to show why this approach could be effective.

Irwin makes central two elements that are not conventionally part of environmental sociological analyses. First, he argues that we need to investigate the institutions that provide the context or 'sites' in which environmental issues are defined and dealt with. This means that science, scientific knowledge *and* institutional regulatory regimes, factors largely tangential to social constructionist accounts, should all be important elements of environmental sociology. Secondly, Irwin argues that technologies and technological development must be analysed as part of our accounts, as it is through technological interventions that the society–nature relationship is mediated. One problem with environmentalist and radical ecological arguments is that they have tended to view all modern technologies as necessarily 'bad', given that all interventions into nature risk producing harmful unintended consequences. Yet this refusal to consider the relative merits of different forms of technology is not merely undifferentiated and overly idealistic, and therefore a rather blunt instrument, but also fails to understand that technological non-intervention is scarcely an option. All human societies, not just modern industrial capitalist ones, develop, create and use technologies in managing their relationships with non-human nature and embedded within these interventions are theories and forms of knowledge, scientific or otherwise.

Exploring hybrid environmental issues also promises to avoid the criticisms levelled at strict constructionism, by developing the concept of 'co-construction'. Co-construction refers to the social construction of both 'the social' and 'the natural'. Hence, investigating environmental issues involves studying the social and the natural together as part of the same 'nature–culture nexus' (Irwin 2001: 174). It is not simply that 'the social' constructs 'the natural', but the social also constructs the social. Hence a co-constructionist analysis bypasses the nature–society dualism (Demeritt 1998). In the analysis of environmental problems, a co-constructionist approach would not only ask some basic social constructionist questions to do with how nature is being discussed, written about and experienced, but it would also draw attention to the way that the social is being written about, experienced and discussed. In this way Irwin believes that the tired old dualism can be circumvented.

Drawing on the work of Latour (1992, 1999; Latour and Woolgar 1986), Irwin uses several examples to illustrate his central point that it has become almost impossible to neatly separate out what is social, scientific or natural in the analysis of any specific environmental issue. If we take the recent outbreak of Bovine Spongiform Encephalopathy (BSE) in the UK (and elsewhere), it may seem that this is a natural problem relating to disease in cattle, which has been identified through science and scientific methods but which had to be dealt with through the political process. However, even cows are not unproblematically 'natural', 'The modern cow is the product of generations of human-controlled cattle-breeding, feeding and housing' (Irwin 2001: 80) and is therefore clearly a social as well as a natural creature. Scientific understandings of BSE are similarly not unproblematic. The practice of science is of course a social activity and the reassurances of scientists that BSE will not cross the species barrier into the human population have been received by the public with varying degrees of scepticism, depending on who delivers the message and how close to government scientists they are seen to be. As Irwin (ibid.: 133) puts this, '"*Science*" *cannot then be counterposed to* "*Society*", *since this is to ignore the social construction of both these categories* [original emphasis].' In cases such as BSE, pesticide use, nuclear energy and many others, we have to accept that the taken-for-granted separation of nature and society does not apply. Such environmental issues are at root, hybrids of nature, science and society, and this calls into question not just the legitimate role of sociologists but also the disciplinary boundaries of science and the ability of specific, compartmentalised disciplines properly to understand environmental issues. It is unlikely that any single discipline would have enough expertise to arrive at a comprehensive explanation of the BSE problem.

Nevertheless, Irwin proposes a specific role for sociologists. This is to open up environmental issues to public scrutiny and thereby bring more democratic accountability to the search for solutions. Inevitably this makes for a critical sociology of the environment and as he says (2001: 134) 'Ultimately, the sociological treatment advocated in this book stresses that environmental decisions are, at their core, a matter of social choice. Rather than limiting or undermining environmental discussion, a sociological approach should shed light on current institutional and technological assumptions.' Now, what is striking about the advocacy of this sociological role is its similarity to that proposed in various social constructionist accounts. Like Hannigan (1995), Macnaghten and Urry (1998) and Burningham and Cooper (1999), in practice it is much less clear how 'the natural' plays a significant part in the co-construction of environmental problems. Instead, what comes through more clearly is the way that 'the social' constructs both the social and the natural, making it very difficult to see how 'nature' plays any significant role in the process. What we see much more clearly are 'contested natures', which are produced through the activities of social and political processes within human societies. In short, despite attempts to move beyond currently polarised positions, both Irwin's and Macnaghten and Urry's theoretical perspectives seem to fall much closer to social constructionism than perhaps they would want to admit.

Conclusion

In recent years sociologists have rediscovered nature as a significant source of contestation and dispute in society. The environmental movement has been instrumental in bringing about this general reorientation, and depending on theoretical perspective this discovery has been seen either as allowing sociology to tackle increasingly vital issues or as an irrelevance to the proper task of the discipline. It has also led to a highly polarised debate and some acerbic exchanges that are understandable given the stakes involved, but which may seem far from constructive. In more recent years however, there have been some hopeful signs that the worst of this is now over as evidenced by several sociological attempts to move beyond polarised camps into more fruitful theoretical positions. What the latter have demonstrated is that sociological analysis can be creative, informative and the basis for empirical research programmes that can add something genuinely interesting to debates around society and nature.

However, these alternatives remain closer to the constructionist pole than the realist one and do not really build in the effectivity of the natural world on social life. It is interesting to observe that despite Macnaghten and Urry's own clearly expressed opposition to simple social constructionism, Irwin (ibid.: 22) labels their approach as 'constructivist', albeit of a different kind to Hannigan's. Similarly, Irwin's own 'co-constructionist' position 'owes a major debt to social constructionism' (Irwin 2001: 173) rather than realism, despite the attempt to build upon constructionist logic in new ways. In this sense the critical realists seem to be genuinely approaching environmental issues in ways that diverge from the sociological mainstream, though of course how successful this perspective is for sociological practice has yet to be clearly demonstrated. Nonetheless, what this conclusion suggests is that, rather than being a 'dull debate', the social constructionist–critical realist debate was and is an absolutely necessary one for sociologists to engage in if the discipline is to have useful things to say about environmental issues. It cannot simply be wished away. What seems likely in the short term is that constructionists and realists will continue to generate alternative research programmes and consequently differing understandings of both the society–nature relationship and the environmental problems themselves. But in the longer term, perhaps we will see more research which will bridge the divide between these alternatives and thus bring environmental issues closer to the sociological mainstream.

4 The Ecocentric Challenge for Society and Sociology

Because sociology is arguably the most institutionally porous of social science disciplines, the substantive concerns of social and political movements tend to find their way into the discipline relatively easily. This has been true of all major twentieth-century social movements in the West. However, there has been something of a time lag in the case of environmentalism with the substantive claims of environmentalists and radical ecologists finding their way into sociological discussions only in the last 10 years or so. This chapter maintains that the primary explanation for this delay lies in the specific nature of the challenge that environmental arguments and ideas pose to the discipline of sociology, which differs in important respects from the substantive issues raised by other social movements. In fact, this chapter suggests that in their strongest incarnations, environmentalism and radical ecology pose a challenge to the continuation of sociology as previously practised. This is because Green politics advocates a fundamental reorientation in social attitudes towards the place of human societies in the wider natural environment, a reorientation that moves in the direction of 'ecocentrism' and away from 'homocentrism' (Merchant 1992). For many sociologists, importing such a reorientation into the discipline is problematic and threatens to dilute the originality of the distinct sociological perspective. To understand why this is so, it is first necessary to grasp the character of the ecocentric perspective.

Ecocentrism

The Promethean 'technocentric' humanist case made by Gellner (1986: 39) is that 'Mankind is irreversibly committed to industrial

76

society and therefore based on cumulative science and technology. Only this can sustain present and anticipated population levels. No return to agrarian society is possible, without mass starvation and poverty.' Once industrialism unleashes technological development to support population growth, it becomes very difficult to see how it could be stopped (Landes 1969). James Lovelock, whose 'Gaian' ideas have a somewhat ambiguous relationship to ecocentrism as they may support more technological intervention not less, echoes this view (Joseph 1990). Lovelock (1979: 121) has suggested for example that, '... given wise husbandry, twice the present human population of the world could be supported without uprooting other species, our partners in Gaia, from their natural habitats. It would be a grave mistake, however, to think that this could be achieved without a high degree of technology, intelligently organized and applied'. Here, Lovelock's perspective does not necessitate a new philosophy of nature or attempts to wrangle with the problems of the 'intrinsic value' of natural environments.

For Greens however, modern industrial societies, whether capitalist, socialist, communist or some mixture of these, alter the traditional human–nature relationship through their focus on expansive economic growth which reduces nature to raw materials or resources 'to be used' and ultimately 'used up'. And though all societies live from nature, the industrial technologies of modern societies allow them to exploit natural resources much more efficiently and systematically, thus speeding up the degradation of nature. In the quest for economic and material development, the problem of nature has been all but lost sight of. Nature is seen simply as the backdrop for human activity, presenting no limits to what can be achieved, given human ingenuity and technological advances. This attitude has often been referred to as 'anthropocentrism', the placing of human beings at the centre of moral concern and valuation, even if this is at the expense of the rest of nature. Ehrenfield (1981: 16) puts this clearly, arguing that

> The principle humanist assumption, which embraces all of our dealings with the environment, and some other issues as well, is very simple. It says: all problems are soluble. In order to make its connection with humanism clear, just add the two words that are implicit; it becomes: All problems are soluble by people.

Anthropocentrism means that human welfare takes precedence over the welfare of other species, a position Singer (1975) refers to as 'speciesism', a concept that extends the modern rights discourse beyond the human boundary, which nevertheless remains controversial (Benton 1988). In addition, 'human welfare' can be defined in several ways, even to suggest that looking after the welfare of other species itself contributes towards human well-being. Even so, from an anthropocentric position, wherever there is a conflict between human and non-human interests, it is specifically human welfare that must come first (Goodin 1992). Such a position reflects a widespread form of common sense humanism.

In opposition to anthropocentrism and technocentrism is 'ecocentrism', the attempt to place nature 'writ large' at the centre of moral concern, politics and scientific study. This is justified because 'there is no valid basis to the belief that humans are the pinnacle of evolution and the sole locus of value and meaning in the world. Instead, ecocentric theorists adopt an ethical position that regards all of the various and multilayered parts of the biotic community as valuable for their own sake' (Eckersley 1997: 28). The originator of the 'Gaia Hypothesis', Lovelock (1979, 1986, 1988), argues that the idea of a human stewardship of nature is unrealistic, since in the long run 'Gaia' – his name for the global self-regulating system of nature – is in control. This is why many Greens have argued that world population levels need to be controlled and ultimately reduced if sustainable communities are to be created because, 'The explosion of human numbers is the greatest long-term threat to the future of human and non-human inhabitants of the earth. While nuclear arsenals present grave potential dangers, the predominant crisis of overpopulation is with us today' (Irvine and Ponton 1988: 17). Again, this is an issue (like the notion of an ecological crisis itself) which has been part of Green thinking since the 1970s, and continues to exercise concern. There is a clear echo here of Malthus's (1798) fears of overpopulation and consequent food scarcity, which formed part of the background for the introduction of the new English Poor Law in 1834. Although the Poor Law was not directly couched in Malthusian terms, '...many of its defenders were 'Malthusians' who wanted restraint on family size to be enforced in workhouses...' (Briggs 1984: 338). Ross (2000) has also examined the way that Malthusian ideas are often used to justify new technological interventions such as the genetic modification of foods, on the grounds that these will solve food scarcity problems and assist developing countries to become more independent. The concern with population is an example of the shift in emphasis which lies at the heart of the ecocentric reorientation.

Ecocentrism undermines the optimistic modernist assumption that humans can concentrate on rationally building society without worrying about natural limits, summarised in French Enlightenment philosopher Condorcet's (cited in Lively 1966: 75) comment that '...we have good reasons for believing that nature has set no limits to our hopes'. For some, the ecocentric re-introduction of the Malthusian idea of natural limits marks it out as a postmodern phenomenon, part of the wide-ranging attack on scientific certainties and continuing modernisation (Hannigan 1995: Chapter 10). However, the situation is rather more complex because the idea of grounding human beings in nature based on an intuitive grasp of their natural affinities sits uneasily with the typical postmodern suspicion of foundations and essences, and the possibility of unmediated access to 'reality'. Nonetheless, the identification of nature as a reality set against the artificiality of human constructions is a key motivating force for ecocentric theorists. Edward Goldsmith's conceptualisation of the society/nature relationship makes a distinction between the 'real' world of nature and the 'surrogate' world of human products and consumer goods. Goldsmith (1988: 185) sees nature as the ultimate source of all value, arguing that 'If the world were a lifeless waste, as is the moon, there could be no industrialization.... It is the biosphere, in fact – the real world – that is being industrialized.' The problem is that the aggressive building up of the surrogate world takes place at the expense of the real world via the extraction of resources and the return of waste from production processes as environmental pollution (Jones 1987). The consequences of this are the satisfaction of needs but the destruction of wilderness (Fraser-Darling 1971). This kind of argument is widespread amongst ecological radicals, though unfortunately Goldsmith is still working with the same society/nature dualism which ecocentrics claim to be transcending and which they identify as a major source of our ecological problems. Perhaps this just shows how deep are the roots of dualistic thinking embedded in modern societies (Horigan 1989; Szerszynski 1996).

It has become commonplace to state that environmentalism and Green politics is characterised by ideological diversity when compared to other political ideologies, though this is far from clear, at least to me. Anyone who has studied the sectarian politics of the socialist and communist left would presumably be able to reach a similar conclusion. Bennie *et al.* (1995: 219) note that 'Any student of green politics quickly realises that 'greenness' itself has become a major conflict point in the politics of green semantics. The many shades of green may express themselves openly in different factions of the green movement, vociferously berating each other – often in terms of the other side being not green enough.' This idea of 'shades of green' identifies factions, ideological disputes and diversity as a central feature of environmentalism and Green politics. However, there is no clear evidence that there are any more shades of Green than shades of red or even blue and the temptation to focus on whatever diversity and fragmentation exists may be more than a little misleading. This is especially so if it ignores obvious areas of fundamental value agreement. At the core of Green politics is a concerted attempt to present ecocentric thinking as an alternative to all 'human-centred' or 'anthropocentric' modes of thought. The ecocentric perspective takes as its founding principle that human societies are embedded in, part of and dependent on a global or 'planetary' natural world or 'biosphere' in which natural forces largely outside human control are operative. Pepper (1996: 329) defines ecocentrism as, 'a mode of thought which regards humans as subject to ecological and systems laws', whilst Eckersley (1997: 49) adds that 'Ecocentrism is based on an ecologically informed philosophy of internal relatedness, according to which all organisms are not simply interrelated with their environment but also constituted by those very environmental interrelationships.' The relational ecocentric perspective also provides a position from which a critique of conservationism, preservationism and other types of 'shallow' or reform environmentalism' can be launched. This ecocentric orientation provides eco-activists with a shared sense of identity and purpose in spite of their disagreements. Ecocentrism therefore foregrounds the question of what constitutes the 'correct' relationship between human societies and the rest of the non-human natural world on which they depend and is concerned with the organisation of social relationships. As shorthand I will refer to all attempts to theorise this relationship as 'the problem of nature', a problem that clearly applies in sociology.

Ecocentric 'Deep Ecologists' have tried to demonstrate that nature has 'intrinsic value', value in its own right, independent of all human valuations. A love of nature, and ideas of the equal worth of natural entities, can easily lead to the view that the value of these entities lies in themselves, in their own properties, rather than emanating from the human mind. This idea is found in the late eighteenth- and early nineteenth-century English romantic poets such as William Wordsworth, William Blake, Samuel Coleridge and Percy Shelley, who sought to expand the boundaries of morality beyond human beings. 'Nature has her proper interest; and he will know what it is, who believes and feels, that every thing has a life of its own' (Coleridge cited in Thomas 1984: 91). This idea is also evident in the American transcendentalist philosophers, for example in Ralph Waldo Emerson's essay on *Nature* (1836), in which he says 'Such is the constitution of all things...that the primary forms, as the sky, the mountain, the tree, the animal, give us a delight in and for themselves' (cited in Pepper 1996: 199). Intrinsic value theories are part of the attempt by deep ecologists today to produce a Green value theory that can be used to give the defence of nature a firmer philosophical basis, but they are not strictly 'new'. Similarly, the current 'transpersonal ecology' strand (Fox 1995: Chapter 5) which encourages the development of an 'eco-logical self' through attempts to experience ourselves as part of nature, bound inseparably with it, is also prefigured in the ideas of Henry David Thoreau. He also expressed a desire to commune with nature, 'I to be nature looking into nature with such easy sympathy as the blue-eyed grass looks in the face of the sky' (cited in Worster 1985: 78). So, it is clear that romantic-inspired 'eco-centric' ideas have a long history, but what might mark out the contemporary period as new could be the extension of such ideas and experiences to the wider population, thus enabling a previously subordinated side of modern culture, its romantic side, to become dominant (Eder 1993: Chapter 7). This question is very much a central one at present though the evidence from attitude surveys and environmental organisation memberships is rather ambiguous.

The challenge of ecocentrism to the existing humanistic political ideologies of socialism, marxism, liberalism and conservatism is clear. As long as political ideologies and scientific disciplines construct theories which take the natural world as the backdrop to human activity, they will be deemed unsatisfactory by ecocentric theorists because they place no value on nature in itself. A similar criticism can be levelled at conservationism, in so far as its arguments are couched in terms of the value of conservation and preservation *for* human beings. This kind of 'enlightened self-interest' is ultimately ineffective though because if self-interest can be shown to lie elsewhere, then an attitude of care towards the natural world will be sidelined.

Ecocentrism is clearly an approach to theory and political activity that marks it out from other political ideologies and we should not lose sight of this fundamental difference, despite its internal diversity. An ecocentric orientation provides the centre for a new political ideology that cuts loose from modern ideologies and carves out a new space, partly in opposition to them (Heywood 1992; Dobson [1990] 2001). However, radical versions of ecological politics also reject conservationism and reform environmentalism, as they stop short of uncovering the real causes of environmental damage. Greens trace the real causes of environmental degradation to modernity's break with nature via classical scientific methods, unsustainable urbanisation and technological interventions. It is important to reiterate though, as we saw in Chapter 2, that the radical ecological perspective is not firmly institutionally embedded in conservationist and environmental organisations, though this does not preclude that individuals joining such organisations may hold to an ecocentric orientation. Empirical evidence in this area is rather sketchy and more research would clarify the overall picture. Bennie *et al.*'s (1995) recent study of the British Green Party upholds the contention that a majority of its members do share an ecocentric perspective and support more radical Green policies. However, the British Green Party is not representative of the wider environmental movement, being a special case both in organisational and in political terms. We should avoid rushing to the conclusion that conservationism and reform environmentalism are being radicalised, as the concern with nature broadens out towards concern for a reconstructed global concept of a planetary nature.

Some commentators have pointed out that the values, ideas and proposals for change of contemporary ecocentrics have quite a long history, traceable at least to eighteenth-century romanticism (Worster 1985; Eder 1990, 1993), nineteenth-century utopian socialism (Pepper 1984, 1996: Chapter 4; Gould 1988) and even to twentieth-century nationalism, right-wing politics and fascist movements (Bodeman 1985/86; Conford 1988; Bramwell 1989). In Anna Bramwell's (1989) *Ecology in the 20th Century*, some direct connections are made between ecological 'primitivism' and far right politics including that of German National Socialism. Such connections form around the ideas of defence of the land or national soil, a bioregional identification and the notion of biologically consistent 'races'. Whilst most commentators note that, in practice, recent ecological politics has tended to be a politics much closer to the left than the right, Bramwell's history is a useful reminder of the way that 'nature' can be appropriated by political ideologies of many kinds. The appeal to nature as support both for right- and left-wing politics seems to show that no consensus exists on the political import of knowledge about natural processes or of giving nature's 'needs' priority (however these are perceived). It also implies that a politics of nature is just as likely to be a politics of the right as that of the left, and although it is easy to see contemporary Green politics as closer to the political left, particularly in the German case (Galtung 1986; Fogt 1989), affinities with the political right can also be found in some of the authoritarian solutions proffered by Ehrlich (1968), Borgstrom (1969), Ophuls (1977) and Hardin (1977), who argued in different ways that some Western liberties may have to be sacrificed if overpopulation and resource depletion are to be tackled. Hardin (1968: 1247) suggested that 'The only way we can preserve and nurture other and more precious freedoms is by relinquishing the freedom to breed, and that very soon.' Again though, acknowledging the ambivalent political character of ecocentrism should not obscure the essential difference between anthropocentric and ecocentric orientations, which marks out ecocentrism as the centre for a new political ideology. As Pepper notes, an ecocentric orientation is a fundamental constitutive feature of what Dobson ([1990] 2001) describes as the political ideology of 'ecologism' and we must now look more closely at the main features of this perspective in the current period.

Ecologism and political ideologies

If ecocentrism is a mode of thought that provides a coherent worldview, then its political corollary is ecologism, arguably a new political ideology (Hayward 1998; Smith 1998; Dobson [1990] 2001).

Dobson's *Green Political Thought* ([1990] 2001) has become a key reference point for students of Green politics, as he makes it clear that 'Unlike any other ideology, ecologism is concerned in a foundational way with the relationship between human beings and their natural environment' (Dobson [1990] 2001: 200) or the problem of nature. For Dobson, this specifically Green political ideology, ecologism, could not have existed before the late 1960s and early 1970s. In part, this is because the kinds of evidence drawn on by Greens have only become available since that time. What he means by this is that '...the gloomy future predicted for us [by ecologists] would have no persuasive purchase if damage to ecosystems had not reached levels that can sensibly be argued to be globally disruptive' (Dobson [1990] 2001: 33). Scientific research into global warming for instance has helped to legitimise the arguments of Greens and to generate a supportive cultural climate for an ecological ideology, which, without such support, would have been literally unintelligible. It has often been said that the origins of ecologism can be found in Carson's influential book, *Silent Spring* (1962), which drew attention to the ecological dangers of the widespread use of modern chemical pesticides. There were other factors such as the use and testing of nuclear weapons (Schell 1982), concerns about the long-term consequences of rising population levels (particularly in developing countries) and worries over the depletion of natural resources, all of which fed into the formation of Green parties and new movement organisations (Atkinson 1991). Dobson ([1990] 2001: 35) argues however that it is only in the 1970s that a new ideology becomes visible so that '...in 1962, ecologism (and therefore the possibility of being Green) did not exist, and that Rachel Carson's book and the period in which it was written are best viewed as part of the preconditions for ecologism'.

Ecologism really comes into being with the publication of the 'limits to growth' thesis of Meadows *et al.* (1974) in which the authors' computer modelling and extrapolation of current trends of resource use pointed to a societal collapse in the twenty-first century. Dobson ([1990] 2001: 80) suggests that the concept of absolute natural limits to ever expanding economic growth is the fundamental principle or 'insurmountable fact of life' at the heart of ecologism. The 'Limits' report for the Club of Rome provided the raw material for Edward Goldsmith's *Ecologist* journal's *Blueprint for Survival* (1972), which the British Green Party adopted as its manifesto. The point of trying to locate the moment at which ecological ideas begin to crystallise into a new ideology is to demonstrate that the Green movement today is not simply a modern version of old ideas, but introduces something genuinely new into social and political theorising. Although Dobson is right to point out that Green ideas have emerged in a social context different from that of earlier periods, this does not mean that ecologism forms a coherent political ideology with an identifiable social constituency of support. Indeed, Greens often argue that the issues that concern them are of concern to everyone, and that it is precisely this universalist character which makes the Green position so distinctive. It is also clear that there is a concerted effort across several academic disciplines to develop a coherent and comprehensive perspective as the basis for progressive politics and the extent of this very attempt is a new feature in the present period.

Because ecocentrism defines itself in opposition to anthropocentric social and political theories, progressive and humanistic social movements find it difficult to reach an accommodation with it. And whilst romantic back-to-nature ideas in the late nineteenth century were part of anarchist and utopian socialist movements (Prynn 1976; Gould 1988), in contemporary ecologism there is a serious attempt to devise a political theory which effectively breaks with humanism. Some links have been uncovered between ecologism and the 'new left', for example (Boggs 1986a,b; Fogt 1989), but a thoroughgoing ecocentrism prioritises the protection of natural diversity and the integrity of nature over social class-based demands for wealth redistribution. Martell (1994) argues that although ecologism adds something new to the political analysis of modern societies, in its own terms it is incapable of prescribing the necessary social arrangements for an ecologically sustainable society. It is possible to try to generate an ecocentric orientation to politics, but much more difficult to see what a form of social organisation based on ecocentric principles would look like. Martell (1994: 160) believes that, '...ecology cannot provide a new paradigm through which a political theory can be constructed on green grounds. Dealing with environmental issues involves drawing on old conservative, liberal, socialist and feminist analyses'. This may well be true, but even so, is hardly unusual. Feminist movements had to draw on liberal and socialist analyses in order to make their own case. What this means is that the field of social movements and of politics, more broadly, is a relational field (Mannheim 1945). Political ideologies and social movements devise their perspectives in relation to others, and they do not emerge from nothing or exist in a vacuum.

The response of socialists and marxists to the emergence of Ecologism and Green political parties was initially quite hostile. Enzensberger's (1974) influential essay accepted that ecocentrism had the potential to attract a mass following but noted that the ecologists' analysis was extremely confused, lacking the grounding of a social-class perspective. A further difference is that from a socialist or Marxist perspective, ecocentrism appears anti-humanist, prioritising the needs of 'nature as a whole'. For socialists like Weston (1986: 3), 'To think that whooping cranes are important (possibly more so than people) one has to be free of the more pressing human problems like that of poverty... [W]hich is why green politics remains a middle-class phenomenon.' The lack of a class analysis leads to the mistaken belief that the ecological problematic holds equal relevance for all social groups, but this ignores the differential experience of environmental degradation, and different ways of defining environmental problems. Greens offer no consistent, sustained critique of the 'environmental' problems of urban areas and the inner cities, for example. Weston argues that the emergence of the Greens is the latest manifestation of a populist political tradition, which gains strength when 'a previously independent group is undergoing fundamental change'. In this sense, Green politics is not novel. It is seen as closely related to the inclusion of 'non-productive' public-sector workers, such as teachers, social workers, doctors and other public-sector professionals within the commercial constraints of capitalism from which they had previously been relatively free. This then feeds into the typically populist recourse to nature as the 'final trump card' (ibid.: 27) in support of Green arguments for de-industrialisation. This holds out no possibility of developing into a transformative mass movement, but merely reflects the ideals of a specific, implicitly reactionary class fraction, the 'new' middle class. Weston has writers such as Goldsmith in his sights here. Goldsmith (1988: Chapter 7) advocates de-urbanisation, the phasing out of consumer products and labour-saving technologies and a programme of re-education. On the latter, he says that, 'Reform of the educational system would also be required to assure the general adoption of the new world-view' (ibid.: 207). Such solutions have an uncomfortably authoritarian feel, especially for those who may not wish to 'adopt the new world view'. An appropriate characterisation of radicals such as Gold-smith might be to see them as 'extreme moderates' (Chisholm 1972: 76), demanding urgent action whilst seeing themselves as simply advocates of 'common-sense' solutions.

More recently, after surveying such ecological political strategies, Martell (1994: 199) declares, '. . . I reject capitalist and laissez-faire solutions to ecological problems and find myself coming more and more back to socialist political economy. I think state intervention, global co-ordination and political action by the green movement are necessary for resolving such problems'. Of course, radical Greens favour decentralised solutions as offering more opportunities for participatory forms of democracy. Pepper's (1991) study of Green communes aimed to gain an insight into whether such experiments offered the potential to transform society in an ecological direction through networks of small-scale alternative ways of living. Although Pepper (ibid.: 219) reports a continuing and strong Green belief system, in practice, '. . . the drift is in the opposite direction, towards becoming part of the society they were originally set up to oppose'. Clearly, such a conclusion raises significant questions about Green strategies for change.

Nevertheless, by the 1980s, some socialists also saw the potential of bringing ecological ideas into a productive alliance with socialism in order to develop a thoroughgoing 'eco-socialist' perspective which concentrates on the way that capitalism destroys local, national and global environments of both human and natural kinds, rather than accepting the Greens' narrow focus on non-human nature (Stretton 1976; Bahro 1982; Steward 1985a,b; Wolf 1986; Ryle 1988). It was even observed that some of the themes emerging within ecocentric thought had a striking resemblance to aspects of early British socialism. Edward Thompson (in Bahro 1982: 8) noted that the position of the German Green activist Rudolf Bahro was '. . . fresh and original. And yet, in a surprising way, it is traditional also. . . . I was astonished to find, on page after page, a reincarnation in modern dress of some of the essential preoccu-pations of William Morris in his socialist writings of the 1880s'. This was before the labour and trades union movement moved towards practical reforms of the existing capitalist system (Przeworski 1986). Similarly in the 1990s, the World Development Movement and environmental justice movements in the USA began to connect environmental degradation, poverty and development, thus laying the foundations for bringing together social movements of different kinds. Notwithstanding such collaborative attempts, the eco-socialist project runs into severe difficulties with strategies for change. Many Greens have proposed a form of 'ecological enlightenment' through education as the best way to achieve lasting changes in values and thereby the treatment of the natural world. What will bring about this experience is unclear, though some have argued that only when environmental damage has advanced to crisis proportions will the non-committed public be receptive to ecologism. Despite some commentators' assertions that the catastrophist environmental writing of the early 1970s was a brief transitional phase, it is quite clear that contemporary ecologism (and many sociological studies too) is still replete with references to 'the ecological crisis'. Therefore, the perceived crisis is still a major motivation for political activists. Goldsmith (1988: 216–17) argues that in the face of increasing ecological damage, 'At some point, panic will set in and people will grope about frantically for an alternative set of solutions. The most attractive is likely to be the most radical – the one that provides the best vehicle for expressing the reaction to the values of industrialism. The ecological philosophy best answers these requirements.' Bahro (1986: 98) arrived at a similar conclusion, 'The accumulation of spiritual forces ... will at a particular point in time which can't be foreseen exceed a threshold size. Such a 'critical mass', once accumulated, then acquires under certain circumstances a transformative influence over the whole society.' Pepper (1986: 125) argues that this amounts to no strategy at all: '... these sentiments are largely hogwash, for they presume that there can be a miraculous creation of the ecologically-conscious human being via some cathartic, unspecified revolutionary experience'.

So, although socialists and radical ecologists acknowledge the need for co-operation, it is difficult to see how this will happen without compromising the ecocentric orientation of radical Greens. If 'ecologism' really does constitute a new political ideology then any movement towards an eco-socialist position represents the unnecessary assimilation of ecologism into an older, anthropocentric ideology. More significantly, the basis of ecologism's originality is, as the term suggests, the privileging of nature's ecology in any analysis or political project, as opposed to the anthropocentric or human welfare orientation of socialism. Differences of this kind lie at the heart of Eckersley's (1990) ecocentric critique of the work of Jurgen Habermas. She argues that his emancipatory project fails the ecocentric test because it restricts 'emancipation' to human beings. Because political ecological ideas emerged outside existing socialist and labour movements, ecocentrism has become an article of faith and a crucial belief system differentiating Greens from all forms of 'grey' politics. However, this worldview is still far from a socialist class analysis.

What should be clear by now is that ecocentrism, as a new worldview, and ecologism, as a new political ideology, throw down a challenge for existing humanistic perspectives and established politics. Although by no means dominant within environmental movements, such ideas force progressive political movements to take account of their critique of 'grey' politics and, in doing so, to re-evaluate their own taken-for-granted assumptions about human beings and their relationship to the natural world. Mark J. Smith (1998: 99) argues that if a form of 'ecological citizenship' is developed then it will mark a radical change in attitudes towards future generations and practices based on these. He suggests that '... the adoption of an ethical standpoint which embraces ecocentrism involves a shift in social and political thought to a new 'politics of obligation'.

What we need to address next is how sociology has responded to the challenge posed by such ideas. Once it is accepted that nature is becoming a central concern in the wider society, two sociological responses suggest themselves. One is to allow the substantive concerns of environmental and Green movements into the discipline, and this response has produced attempts to generate an 'environmental sociology'. The second is to re-examine existing theoretical traditions to explore what resources are available within the discipline for the analysis of environmental issues. This can be called a sociology of the environment. Both alternatives have produced some useful research and we will see the outline of each in turn.

Environmental sociology

One possibility is to work towards an 'environmental sociology' which would take seriously the scientific findings of biology, ecology and the natural sciences more generally, building the theoretical yield from these into the fundamental knowledge base of sociology itself. This is the approach taken by environmental sociologists in the United States who accept the concept of natural laws and natural limits to human action. This approach has been productive and encourages interdisciplinary work across the social and natural sciences, providing a useful bridge between disciplines. Of course the danger for sociology is that disciplines do not stand in an equal relationship to each other, having developed and become institutionalised at different times. Amongst the hierarchy of scientific establishments (Elias 1982), the natural sciences clearly stand higher than the social sciences so that any accommodation between them is likely to be on terms dictated by the more powerful group, leaving sociological knowledge gains at risk. It is widely accepted that sociology has struggled to establish itself both institutionally and in terms of its distinct subject matter. The sociological revolution in knowledge in Europe in the post-Enlightenment period constituted a genuinely new departure in the available stock of knowledge concerned with interdependent human beings and their lives together (Kilminster 1998). Simplifying somewhat, the concept of 'society', which was developed to express the fundamental basis of the new discipline, had to be fought for against other disciplines working from a more involved perspective (political economy), a more individualistic perspective (mainstream psychology), a more abstract perspective (philosophy) and a more idiographic perspective (mainstream history). The early sociologists' attempts to found a new discipline had to be concerned to establish the social as a level of reality in its own right. Understandably therefore, sociologists can be expected to be wary of all attempts to backtrack on this clear gain in human knowledge.

Nonetheless, in the early 1970s, Riley Dunlap and colleagues working in the USA came to see existing sociological approaches to the study of nature–society relations as inadequate, having failed to integrate knowledge from the biological sciences, particularly ecology, into their analyses. Instead, sociology 'was virtually blind to the biophysical environment' (Dunlap 2002: 346) and seemed to suffer from an adherence to what Catton (1978) and Dunlap (1980) called the 'Human Exemptionalism Paradigm' (HEP), which did not allow for an environmental sociology. As a paradigm, the HEP guided approaches to research and dominated the teaching and training of sociologists, propagating a kind of worldview or vision of social reality. This worldview infused all sociological traditions and had little to say about nature–society relations, taking for granted that the role of the sociologist was to explore social not natural relations. Not to do so was to run the risk of being accused of reductionism. However, this also led to the misguided view that human societies were, to all intents and purposes, exempt from biological and ecological laws that applied to all other forms of life. Catton and Dunlap argued that they are not and therefore the HEP needed to be transcended. Instead, they proposed a shift towards a 'New Ecological Paradigm' (NEP) that assumed human societies are dependent on functioning ecosystems and therefore sociologists needed to re-examine the fundamental assumptions of their discipline.

What Catton and Dunlap proposed was an environmental sociology that would not necessarily replace existing theoretical perspectives but would demand that they are modified to incorporate the NEP. One example of this is that marxist theorists have looked at the realist underpinnings of Marx's method as a way of avoiding strict constructionism and bringing the reality of nature's forces and powers back into the picture. In the same way, Murphy (1994a,b, 1997, 2002) has interpreted Max Weber's perspective as a form of 'ecological materialism'. These explorations are exactly what Catton and Dunlap had in mind when they proposed moving sociology away from an exemptionalist paradigm and although still relatively underdeveloped in terms of empirical research, in future they may well produce ongoing research programmes. It is clear therefore that environmental sociology will not resolve theoretical disagreements but may indeed simply reproduce them. Provided that the reality of ecological laws is accepted, this would not undermine the environmental sociology project.

In a recent assessment of the trajectory of environmental sociology, Dunlap (2002) suggests that there has been much progress. First, environmental sociology has become a recognised sociological specialism in many parts of the world and continues to stimulate research. Secondly, some version of the NEP is now widespread in sociological work on the environment showing that the call to abandon the HEP has not gone unheeded. Thirdly, the study of environmental issues has made its way into mainstream sociology and social theory, ensuring that the environment will not be ignored or taken as unimportant. Dunlap cites this as the most significant result of the push for an environmental sociology. This assessment, though not exactly inaccurate, is nevertheless perhaps too optimistic. Environmental sociology has certainly become a legitimate specialism, but as such it has not really made an impact on standard sociological subjects such as the study of social class, 'race' and racism, gender relations, crime and deviance and so on. Environmental sociology is still very much restricted to the study of society–nature relations and clearly identified environmental issues rather than transforming mainstream sociology. The NEP is certainly prominent amongst such environmental sociologists, but again it is not clear how far mainstream sociology has moved towards this paradigm. Finally, social theory does routinely discuss environmental issues and to that extent the latter are now part of mainstream sociology. However, this fact alone does not support the contention that Catton and Dunlap's arguments have received widespread support. Indeed the reverse may well be the case. What might be happening is that we now have a sociology of the environment rather than an environmental sociology, and if so, then the proposed 'greening' of sociology around the adoption of a NEP may have failed.

An alternative approach therefore would involve working towards a 'sociology of the environment'. This would mean bringing a sociological perspective to bear on environmental issues and concerns, showing how these always involve scientific findings, institutional regulatory regimes, belief systems and changing sensibilities. The benefit of this approach would be that it takes the establishment of sociology for granted and proceeds from the idea that natural science is of course itself a social activity whose knowledge cannot be taken at face value, but has to be subjected to critical evaluation. A danger here, though, is that the effectivity of the non-human natural world, the very issue around which environmental movements have organised, could be lost.

In assessing whether we are moving towards a sociology of the environment, it is important to recognise that there have been several attempts to re-examine existing sociological theories and traditions. This has begun in relation to the work of Marx (Parsons 1977; Grundmann 1991; Dickens 1992, 1996, 2002; Benton 1996a,b; O'Connor 1998; Foster 2000), Durkheim (Turner 1996, 1999; Catton 1998, 2002) and Weber (West 1985; Murphy 1994a,b, 1997, 2002). Dickens (1992) points out that other figures outside the classical sociological canon such as Herbert Spencer, Ferdinand Tönnies, the Chicago School and Talcott Parsons also had interesting things to say about modern societies and the problem of nature, and we might also expect these to be re-examined in the light of the ecological problematic. Goldblatt (1996) argues that in the early sociological ideas of August Comte and Herbert Spencer, sociology was seen as subordinate to biology, reflected in their use of biological metaphors and analogies in the representation of social relations. For Spencer and other social evolutionists in particular, evolution and natural selection potentially provided unifying ideas for the social and natural sciences, though as Dickens points out (1992: 20–7) Spencer's theorising began *before* Darwin's *Origin of Species* had been published, hence he cannot simply be accused of trying simplistically to apply biological theories to studying society. In this early sociology it seemed self-evident that the study of society could not be divorced from biology as human beings were still governed to some extent by biological laws.

However, in the latter part of the nineteenth century, the gloomy prediction of Malthus (1970) that food production could not keep pace with an expanding population, seemed to recede with rapid industrialisation and economic growth (Goldblatt 1996). Thus in the work of Marx, Durkheim and Weber and their followers, the focus moved to studying social relations and society with little or no reference to biology. From this starting point the study of sociology and biology, society and nature would take place in increasingly separate academic disciplines. This does not mean that Marx, Durkheim and Weber had nothing to say on environmental issues, but as Catton and Dunlap argue, these never became central to their theoretical endeavours. Hence recent scholarship, which attempts to extract such a theme more explicitly, reflects the structure and concerns of contemporary sociological theory rather than that of the late nineteenth century. It may well be possible to make use of Marx's 'critical realist' method, Durkheim's flawed concept of 'organic solidarity' as a form of mutualism (Catton 2002) and Weber's incipient 'ecological materialism' (Murphy 2002) as routes from sociology into environmental issues. However, for some, there are good reasons to think that such a project will yield strictly limited useful results. Nineteenth-century sociological theory drew on the existing biological knowledge of the time, which by contemporary standards was itself limited and flawed and this means that returning to the classics may be a fruitless enterprise. In addition, such sociological theory was not devised to explore and understand how environmental problems are generated, but to try to explain how modern societies had been able to *break with* the environmental restrictions of traditional societies (Goldblatt 1996: 4). The problem of explaining modernity and the revolutionary productivity of capitalism were central questions, not the possibility of natural limits to economic expansion.

Given this unpromising analysis of classical sociological theory, it may be more productive to examine some of the more recent sociological theories, which *do* try to tackle environmental issues head on. There are many possibilities to choose from here including Giddens's ideas on reflexivity and de-traditionalisation (1990, 1991, 1994, 1999), Beck's theory of the emergence of the 'risk society' (1992, 1994, 1995, 1999), Gorz's version of post-industrial socialism (1980, 1985, 1989, 1994), Habermas's theory of environmental movements as resisting the 'colonization of the lifeworld' (1981, 1987, 1989, 1990) and Eder's theory of the transformation of the dominant cultural paradigms of modernity (1982, 1985, 1990, 1993, 1996). Although the classical tradition has not been abandoned wholesale in these theories, their motivations and 'central problems' are significantly divergent, inspired to varying degrees by contemporary substantive environmental issues. In short, contemporary sociological and social theory *has* started to take on the ecocentric challenge outlined in this chapter. This is because, unlike in the late nineteenth century, a mass-membership international environmental movement continues to keep society–nature relations at the forefront of politics, and if sociological theory is to maintain its relevance then it will need to be able to contribute to the analysis of environmental problems.

Conclusion

With some caveats, Benton (1991) argues that the social sciences should give the rise to prominence of biology and issues around genetics and nature, a 'cautious welcome'. These issues are welcome in so far as they make visible some of the problems of working with dualistic ways of thinking, such as society/nature, which require a division of labour between different disciplines. Environmental issues point in the direction of dissolving such dualisms in order to properly understand how environmental problems are generated. The 'ecological turn' has also been enormously productive in forcing sociological theorists to concentrate on real world problems and to reflect on the fundamental assumptions of their own sociological work. However, Benton's welcome is a necessarily cautious one if a simple return to an older biological reductionism is to be avoided.

The emergence of an environmental problematic alongside activist and increasingly internationally organised environmental networks poses some unique difficulties for sociological theorising. This problem can perhaps best be captured in the way that sociologists have found it extremely difficult to deal with a range of issues raised by the emergence of environmental, ecological or Green movements that privilege the natural over the social. In bringing nature back into central focus, environmental political movements have thrown down a significant challenge to the discipline of sociology, to reconsider some of its defensive boundary maintenance strategies in order to take on board environmental concerns (Irwin 2001). So far, this has had limited success with the relative marginalisation of a specifically environmental sociology as evidence of this, as is the strong current of social constructionism in the study of environmental issues, which represents something approaching a 'business as usual' strategy.

Nonetheless, it would be a shame if sociology were to bypass or ignore the ecocentric challenge rather than to work through it. Research rooted in environmental sociology and the sociology of the environment contain much that is useful and worthwhile, and we should not be forced to choose between the polarised alternatives of realism or social constructionism as combatants to the death in the study of environmental issues. There is no need to reduce sociological problems to the level of biology, nor is there a need to believe that human biology has been entirely transcended in social life. What emerges from the current debate on the best way forward for sociology in respect to the environment is that such a debate asks us to question what kind of creatures human beings are. And although this question is perhaps under-theorised and under-researched at present, the study of identity formation could benefit from an engagement with ecological ideas of humans as natural beings with 'ecological selves'. Such an engagement might illuminate the current division between ecological, psychological and sociological theories of the self and identity formation and is the theme of Chapter 5.

5 Living with Gaia: Deep Ecological and Social Selves

The sociological study of identities has become more important in recent years with the emergence of expressive forms of politics in the so-called 'new social movements' and their construction of grassroots collective identities. The social construction of identity has also been a theme within debates on consumerism and the consumer society, which enables and encourages the purchase of elements for the construction of social identities. The dominance of broadly social constructionist arguments in this field has not allowed for a systematic discussion with the alternative arguments presented by deep ecologists and ecofeminists, many of whom claim a strong connection between self identities and the rest of nature. Their concept of an 'ecological self' is vigorously contested in academic debates, feminist scholarship and within environmental and Green movements. Whilst some see such a concept as essentialist and politically regressive, harking back to arguments that propose 'natural' gender divisions, others believe that amongst the alternative proposals for the solution of environmental problems, the most effective is likely to involve encouraging people to recognise their rootedness in natural ecosystems and hence their intrinsically ecological self-concept. This chapter outlines the terms of this debate and brings ecological theories into contact with sociological theories of self formation and the creation of self identities. In doing so, the extent to which ecological and sociological theories are potentially compatible may become a little clearer.

Theories of ecological selves

Why do some people risk imprisonment, injury and even death to prevent trees being felled, natural areas being despoiled by new roads and airports, the abuse of animals or to prevent the pollution of the marine environment? Notwithstanding the pleasures to be gained from the excitement and thrill of such activities, one feasible answer might be that people identify in some way with trees, animals, plants and oceans in ways that are not dissimilar to their identification with human relatives, friends and colleagues. We may surmise that the defence of these human–human relationships is partly because these relationships are constitutive of their own self identity. In this way, altruistic actions in defence of others may be a form of self defence too. Of course, this way of answering the question is relatively easy to understand when applied to human beings, but could it also be applied to non-human animals and the rest of nature? Theorists of ecological selves believe that it can and that encouraging people to explore their ecological self is the best way to tackle environmental problems in the long term. As Devall (1990: 37) argues, 'Before changing paradigms or political ideologies or social institutions, it seems to me, we must change the way we experience life.'

Ecocentric theorists have produced a series of arguments which suggest that anthropocentric modern societies do not encourage people to realise and experience their ecological selves, quite the reverse, they focus attention on the radical *difference* between human beings and the rest of the natural world. This allows people to experiment on and kill animals for fashion, to pollute the environment and to turn forests, oceans and natural areas into 'resources' in the pursuit of profit and material prosperity. In such societies the idea that human beings could identify with or see themselves in nature seems vaguely ridiculous. Modern humans use natural things for their own ends, they do not have an ecological self, instead nature has come to be seen as the 'other' against which human societies define themselves (Tester 1991). In this context, the self identities of people are formed in specifically social relationships in which nature or ecology plays no significant part.

The deep green position is that this rupture between humans and nature has to be healed and probably the most effective way of doing this lies in transforming individuals and their ways of thinking about themselves and their relationship to nature. Green politics insists that human societies are inseparable from non-human nature and they must therefore take nature's laws into account. People need to live as if nature *does* matter (Devall and Sessions 1985). Environmentalists seek to solve the problem of nature and move towards sustainable societies that do not destroy the natural base on which they depend. Environmental movements have pursued this goal in a variety of ways from consciousness raising in the general public, to transforming the institutional structures of modern societies in an ecocentric direction. This means changing state policies, organisational structures, the operation of business enterprises, production methods and so on. However, although this provides activists with a focus for political lobbying and campaigning, in some ways it may not be the most successful strategy if it fails to change values and attitudes. For some within the environmental movement, it is not enough to focus simply on the institutional level. Change has to be at the level of identifications and self identities. For this group, the promotion and exploration of people's 'ecological selves' is the surest way to prevent ecological damage and cement a new set of ecological values.

Reference to the ecological self is meant to alert people to an aspect of their 'self' of which they may not be fully aware. If human beings are a part of nature and nature is their 'inorganic body' (Marx 1844), then their selves should be natural and ecological as well as social. So, although people do not routinely see or experience nature as part of themselves, deep ecologists argue that this misidentification or 'alienation' lies at the root of ecological degradation. What makes deep ecology different from many forms of reform environmentalism is the movement from ethics to ontology, or the insistence that ethical argumentation and persuasion, though necessary, will not be sufficient to transform the ingrained anti-ecological character of modern societies. The influential ecophilosopher, Naess (1985: 264) for instance, sees clear limits to environmental ethics, arguing that 'The history of cruelty inflicted in the name of morals has convinced me that increase of identification might achieve what moralizing cannot: beautiful actions.' The enormous philosophical literature on environmental ethics centres on the questions of why and how we should defend nature. One telling debate has been the question of whether this defence is because nature has intrinsic value, that is, value in and of itself quite separately from human judgements, or whether the act of valuing is a specifically human capacity, and if so then can nature be defended against the other interests of human groups? Such debates normally take place before action is taken and run the risk of doing nothing in the meantime, allowing environmental degradation to continue. What ecophilosophers like Naess and Warwick Fox look to do is begin a process of self-realisation that is simultaneously bound to activity. Self-realisation is not a passive, reflective activity but demands actions in the world. As Drinkwater (1995: 97) makes clear, 'Deep ecology doesn't hold law, reason, order, the *logos* as its highest ideal. It has much more faith in natural sympathies, feelings, identifications. It is down to earth. It defends living things. This is important, because we can actually *do* something about life on Earth.'

This intuitive feeling of connectedness is fundamental for deep ecologists and may mark a process that some have described as the 're-enchantment of the world' (Moscovici 1977). Because it is ultimately based on intuition rather than rational and ethical argumentation, the approach is bound to remain controversial. Even within the broad environmental movement, some believe it may be a hindrance rather than a benefit (Dryzek 1987). This is evidenced by the social ecologist Bookchin (1987), who once disparagingly described the deep ecological tendency as 'eco-la la', a retreat into self-experience and self-expression when it is the institutional structures of modernity that require urgent change. Nonetheless, there is now a body of ecocentric work that promotes expansive 'self-realisation'. This means that people should aim to achieve as wide an experience of self as possible, to include other people, animals, bioregions and even nature as a planetary whole. This does not mean submerging or losing the individual self in wider nature, but rather seeks the self's ennobling or maturation by re-connecting the self with nature. Naess (1985: 261) argues that 'Self-realization in its absolute maximum is, as I see it, the mature experience of oneness in diversity.... increased maturity involves increase of the wideness of the self.'

Warwick Fox has termed the attempt to connect self and nature, a form of 'transpersonal ecology'. Fox's perspective (1984, 1995) is based on the notion that the best way to prevent human destruction of the natural world is to encourage people to cultivate their 'ecological self' and to experience themselves as part of nature.

This means encouraging a different way of thinking about environmental problems, which goes beyond the modern dualism, implied by the separation of society and nature. As Shepard (1969: 2) has argued in a famous passage, this implies, '.... a kind of vision across boundaries. The epidermis of the skin is ecologically like a pond surface or a forest soil, not a shell so much as a delicate interpenetration. It reveals the self ennobled and extended rather than threatened as part of the landscape and the ecosystem, because the beauty and complexity of nature are continuous with ourselves.' In this way, damage to nature comes to be perceived as damage to the self, and it is this which offers the best hope for the salvation of all life, including human beings. Transpersonal ecology aims to expand the notion of care beyond human beings, out into non-human nature so that humans can begin to feel connected to nature in such a way as to evoke feelings of care. Eckersley (1997: 62) argues that '... transpersonal ecology is concerned to expand the circle of human compassion and respect for others beyond one's particular family and friends and beyond the human community to include the entire ecological community'. It therefore puts its hopes for the transformation of industrial societies in the cultural process of changing individual selves and self-perceptions through increasingly wider identifications. Devall (1990: 52) states this idea clearly, arguing that '... the more we know a place intimately, the more we can increase our identification with it. The more we know a mountain or a watershed, for example, and feel it as our *self*, the more we can feel its suffering'. For Devall and others, there is no sentimentality or romanticism in such statements, which are instead seen as extensions of the knowledge that living beings can experience suffering. If there really is human–animal continuity then it may be entirely possible for people to experience such identifications and feelings. The problem with 'ecological identities' of this kind is that they may be limited to those few people who are actively seeking to get in touch with their ecological self (Light 2000) and are not easily extended to the non-committed public. If so, then it may be difficult to develop that critical mass of activists needed to transform society and in the meantime environmental degradation continues apace.

What human ideas and actions might such a process of expanded self-realisation encourage? It may involve 'ecological practice', a way of living and being that leads to wider identifications and natural knowledge. Everyday activities such as eating and drinking can be problematised by considering how and where food is produced, thus bringing into conscious awareness those social and economic processes that usually remain hidden or taken for granted. Devall (1990: 42) suggests that 'When we drink water, we trace it to its sources – a spring or mountain stream in our bioregion – and contemplate the sources of energy as part of our body. The "living waters" and "living mountains" enter our body.' The proposition here is that people should explore their own bioregion or water-shed in order to know it better and to forge a wider identification with it. If we know our home place intimately, then we will not tolerate the pollution or destruction of it. 'It' has become part of 'our' own self. Similarly, Drinkwater (1995: 86) says that 'The Earth is my home, so I experience concern for those beings that share it with me and with whom I am inter-dependent. That *may* include the bioregion, although for most of us, being at home in our bioregion is a somewhat future state of affairs.' For modern urbanites, used to purchasing fresh fruit and vegetables all year round regardless of natural seasons and having access to water, literally 'on tap', we also have to ask the motivational question, why should they *want* to identify with a bioregion that probably seems remote from their everyday life experience?

Deep ecologists also promote a return to simpler lifestyles or a 'voluntary simplicity' that uses up fewer of the earth's resources. Such lifestyles would conserve resources wherever possible, use local products to avoid excessive transportation and pollution and ultimately redefine 'quality of life' in ways that do not depend on high levels of conspicuous consumption. Devall (1990: 83) says that 'I try to base my own style, as much as possible, on products produced in my own bioregion. I buy milk and cheese from local dairies, salmon and other seafood in season (not frozen) caught in local waters, beer from a local brewery, house furnishings made by local craftsmen and artists. Rich experience does not have to be expensive.' Leaving aside the contentious question of whether all communities have access to their own local salmon and brewery, or whether such 'simple living' really is less expensive compared with the economies of scale that can be achieved by large supermarket chains, this kind of alternative to the consumer society could lead in the direction of a genuinely 'postmodern' or 'post-industrial' society, in contrast to the high technology, service-based post-industrialism described by sociologists (Marien 1977; Rose 1991). The alternative post-industrialism rejects high technology industrialisation and works for a different type of society in the wake of a *failed* industrialism. Such ideas are by no means unique. Many nineteenth-century communes in Britain (Hardy 1979) and elsewhere tried to live simply and in closer contact with nature, with communalist socialists such as Edward Carpenter attempting to bring about a 'simplification of life' to combat what they saw as the artificiality of civilised lifestyles (Roberts 1915; Rowbotham and Weeks 1977). However, in the contemporary context such ideas do demonstrate the main differences between radical Green political activity and mainstream politics. Wilson's (1992: 17) survey of the 'culturing of nature' in the USA makes a plea for re-connecting with nature in somewhat similar terms: 'We urgently need people living on the land, caring for it, working out an idea of nature that includes human culture and human livelihood.'

For critics of all radical ecological solutions that involve living life closer to nature, such proposals are fundamentally misguided. Lewis (1994) argues that there are two groups of people whose stance constitutes an obstacle to solving environmental problems. The first group covers all of those who deny the existence of serious and increasingly global ecological problems, arguing instead that the 'ecological crisis' is something of a myth. The Swedish statistician Lomborg (2001) has recently been perceived as an exponent of this view, arguing that environmental claims are really political claims as much as, or even more than, scientific ones, and that most global environmental claims, concerning biodiversity loss, global warming and so on, are grossly exaggerated. Lomborg's main point however is not that there are no serious ecological problems but that there are many other more harmful problems too and that the focus on the environment may lead to more misery and deaths from distributional issues such as global poverty and gross inequalities in the developing world. For Lomborg, it would be better to put our efforts into attacking those problems first. The second group of critics, though, are those radical ecologists who reject reform environmentalism as insufficient, instead calling for radical social and political changes. Lewis takes the view that both groups are wrong and that reform environmentalism is, at the same time, the most 'radical' and 'realistic' position in relation to environmental issues. The resource optimists fail to take into account the effects of industrial activity on non-human nature, concentrating instead on the effects on human beings. This is a somewhat blinkered view that does not take seriously enough the connection between humans and nature. If environmental problems are not tackled, then the damage done to natural ecosystems will, sooner or later, force human societies to change. On the other hand, many radical ecologists argue that in order to solve the ecological crisis (which they see as all too real) people should be encouraged to get closer to nature, in various ways, so that they will not accept environmental degradation. However, Lewis believes that the latter is a self-defeating strategy, which, if taken seriously, would produce more, not less, environmental damage. He argues that 'If all Americans were to flee from metropolitan areas, rural populations would soar and wildlife habitat would necessarily diminish' (Lewis 1994: 8). Similarly, advocating 'natural' wood burning as an alternative to nuclear power is not a pollution-neutral option, but would turn the USA into '...a deforested, soot-choked wasteland within a few decades' (ibid.: 9). Lewis's 'environmentalist' solutions are based on the principle of 'decoupling' human societies from non-human nature. Rather than getting closer to nature, decoupling requires a further distancing of humans from nature in order to preserve the latter from damage by human populations. This could only be achieved by making creative use of technologies and turning the forces of dynamic capitalism to work *for* environmental protection rather than *against* it. Lewis's critique may itself be too optimistic for many radical ecologists, but it does show that there may be some middle ground between eco-radicalism and optimistic humanism that nevertheless remains in a real sense, 'environmentalist'.

Ecofeminism and nature

The 'ecofeminist' label covers a wide range of activities, many of which do not necessarily involve the transformation of personal and self identities. Nevertheless, many ecofeminists have argued that there is a special connection between women and nature and therefore also the possibility that, rather than being a hindrance to feminist politics, may even be a uniquely positive feature of it.

Indeed, despite its often remarked upon internal diversity, it is reasonable to suggest that if *eco*feminism is to bring anything genuinely new to wider feminist scholarship, then it has to explore the relationship between women and nature as its central theme. The internal diversity of ecofeminism has been said to include liberal ecofeminism, social ecofeminism, socialist ecofeminism, cultural ecofeminism and 'Third World' ecofeminism (Merchant 1992). Whilst some are impressed by this diversity, seeing it as ecofeminism's key feature, it is important not to lose sight of the 'eco' in ecofeminism under the welter of additional political and theoretical arguments. In addition, ecofeminism is a diverse body of work taking in poetry, novels and artistic works as well as academic texts, and although there now exists a substantial ecofeminist literature (Daly 1978; Griffin 1978; Merchant 1982, 1992; Plant 1989; Diamond and Orenstein 1990; King 1990; Warren 1990; Gaard 1993; Mies and Shiva 1993; Plumwood 1993; Salleh 1997), the status of ecofeminism is by no means assured.

The ecofeminist strand of ecocentrism is rooted in an understanding of the apparently uniquely close links between women and the natural world, and introduces something potentially unique to environmentalism, namely the idea that women have a special interest in the politics of nature. Consider the following from Griffin (1978: 40); 'We know ourselves to be made from this earth. We know this earth is made from our bodies. For we see ourselves, and we are nature. We are nature seeing nature. We are nature with a concept of nature. Nature weeping. Nature speaking to nature of nature.' Such a statement embodies a theory of ecological selves, but also aims to raise awareness of the connections between women and nature. Sargisson (2001: 63) argues that 'Much of the content of ecofeminist thought is deeply essentialist: insisting on profound, intractable and significant differences in the nature of men and women.' However, ecofeminists reverse the relative valuations attached to these complex differences in order to promote a positive valuation of both women and nature. This marks out the ecofeminist perspective as distinct and different from other versions of ecological selves.

For example, Eckersley (1997: 64) says that

unlike transpersonal ecology, ecofeminism has taken the historical/ symbolic association of women with nature as demonstrating a special convergence of interests between feminism and ecology. The convergence is seen to arise, in part, from the fact that patriarchal culture has located women somewhere between men and the rest of nature on a conceptual hierarchy of being (i.e., God, Man, Woman, Nature). This has enabled ecofeminists to identify what they see as a similar logic of domination between the destruction of nonhuman nature and the oppression of women.

Ecofeminism begins from the acknowledgement that patriarchal cultures enable the male domination of both nature and women and this potentially opens up a space for an identification of women with nature. Ecofeminists argue that even deep ecological philosophy has tended to adopt a male-dominated perspective, with 'ecotopias' failing to take account of feminist questions about equality (see Callenbach 1978), instead producing male fantasies of women's 'natural' role in an ecotopian society. This argument is familiar to many mainstream feminist theories, which recognise that such a symbolic division of the world can be found in many areas of social life including academic writing, wherever women's natural role as nurturing mother and carer is referred to, or wherever biology is called on to explain the behaviour of women. However, what marks out ecofeminism as different from other feminisms is that it stays with the woman/nature identification. To some theorists this means that ecofeminism is misguided, suspect, naïve or dangerous, and quite possibly all of these. Rather than challenging the connection between nature and women, some ecofeminists seem to want to celebrate it. The attempt to dominate nature has its corollary in society with men's attempt to dominate and subjugate women. The two forms of domination are intimately connected. This means that women have a special interest in ecology, but also that attempts to defend nature must be attempts to defend women against patriarchal domination. In short, radical ecology is as much about women as it is about nature. However, whether women actually *are* involved in environmental and Green politics in greater numbers than other 'grey' forms of politics is not yet clear and requires more empirical research. Whatever evidence there is suggests that women are not involved in environmentalism and Green politics in any greater numbers than are men (Kolinsky 1988; Blocker and Eckberg 1997).

In an influential ecofeminist historical account, Carolyn Merchant's *The Death of Nature* (1982) attempts to trace the historical 'logic of domination', arguing that in Europe the period of the 'scientific revolution' between 1500 and 1700 is crucial for understanding the specifically feminist interest in ecology, thus implicating western scientific method in the domination of women. During this period, came the emergence of, '. . . a world view and a science that, by reconceptualizing reality as a machine rather than a living organism, sanctioned the domination of both nature and women' (ibid.: xvii). In particular, Merchant finds a connection between patriarchal culture and the scientific attitudes of men like Francis Bacon, whose *New Atlantis* (1624) 'replaced politics by scientific administration' (ibid.: 180) where, 'A new experimental method designed to constrain nature and probe into her secrets would improve and "civilize society"' (ibid.: 148). Thus as nature became devalued, so did women, who were seen as intimately connected to natural processes through their biological constitution. Whereas the mediaeval 'organic' image of nature was partly of the female as 'wild and uncontrollable' (and helped to justify the persecution of women as witches) another aspect of this organicism was the image of nature as a 'nurturing mother' providing for human needs. Similarly, Shiva (1988), formerly a physicist working in India's nuclear power programme, criticises the so-called 'green revolution' designed to revolutionise agriculture in developing countries by introducing industrial farming methods and technologies as involving 'the worldwide destruction of the feminine knowledge of agriculture, evolved over four or five thousand years, by a handful of white male scientists in less than two decades' (cited in Pearce 1991: 270). Shiva argues that women's knowledge has been undervalued and attacked by male-dominated science.

Much ecofeminist writing is concerned with promoting ecological spirituality as a means of raising consciousness of the intimate connection between women and nature. This often takes the form of, 'retrieving the insights of non-hierarchical pre-Christian cultures or reviving other Earth-based traditional practices (e.g., celebrating the Goddess-oriented culture of Old Europe, pagan rituals, Gaia, the body, natural cycles, and the experience of connectedness and embodiment in general)' (Eckersley 1997: 64). This is not necessarily a unique feature of ecofeminism however, as the recourse to ritual as a way back from the profane industrialised world into the sacred arena of nature seems to apply to deep ecology in general (Spretnak 1986). Indeed, Spretnak and Capra (1984: 50) argue that

> We feel that deep ecology is spiritual in its very essence. It is a world view that is supported by modern science but is rooted in a perception of reality that goes beyond the scientific framework to a subtle awareness of the oneness of all life, the interdependence of its multiple manifestations, and its cycles of change and transformation. When the concept of the human spirit is understood in this sense, as the mode of consciousness in which the individual feels connected to the cosmos as a whole, the full meaning of deep ecology is indeed spiritual.

This feeling of the interconnectedness of living things remains an intuitive motivation for ecocentrics of all kinds.

However, in some of its more essentialist formulations, ecofeminism has little to say about the connection between *men* and nature, thus restricting the pool of support for essentialist ecofeminism. This is probably why the position remains a minority one in the radical ecological movement and causes suspicion amongst those who see the unique basis of the movement as holistic and inclusive. Salleh (1997) makes the additional point that ecofeminists have themselves been marginalised within the 'deep ecological' tradition itself, with labels such as 'essentialist' serving to maintain the distance between a male-dominated deep ecology and a marginal 'essentialist' ecofeminism. Not all ecofeminism can be described as essentialist though, and some ecofeminists have attempted to move away from essentialist positions whilst also hanging onto important ecofeminist insights into the connection between women and nature. Cultural ecofeminism is much more interested in the cultural construction of associations that connect women to emotions and nature and men to reason and culture. Plumwood (1986: 122) suggests that although ecofeminism has not emerged in a vacuum and therefore has to draw on other aspects of existing feminist ideologies, it nevertheless marks a 'positioning' of women with nature 'against a destructive and dualizing form of culture'. Plumwood (1988) argues that rather than privileging such 'female' attributes as caring and emotionality on the grounds that they are alternatives to destructive male attributes, what is required is a general 'human ideal' that applies for both men and women, but which rejects the 'masculine' domination of nature. Taking a radical democratic position, Sandilands (1999) also takes issue with essentialist ecofeminism as insufficiently critical of the imposition of the supposedly obvious categories, 'nature' and 'women'. These categorisations serve to close off rather than open up debates about the relationship between women and nature. She writes that:

> Ecofeminist myths of unity rest on the idea that humans can return to an organic state of grace by transcending the ways in which nature has been constructed in patriarchal development. Such a quest for organic harmony is impossible and dangerous: impossible because we can never know nature apart from culture, ... dangerous because it draws attention away from the fact that ecological degradation is a complex social problem (Sandilands 1999: 70).

Instead, Sandilands (1994, 1995) proposes that the importance of ecofeminism lies in its insistence that movements for democratisation must bring nature into the conversation alongside other (human) participants (Sturgeon 1997). In so doing, ecofeminists stand at the forefront of the expansion of democracy.

For deep ecologists, transpersonal ecologists and essentialist ecofeminists, natural identification is a vital prerequisite for a sustainable society. However, the very fact that such an identification does *not* currently exist strongly suggests that *social* processes of identity formation have been and continue to be much more significant. Recognition of this means that if theorists of ecological selves are to do more than simply exhort people to 'find themselves in nature', then it will be necessary to understand how social selves and social identities are being constructed.

Sociological theories of social selves

From the standpoint of theories of ecological selves, sociological theories of self formation and self identity are denuded and one-sided, concentrating on selves as emerging only within human–social relationships. This is of course partly true. Sociologists have sought to understand how human beings come to experience a sense of self and how personal and social identities are socially constructed. What such theories suggest is that people are not born with a self that then develops in social interactions, but that self experience arises out of social experience without which the self-reflexive character of human individuals would not exist. This robustly sociological starting point does perhaps underplay the role of human biological inheritance, and clearly does mark out sociological theories from psychological theories of self and philosophical theories of the mind. However, apart from some poststructuralist and strict constructionist theories of self identity, the biological capacities of human beings are in fact embedded in most sociological theories of self formation and to that extent the ecocentric critique of sociology misses the mark.

Many sociological theories of self formation take their lead from the work of the influential 'social behaviourist', Mead (1934). Mead was concerned to demonstrate that any satisfactory theory of the self had to begin from the overall *social process* not the isolated *individual*, as the former logically precedes the latter. Modern individuality is explicable in this way as the product of a particular set of social relationships. Mead's theory saw the self-concept as twofold, involving both the 'I' and 'me'. In this formulation, the 'me' represents the social self, that part of the self that is constructed from the generalised attitudes of others towards the person. This is quite close to Cooley's (1922) concept of the 'looking glass self', which identifies the way that people's social self is constituted by the organised reflections they glean from other people, as if seeing themselves reflected back in a mirror. However, Mead recognised that for the 'internal conversations' we have with our 'selves' to take place, a second element, the organismic 'I' had to be a partner in the conversation. Together, the 'I' and the 'me' make up the self-concept, allowing people to see themselves with a degree of relative detachment, as it were, from the outside looking on. Hence, although Mead's theory clearly *is* a genuinely sociological theory of self formation and development, it still allows for the influence and effectivity of people's biological or organismic self to influence behaviour. As Burkitt (1998: 31) puts it, 'In Mead's theory, then, humans are to be thought of as possessing a nature, just like the other animals of the world. The difference between Mead's understanding of human nature and the way it is generally used, is that Mead sees the nature of humans as social.' And of course, this must also mean that theories of the self have to take this into account. It is not enough to concentrate on the natural or biological side of the self without also considering the significant social element.

Similarly, Elias (1991) argues that individuals in modern industrialised societies tend to experience their personal selves a little like 'pearls in a shell', with the unique 'inner' self separated from other selves by an impenetrable barrier. This image of people he calls '*Homo Clausus*' or 'closed people'. Sociologically however, and following Mead, people should be seen as *Homines Aperti*, or 'open people', whose selves and self identities are partly generated through the wider social process. Philosophical and psychological theories that take the socially created *Homo Clausus* experience as constitutive of a *universal* human self experience fail to explain why other societies do not share it (Westen 1985). In addition, Elias accepts that humans are also biological creatures with specifically human capacities and abilities and that these shape, limit and enable people in particular ways. This brings Elias's theory close to the critical realists' ideas we saw in Chapter 3, though it would not be correct to describe Elias's position as a critical realist one.

What becomes clear, even through this necessarily cursory outline of the basic shape of sociological theories of the self and processes of identity formation is that it simply is not the case that sociological theories routinely eliminate the effectivity of biology or nature. One of the best-known of all sociologists of the self and identity, Erving Goffman, insisted in his work that the self is an 'embodied self' not simply a virtual or entirely socially constructed one. Jenkins (1996: 69) reminds us that, 'Goffman's unit of analysis is the embodied individual, and the embodied self has its territories, preserves of space which can be respected or violated.' In this way, Goffman is able to connect bodily features and capabilities with socially generated motivations and behaviours, which come together in interactional situations. Similarly, Pierre Bourdieu's concept of the 'habitus' is a useful way of theorising 'embodied habit' or 'practical dispositions' (ibid.: 71), which refuses to eliminate the human biological inheritance from the picture. Even so, Bourdieu is equally insistent that habitus is only operative in particular social 'fields', which thereby allows him to theorise both the natural and the social levels in relation to selves and personal identities. If any of these sociologists *have* tended to spend more time discussing the social elements of people's identities, then this is because the social level of reality practically *is* more influential in shaping people's individual self experience. Sociologists simply report this in their empirical and theoretical work.

In sociological theories of the self, theories of mind and self identity formation, a distinction is made between the formation of a 'self-concept', or a sense of self and the personal identities that are constructed from this. Mead, for example, was concerned to show how the self-concept develops in early life, allowing people to see themselves reflexively and thus open to the influence of others. In contrast, theories of ecological selves have tended to focus simply on changing personal identities by encouraging a series of wider and more 'natural' identifications. There is of course a good reason for this. Greens want to change the attitudes of really existing adult people and this means encouraging them to explore the possible identification with nature and natural things, which they may then come to experience as part of their own self identity. Whilst this is a legitimate political project, it does leave theories of ecological selves somewhat under-theorised in relation to an explanation of how the self-concept initially develops. We could say that they are sociologically underdeveloped. They also seem to operate with a rather unsophisticated knowledge of sociological theories of self formation, which makes their arguments and critiques less convincing than they might otherwise be.

Conclusion

Deep ecology and ecofeminism have been able to tap into modern 'romantic' ideas concerning human beings, whose 'proper' place as natural beings has been distorted by an artificial and alienating society. This has been a recurring theme from Jean Jacques Rousseau to Herbert Marcuse and Bill Devall. Encouraging people to find or identify with their real, authentic selves in nature, bioregions or ecosystems is a strategy that grounds radical ecological politics in a way that is not open to most other social movements. Devall (1990: 40) argues that

When sociologists discuss *self* they usually are referring to the social self. When asked "who are you?", most people respond by saying: "I am a Christian" or "I am a male" or "I am a carpenter" or "a mother" or "an American." Sometimes people say "I am an environmentalist." A person expressing ecological self would say "I am a forest being."

What are sociologists to make of such a statement? Why 'a forest being'? Presumably because of the idea of getting in touch with the evolutionary origins of the human species. But what is significant about forests? How far back into the evolutionary process should we go in recognising these origins? Why not 'I am a cloud of dust and gas being'? Sociologists cannot accept the idea of some pre-social state of an 'original' or 'authentic' human relationship to nature without society. From a sociological perspective, 'man is inconceivable outside social relations or severed from biological nature' (Kilminster 1991: 88; see also Moscovici 1976). The modern romantics' recourse to 'natural' man as a critique of their perception of modernity's attempt to constitute man beyond nature, ironically reproduces the very modern dualism they want to eliminate. The serious problem with such formulations is that despite their criticisms of modern dualistic thinking, they wind up reproducing perhaps the most fundamental of these, the nature/culture dualism. Theories of ecological selves also seriously misrepresent sociological theories of social selves. Such theories are not typically of a strict social constructionist kind but actually do take into account both the biological and the social nature of human selves.

So, it may well be politically advantageous to argue for an ecological identification, and when deep ecologists, transpersonal ecologists and ecofeminists encourage people to see themselves as part of nature, they do this in the hope that this is the best way to achieve ecologically sustainable societies. However, the theory of human selves and self formation embedded within most such arguments is essentialist and misleading. In this respect at least, sociological theories of self formation appear as paragons of holistic virtue, seeking to combine biological inheritance *and* social relationships. If deep ecology is to become practical then it needs to take the social side of self formation processes much more seriously. After all, if specifically *social* relations were not effective in the process of identity formation, then there would be no need for ecocentric theorists. The very fact that people need to be shaken out of their social identities in the first place suggests that the social self *is* the primary reality for most people. Ecocentric theorists are right to argue that human beings are *natural* beings, but they are wrong to suggest that the biological is somehow more 'real' than the social. Such a view remains a serious obstacle to ecocentric theories of self and society as well as to any accommodation between ecocentric and sociological approaches to environmental issues.

6 Environmentalism in a Risk Society

Since Daniel Bell's post-industrial theorising in early 1960s America, social theorists have produced a quite staggering series of analyses claiming to have uncovered 'the secret of these new times'. Sociologists are now familiar with theories of the post-industrial society (Bell 1974), the programmed society (Touraine 1971, 1981), the self-service economy (Gershuny 1978), postmodernity and postmodernisation (Lyotard 1984; Bauman 1992, 1993; Crook et al. 1992), post-Fordism (Amin 1994) and neo-Fordism (Aglietta 1987), disorganised capitalism (Lash and Urry 1987), the information society (Castells 1996), the knowledge society (Stehr 1994) and the post-traditional society (Giddens 1994, 1999), to name only the most well-known. And we now have Ulrich Beck to thank for introducing us to the 'risk society' (Beck 1992). The impression cannot be avoided that although sociologists agree that we are in the midst of some significant social transformation, they do not agree on what this is.

This chapter focuses on Beck because his thesis of social transformation stands alone in placing environmental concerns at its centre. In a recent comprehensive review of risk theories and their relationship to environmental issues, Strydom (2002) helpfully divides the risk debate into 'critical' and 'sceptical' theories, or between those who see risk theory as a *critical* theory of society and others, including Luhmann's (1989) systems theory, which take a more sceptical view not just of the risk thesis, but also of the possibility of dealing with the increasing risks generated by modern societies. Strydom (2002: 1) leans towards the critical position, arguing that, 'A new society is emerging that will in all probability come into its own during the next three to four decades.' Leaving

115

aside the portentous tone of this statement, which has been made in very similar language in most of the disjunctive theories listed above, the new society will be above all else, a risk society, and if so then its foremost interpreter will be Ulrich Beck. Because I am primarily concerned with what the risk thesis can add to our understanding of environmentalism, this chapter will centre on Beck's influential work, drawing on related theories and evidence where necessary.

Ulrich Beck's risk society thesis

Since the translation of Ulrich Beck's *Risikogesselschaft* (1986) into English in 1992 as, *Risk Society: Towards a New Modernity*, the concept of 'risk' has become central to many sociological studies of environmental issues and politics. However, it should also be recognised that risk discourse is wider than this, taking in many other fields and that risk has become a flexible concept that, depending on context, refers to real world risks, perceptions of riskiness or ways of dealing with hazards. The spread of the discourse of risk in this way, arguably lends substance to Beck's general thesis that we are moving towards a 'risk society', a society increasingly concerned with risks. However, this chapter investigates the contours of the risk society only from the standpoint of its relevance to an understanding of environmentalism. In doing so it is also necessary to examine Anthony Giddens's recent work which treads a similar, though not identical, path to Beck (see O'Brien *et al.* 1999). Clearly the concept of risk is relevant to an understanding of environmentalism, but the question is whether this is the most productive way of examining environmental issues and if not, how might risk be incorporated into other theoretical perspectives?

Goldblatt (1996: 155) rightly points out that the ideas of Ulrich Beck have '... a particular importance for anyone concerned with the response of social theory to environmental degradation and environmental politics'. This is because Beck does not discuss environmental issues in an ad hoc way, nor does he see them as restricted to a specialised sub-discipline called environmental sociology or to a sociology of the environment. In addition, he does not believe that existing bodies of sociological theory can deal adequately with environmental issues. Instead,

Beck's theoretical ideas depend for their force on the pressing need to understand contemporary environmental degradation and pollution, which is allotted a central role. His thesis of the emergence of a risk society (1992, 1995, 1999) is an attempt to shift the terms of the debate around the direction of social change away from a comparison of modernity with postmodernity or industrialism with post-industrialism. By introducing the concept of risk, he is able to find a way around such static, dualistic theories by positing not a break with, but a continuation of, existing and longstanding industrial and modernising trends as the main source of the problems faced by human societies. The following account concentrates on two main aspects of the risk society thesis. First, the way environmental issues are theorised within it, and secondly what environmentalism tells us about the character of modern societies.

Beck has produced a framework for thinking about why risk and risk consciousness have become such prominent features of modern life. Using the theory of 'reflexive modernisation', Beck takes issue with postmodern theorists, ultimately rejecting the concept of postmodernity. Whereas the latter is often taken as in some ways marking a break with the central trends of modernity, the reflexive modernisation thesis argues that risk societies have been generated through the ongoing processes of industrialisation and modernisation. So although Beck argues that risk societies are in some sense 'new' types of society, he also says they are the products of the industrialisation. The three-stage periodisation Beck works with centres around the historical break with tradition produced by modernity. However, he argues that we are currently entering a new phase of modernity, which he describes as its 'reflexive' phase.

Pre-Modernity   →   Simple Modernity   →   Reflexive Modernity
(feudal/agrarian)   (modern/industrial)   (modern/risk society)
(Lash and Wynne 1992: 3)

Although this is a chronological scheme, it should be noted that no specific dates are attached to the typology; and in truth, Beck is only concerned with the change from a 'simple' industrial form to a 'reflexive' or risk form of modernity. Lash and Wynne (ibid.), tellingly making use of Daniel Bell's concept of 'axial principles', argue that for Beck, modernity is very much coextensive with industrial society and the new reflexive modernity with the risk society. Industrial society and risk society are for Beck distinct social formations. The axial principle of industrial society is the distribution of goods, while that of the risk society is the distribution of 'bads' or dangers. Further, industrial society is structured through social classes while the risk society is individualised.

So, the activity of industrial societies centres around the production of useful material goods, but over time their normal production processes and institutionalised modes of development produce increasingly deleterious side effects in the form of waste and pollution, which gradually come to dominate social life at the expense of goods production. More time and energy is spent trying to manage and control the *effects* of industrial production than with producing goods, hence it is justified to speak of the emergence of a 'risk society' in which various forms of pollution and high consequence environmental problems have to be dealt with. Instead of conflicts over material inequalities and quarrels over the distribution of the 'wealth cake', a realisation dawns that the cake itself is poisoned (Beck 1995: 128). As Beck (1992: 20–1) says,

> the knowledge is spreading that the sources of wealth are 'polluted' by growing 'hazardous side effects'. This is not at all new, but it has remained unnoticed for a long time in the efforts to overcome poverty... To put it differently, in the risk society the unknown and unintended consequences come to be a dominant force in history and society.

What Beck (1994: 2) is theorising here is the 'creative (self-)destruction for an entire epoch: that of industrial society'. However, this occurs not through a revolutionary movement or directed political project as envisaged in marxist theories. Instead, the industrial society is effectively dissolved through an unplanned and unpredicted development occurring 'behind the backs' of everyone. And although initially the unplanned nature of this development was not explicit in his work, later Beck has made it clearer that 'reflexivity' is not the same as 'reflection'. He suggests that we should '... call the autonomous, undesired and unseen, transition from industrial to risk society, reflexivity' (ibid.: 6), whilst 'reflection' is the secondary activity of scientific, political and public awareness of and attempts to regulate risk. This means that 'reflexive modernity' marks a shift in the form and character of the modernisation process, producing a new societal condition, which first comes into existence and only later becomes the subject of public and academic debate. Arguably the latter has still to fully develop and the institutions of society lag behind social change, unable adequately to regulate the emerging reflexive modernisation process. Indeed this is the source of much of Beck's frustration and irritation.

The emergence of the risk society displaces industrial society and yet risk societies are still highly technological, industrialised societies. This is because it remains the case that industrial processes and the production of consumer goods continue to create the bulk of modern risks, wherever those processes happen to take place or its products consumed. The movement of manufacturing industries to regions outside the highly industrialised world does not mean that the latter are immune from industrial pollution, which does not respect national boundaries. It is clear that Beck has his finger on an important insight here that expansive industrial capitalism does not simply spread to all parts of the world, but in doing so the human world becomes more interdependent and susceptible to regionally polluting practices. However, the evidence that risks have in fact come to dominate production in the industrialised world is very difficult to demonstrate. It could also be argued that if risks are the product of industrialism then industrial societies are and have always been risk-producing societies, and this is therefore not a major change.

One response to such a criticism is the argument that today's risks are simply 'higher consequence risks' (Giddens 1991: 4), which threaten people far removed from the site of risk production. For Giddens (1999), modernity has produced a 'runaway world' in which most of the risks we face are 'manufactured risks', the product of decisions made in corporations and governments, though also by individual consumers. On this point he is in agreement with Beck. However, modern societies and their institutional modes of self-reproduction are complex systems that routinely produce 'normal accidents' (Perrow 1984). Such 'accidents' now form the backdrop for an acceptance of the risk discourse, and include high consequence accidents at nuclear power plants, such as those at Three Mile Island in the USA (1979) and Chernobyl in the Soviet Union [*sic*] (1986), industrial disasters such as the 1984 Bhopal chemical plant explosion in India as well as a variety of oil 'spills' such as that of the Exxon Valdez (1989) and many more. The point about these examples is that they show such accidents are indeed 'normal', to be expected. The problem is that it also shows there is no complete control over such events (Strydom 2002: 58), undermining some of the sanguine forecasts of scientific optimists and the public's confidence in scientific expertise. Giddens's runaway world is a world largely out of human control which produces uncertainties and risks of greater consequence. And even if there is now more knowledge of those risks, the heightened awareness that they are always escaping social control tends to reinforce and extend people's feelings of uncertainty and 'ontological insecurity'.

Public attitudes towards risk and environmental issues seem to be divided. The Eurobarometer Survey of 2002 (European Opinion Research Group 2002: 7) found that 44 per cent of Europeans surveyed agreed that 'human activity has led to irretrievable damage to the environment', whilst 45 per cent believed that 'the deterioration of the environment can be halted by changing our way of life'. Nonetheless, both the groups are in agreement that the environment *is* deteriorating despite their relative optimism or pessimism about the possibility of halting this. There are of course some significant national differences within these figures, notably that environmental problems are seen to be more serious in the south of Europe than the north. The survey suggests that as countries in the south industrialised later, environmental risks from air and water pollution and awareness of the disparity between economic development and environmental quality were more keenly felt, whilst the countries of the north had experienced such a disparity much earlier. Another interesting finding is that 'without exception, women are more worried than men' (ibid.: 21), perhaps supporting some of the arguments of ecofeminists which we explored in Chapter 4.

One problem with Beck's framing of the problem is that in order to make the explicit case for the emergence of a risk society, he is drawn into a form of theorising in which societies are seen as 'things' – the industrial society, the risk society – rather than focusing on the social process of continuing industrialisation. This is unfortunate because it means losing some of the potential gains he makes over similarly static post-industrial theories. If we see that the expansive industrialisation process gradually leads to more and higher consequence risks, such as global warming, which then become major social and politically contested problems, then it is possible to avoid thinking in terms of static societal types. As an illustration here, even if, as many sociologists have shown, a majority of workers in some industrialised societies are now employed in service occupations rather than directly in manufacturing industries, this does not mean they can avoid or opt out of the consequences of industrialisation at the international or global level. The concern with increasingly global environmental problems is one aspect of a heightened sensitivity to transnational connections in the current period (Sklair 1994), and a source of support for environmental and Green social movements. As Richard Kilminster (1997: 258) puts this, 'The more extensive and intensive people's dependence on each other becomes globally, the more it is in their mutual interests to mitigate the unintended harmful environmental effects as well as to reduce the risk of a nuclear war.' The spread and intensification of human interdependencies brings with it the possibility of closer collaboration to deal with environmental issues. None of this means we are entering a 'risk society' which can be contrasted with its predecessor, the 'industrial society'.

A further problem with the theory of reflexive modernisation is precisely Beck's concept of 'risk' itself. He defines risk as 'a systematic way of dealing with hazards and insecurities induced and introduced by modernization itself' (1992: 21). But if risk is a way of *dealing with* hazards, then risk does not refer to those hazards themselves. However, at other times he also seems to be saying that risks *are* real social hazards such as industrial pollution and radioactive leaks which people *really* face, whilst also noting that risks are 'particularly open to social definition and construction' (ibid.: 23). This is rather confusing, though of course, Beck is not alone in trying to wrestle with the problems of realism and social constructionism. The debate between these two seemingly intractably opposed positions has become more openly contested in recent years, though, as we saw in Chapter 3, there have been some attempts to move away from such polarised positions. In short, Beck seems to take up an ambiguous position in this debate in relation to the reality or otherwise of modern risks. Strydom (2002: 46) notes that realist and constructivist epistemologies have proved to be very controversial and that 'Even as late as the year 2000, Beck still considered it necessary to make his own epistemological position clear.' Strydom sees Beck's position as one of 'weak constructivism' or 'constructivist realism' that falls between 'naïve realism' and 'naïve constructivism'. Whether this actually clarifies his position is questionable and does not answer the central question, are the risks we face really more global and serious than before or are we simply more aware of risk?

Nevertheless, and moving against his own position somewhat, what we can usefully derive from Beck's work is that industrialisation remains one of the dominant forces or processes in an increasingly globalising world. This conclusion is an advance over those post-industrial approaches which posit a radical break with industrial society and culture in a postmodern age, and allows us to take a more developmental view of the industrialisation process and its consequences. The next question is how does Beck's risk society thesis deal with the politics of nature?

Risk and the politics of nature

Beck suggests that contemporary ecological protests have taken on an increased significance because nature, previously considered to be outside society and politics, has become a social and political issue. Nature has been drawn into the reflexive modernisation process itself, meaning that what we previously thought of as natural is at an end, though Beck (1995: 39) says that 'Upon close inspection, all who talk of "nature" in the sense the word pretends to, namely that which is untouched, free of human creation and destruction, have always refuted themselves.' This is because speaking of nature 'conjures up the whole dichotomy' of nature and culture and the interrelations between them. It is just that today the 'naivety of the given' is becoming less easy to sustain. As Giddens has also argued (1994: 77), 'Nature has become socialised. Today, among all the other endings, we may speak in a real sense of the end of nature – a way of referring to its thoroughgoing socialization.' For both Beck and Giddens then, nature has lost its capacity for 'otherness' in relation to human societies. The dividing lines between the natural and the social have become blurred to such a degree that we cannot take nature's obvious meaning for granted any more. This assessment really restates, though in a sociological idiom, an earlier argument advanced by McKibben (1990: 55), that the effects of industrial activity have reached a point where they partially shape natural cycles themselves, so that 'A child born now will never know a natural summer, a natural autumn, winter or spring. Summer is going extinct, replaced by something else that will be called "summer"'. An awareness is growing that human societies are changing the cycles and processes of nature but without being able to exert control over them. This produces uncertainty, anxieties and fear. The risk society thesis sees environmentalism and Green politics as one of the products of such a situation, creating the conditions for collective actions in defence of a fast disappearing natural world. The thing called nature that environmentalists defend is now not, according to Beck and Giddens, something that exists outside or beyond human interference (Evernden 1992). Advances in genetic engineering, in vitro fertilisation techniques and human-generated changes in global weather systems all point in the direction of acknowledging this point. Beck (1994: 27) puts it well:

> It is already becoming recognizable that nature, the great con-stant of the industrial epoch, is losing its pre-ordained character, it is becoming a product, the integral, shapeable 'inner nature' of (in this sense) post-industrial society. The abstraction of nature leads into industrial society. The integration of nature into society leads beyond industrial society. 'Nature' becomes a social project, a utopia that is to be reconstructed, shaped and transformed. Renaturalization means denaturalization. Here the claim of modernity to shape things has been perfected under the banner of nature. Nature becomes politics.

Although modernity does partly 'shape things', Beck's argument perhaps does not do enough to acknowledge that humans do not dominate or control natural processes. It is simply that nature has been dragged into the field of politics, so what Beck is hinting at here is not the end of but the paradoxical triumph of modernity. It is a triumph because nothing is now beyond human societies, but this is also paradoxical because despite integrating nature into society, modern development now produces risks which cannot be scientifically calculated with any certainty. As such, scientific experts in specialised fields can be legitimately challenged by lay actors with specialised local knowledge, as demonstrated in Wynne's (1996) study of Cumbrian sheep farmers' interactions and conflicts with experts after the Chernobyl nuclear accident in 1986, or in the sceptical reactions of people to the UK government's response to the recent foot and mouth outbreak in the UK. Risks which might previously have been seen as 'natural' are now seen to emanate from human activities and it is these which are becoming political concerns. At the radical extreme, of course, are Greens advocating de-industrialisation as the only long-term solution to environmental dangers. Workers' movements tied into industrial processes, whose livelihoods depend on them are in no position to provide an effective, critical opposition to the new situation. Hence new social and cultural movements have become more visible as well as have greater significance for the future development of society.

Beck is clearly aware, as we saw in Chapter 2, that many con-servationist and preservationist organisations trace their origins back to the period he describes as one of 'simple modernity' (industrial societies) rather than 'reflexive modernity' (risk societies), but he argues that there are significant differences between the 'old' and the 'new' forms of nature politics. Beck (1992: 162) notes that,

> Conservation movements have existed since the beginning of industrialization. Yet the selective critique expressed by conser-vation organizations (which in addition involved neither large costs for nor a fundamental critique of industrialization) was never able to shake off the nimbus of hostility to progress and backwardness that surrounded it. This only changed when the social evidence of threats to nature through industrialization grew and at the same time scientific interpretations completely detached from the old ideas of conservation were offered and accepted.

His argument here is now well rehearsed, that the old conserva-tionist critique was selective, localised and unrelated to scientific research whereas the new Green politics produces a more general critique of the industrialisation process as such, and *is* connected to findings from scientific research. What Beck has in mind are new disciplines or sub-disciplines such as conservation biology, ecology and marine biology, which have provided significant scientific evidence of the harmful effects of industrial processes on the natural world, thus legitimising the protest movements, taking their concerns into established political systems. In this sense, contem-porary Green movements can be seen as signs of the emergence of the reflexive phase of modernity, as they are concerned with the 'dark side' of industrialisation, rather than its formal, public and institutionalised face. More starkly, we could say that Green movements signal the inevitable end of industrial societies. Beck (1992: 11) puts this in his inimitable way in the following passage.

> in its mere continuity industrial society exits the stage of world history on the tip-toes of normality, via the back stairs of side effects, and not in the manner predicted in the picture books of social theory: with a political (revolution, democratic elections) explosion. Furthermore, this perspective implies that the countermodernistic scenario currently upsetting the world – new social movements and criticism of science, technology and progress – does not stand in contradiction of modernity, but is rather an expression of reflexive modernization beyond the outlines of industrial society.

In one sense, this type of account is very attractive and persuasive as it describes significant social change as part of the process of 'normal' industrial development, which does not require recourse to radical social and political movements or rapid, disjunctive social-structural theories. This does not mean that the latter should be ruled out as explanations of course, only that they should be reserved for genuinely rapid, revolutionary periods. In relation to the emergence of a highly visible politics of nature since the 1970s, Beck makes some salient points. Nonetheless, his dismissal of earlier periods of environmental concern prevents the risk society thesis from addressing the environmental movement's development over time and therefore misreads the place of contemporary Green and radical ecology movements within the longer history of environmentalism. For instance, it is simply not the case that the early environmentalism was unconnected to science and scientific research. The enormous growth of nineteenth-century natural history societies which categorised and classified plant species, thus bringing home the consequences of unchecked population growth and industrial and urban development on natural environments, was influential in motivating conservationists to action.

There is also little awareness in Beck's thesis of the possibility that there may be cyclical processes in modern societies that alternate between scientific optimism and pessimistic critique. For instance, Brand (1990) has studied the cyclical recurrence of 'modernisation critiques' in numerous countries, finding that they occur quite regularly, though in different forms, during times of economic optimism and pessimism. Similarly, in an earlier piece of research, Toulmin (1972) argued that anti-science movements seem to recur because people find the relatively detached, cold and calculating perspective of modern science difficult to reconcile with their emotional commitment to humanistic values, both of which are products of modernity. This means that we should not read too much into particular periods of modernisation critique, which may subside and be replaced by renewed optimism in science and technology. Such cyclical movements, if clearly demonstrated, would seriously question Beck's chronology of modernity and its phased progression. In their different ways, both Brand and Toulmin make the case that anti-industrial and anti-scientific sentiments have been expressed in a variety of social and cultural movements throughout the last 300 years or so. Such movements seem to move in cycles, swinging between optimistic and pessimistic assessments of modern, scientific development. It appears unlikely that the definitive break that Beck seeks to convince us of can be satisfactorily and empirically demonstrated, unless and until the risk thesis can bring within its remit some of the more historically informed research on social and counter-cultural movements and the social conditions which lead to their emergence (Zald and Ash 1966; Tarrow 1998).

One problem that has emerged during this reconstruction of Beck's risk thesis is that it is not really clear why Beck feels the need to oppose the concept of a risk society to that of industrial society. As he himself at times implies, industrial societies can also be seen as, and in a real sense always have been, 'risky' societies. This must be so to the extent that industrial culture demands technological solutions to deal with the side effects or consequences of industrialisation. These have always gone hand in hand with a simple industrialisation process, though of course we may well be more aware of this linkage today than in the past. To argue that modernisation has become dominated by an ecological orientation is speculative and not yet adequately demonstrated. Hajer (1996: 246) seems to be much more realistic in suggesting that '...it is better to refrain from speaking of today's predicament in terms of "our ecological crisis" (which suggests it is time-and space-specific) and to speak of the ecological dilemma of industrial society instead'.

This is a much more realistic assessment, which leads to the conclusion that this dilemma is embedded within industrial development and has provoked continuous reflection and critique since at least the creation of formal environmental organisations in the latter half of the nineteenth century. In relation to contemporary nature politics, in both its reformist and radical versions, Lash (in Beck *et al.* 1994: 211) argues that 'one can surely agree with Beck and Giddens (and David Harvey) that environmental politics is in the end about damage limitation'. We might well agree, but if this is the case then there would appear to be little difference in principle, between late twentieth-century Green politics and late nineteenth-century environmentalism, both of which have sought to prevent damage to nature, whether this is perceived as valued local environments, wildlife habitat or the planetary biosphere. This assessment also does not sit well with Beck's thesis that reflexive modernisation marks a new phase of modernisation, taking us beyond industrial society and a simple phase of modernity. The balance of the historical evidence suggests that environmental politics *is* about damage limitation, and it is difficult to see how it could be anything else, given that human societies exist in constant interchange with non-human nature. But this appraisal in itself tells us little about the character of environmentalism in different periods, nor does it help us to understand how environmental movements have developed over time or how its range of concerns has broadened. Despite the important insights concerning the institutional inadequacy of regulatory regimes in dealing with environmental risks and Beck's attempt to show how a reflexive form of modernity has emerged out of a simple form, the conclusions he draws from the risk society thesis are not adequately substantiated by empirical studies.

Risk discourse and Green politics

On the surface, Beck's discussion of the risks produced by industrialisation and modernisation interlocks well with the concerns of contemporary Greens, especially in so far as the destruction of valued environments, industrial pollution of rivers and waterways, fears around modern food production methods, the production of climate change and so on is central to his perspective. Like radical ecologists, he argues that 'Advanced industrialism in the confusion of centuries is now toying with life, with the lives of entire regions and generations' (Beck 2002: 164). This statement is certainly consonant with the dire warnings of environmentalists, which were seen as eccentric and grossly overstated in the 1970s, but are now taken seriously by academics and governments as key problems demanding international co-ordination and co-operation. Indeed, much of the force of Beck's argument stems from the proposition that regulatory frameworks in the environmental field are inadequate for the task of regulating the emerging global risk society. This is framed in pseudo-marxist terms and with some wit, as the incompatibility between the 'relations of production' (of risks) and their 'relations of definition' (constructions) (1995: 130). Whilst *risk production* has moved to a new level of dangers that spread outwards from the industrialised world to encompass all human (and non-human) life, *relations of definition* are firmly stuck in the early industrialising phase. Historical memories (Bauman 1982) of how to deal with risks are simply inadequate when the risks have broken their geographical bounds and cut loose from the simple wealth creation process to take on a life of their own.

An additional problem arises therefore that we no longer know who to blame for the production of risks. Corporations which adopt polluting production methods, workers who defend their right to work in such places, consumer groups who use the products, or governments which allow such production to take place? We blame everyone and therefore no one, perhaps taking it upon ourselves to do what we can to improve our environment. As Beck puts this (1995: 135), 'A society in which anyone who pinches a radio from a caravan can be fined twice as much as an unscrupulous factory owner who permanently contaminates the surroundings with radioactive substances, cannot assume that the injunction to do what one can will counteract the devaluation of its legal principles.' To the extent that those legal principles lie in individual culpability, legal systems will continue to fail to address issues of risk.

However, Beck's theoretical perspective is not really as sympathetic to the environmental and radical ecology movements as it may seem. Indeed, Beck is probably one of the sternest critics of a form of Green politics that relies on the defence of nature, which he sees as misguided and completely unable to deal with risk. Worse, nature politics essentialises the natural when all the evidence shows that there is no separate or essential nature. As Beck (1995: 38) caustically puts this, 'Today more than ever, now that it no longer exists, "nature" is becoming rediscovered and pampered.' In this context, environmentalism propagates an ideology that obscures rather than enlightens. Taken as a whole in fact, Beck's corpus of work so far contains remarkably little reference to research on environmental movements and does not systematically engage with the substantive arguments from within environmentalism and Green politics. Indeed, in *Ecological Politics in an Age of Risk* (2002), reference to the development of such movements is extremely difficult to locate. Thus, Beck's ongoing dialogue with environmentalism appears to be conducted at a high level of generality which does not do justice to the continuing development of arguments produced from within the movement. The danger for the risk thesis therefore is that of conjuring up a 'straw man' rather than engaging with environmentalism as lived and practised.

Nonetheless, Beck is right to note that the idea of defending an unspoiled nature has been and remains a motivating factor for many Green activists whose campaigns, rather than simply misunderstanding the way social processes transform natural cycles and weather systems, are designed to minimise such disruption. Of course, we may think such campaigns are doomed to failure, but that would be to reject the radical proposal for de-industrialisation as unrealistic. This is quite different from accusing Greens of essentialism. And of course, such an environmental perspective is not restricted to politically motivated but misguided activists, but also finds some support from realist social theorists and environmental sociologists. Again we return to the same point about the risk thesis, namely that although provocative and sometimes insightful, it tends to caricature environmental political movements rather than engaging in debate with them, and as such the thesis lacks a solid empirical grounding.

Conclusion

The concept of risk has a special place in discussions of environmental issues and risk theorists find much useful material in such issues that help them to make their case for seeing modern societies as risk societies. Risk theories are also useful because they provide part of an explanation for the receptive audience for environmental movement concerns. Once people become sensitised to risks and aware of the conflicting and uncertain advice of scientific experts, the often gloomy predictions made by some environmentalists and Greens begin to make more sense. In this way, the social conditions for an expansion of environmental movement membership and support are created. However, as a theory of society, Beck's risk society thesis, ultimately is not convincing. Like many other disjunctive theories, the persistent tendency to portray 'before and after' pictures of social change, whilst telling us something about living in the modern world, consistently overstates the case beyond what empirical evidence will support. Critics of Beck's risk thesis complain not only that it lacks empirical support but also that it is overly rationalistic and fails to take account of cultural variability in risk-defining processes (Douglas 1984, 1994; Scott 2000). It also works with a denuded characterisation of environmental movements and the developing discourse of ecocentrism and ecologism. The concept of risk certainly *has* become more prominent in the social sciences, and there is some interesting work in the areas of risk perception and risk analysis. However, the claims for the emergence of a risk *society* in the terms laid out by Beck are not yet made.

There are also other ways of theorising modern societies that stand as alternatives to the risk society thesis and although this is not the place to engage in an extended discussion of these, it is at least possible to point towards one potential alternative. Rather than using the concept of 'risk', it may be more useful to think of modern societies as producing higher level 'vulnerabilities' (de Vries 2002). This distinction is not simply terminological but marks out a different way of thinking about social development and change, which can be gleaned from the world history of William McNeill (1975, 1979) and the long-term developmental sociology of Johan Goudsblom (1989, 1992), who both argue (in rather different ways) that the increasing human control over natural forces and non-human animals is always gained at a price. Part of that price is an increasing dependence on the social relations and technological means which enable human control to be established. This has the further consequence that as the division of labour and human interdependencies geographically extend over larger areas, so societies generate vulnerabilities at higher and higher levels. Modern societies are vulnerable to breakdowns in the systems of control that allow people to live relatively peaceably and safely. If we consider the higher level vulnerability created by the increasing reliance on information technologies in routine administration, international banking, air traffic control systems and so on, it becomes easier to see the force of such a proposition, which McNeill (1979) calls 'the Law of Conservation of Catastrophe'. 'Law' is probably too strong a characterisation, but what McNeill means here is the storing up of the potentially 'catastrophic' consequences of higher levels of social organisation, which if released affect more people and threaten to render inoperative more elements of society's infrastructure.

Introducing the notion of transformations in the level of vulnerabilities provides a useful alternative to risk, which recognises that whilst modern societies are certainly producing higher level vulnerabilities, this does not mean that they are 'high risk' societies. This may sound strange when we consider the potential price of high-consequence environmental problems such as global warming and ozone depletion. But risk is an inherently political concept, which embodies the idea that measures should be put in place to minimise or eliminate such risks. Vulnerability on the other hand involves an understanding that the increasing scale of human interdependencies produce *both* gains and new problems and that these always go hand in hand. Whilst information technologies enable easier and perhaps safer travel systems, they also make such systems more vulnerable to a breakdown that affects large parts of or even the entire system. However, recognising that the system is more vulnerable to a general disruption does not simply make travel more risky. Taken as a whole, it may well be that modern travel systems have brought about a reduction in many kinds of previously taken-for-granted risks for travellers.

To summarise then, theories of an emergent new type of 'risk' society hold out exciting, yet illusory prospects for sociologists, closing off as many research avenues as they claim to open. Disjunctive theories of this kind tend to produce one-sided accounts of social change and are therefore somewhat unrealistic and even unhelpful. Whilst sociologists must discuss contemporary issues and fears, it surely becomes problematic when arguments are made that we need, say, a postmodern sociology, a global sociology, a risk sociology or even an environmental sociology. What we really do need is a sociology that is able to analyse and make sense of post-modernism, globalisation, risk and environmental issues and we return to this conclusion in more detail in Chapter 9.

7 Modernity as an Unfinished Ecological Project

Given the identification of continuing environmental degradation and socially created environmental problems at increasingly higher levels, the logical question is to ask how these can best be tackled. In this chapter three broadly based frameworks are outlined, all claiming to be effective in addressing environmental problems. These are discussed under the general headings of Green consumerism, sustainable development and ecological modernisation. Though each is internally divided and there are clearly differences between them, the argument here is that a case can be made for seeing all three as sharing a common assumption. This is simply the belief that the basic pattern of modern industrial and technological development can continue, albeit in less ecologically destructive forms. This means that social and institutional reform will be enough rather than the need for the wholesale transformation of modern societies. All three perspectives are rooted in the peculiarly modern mentality, which insists that social and environmental problems of all kinds can be solved without sacrificing Western standards of material prosperity and quality of life. The basic questions posed in the chapter therefore are, can there be a Green consumerism under capitalism, is continued economic development ecologically sustainable and can there ever be an ecological form of modernisation?

Green consumption in capitalist societies

Sociologists have argued that over the course of the twentieth century, the central orientation of industrial capitalist societies has shifted from a production paradigm towards a consumerist one, and it is now commonplace to see the relatively rich societies referred to as 'consumer societies' (Campbell 1987; Featherstone 1991; Lury 1996). Although this is another example of those theories that work with distinct, static societal types, as we saw in the previous chapter, such theories do make several central claims. First, productive work is becoming less influential in providing people with ready-made identities and is less central to the process of identity formation. Instead, it is conspicuous consumption that provides people with the opportunity to construct a personal identity by purchasing the elements to do so in the marketplace, giving at least the perception of more free choice and individuality. A process that Zygmunt Bauman describes as the purchase of 'identity kits' (Bauman 1998). Secondly, corporations are much more concerned to tap into and produce for a more flexible and differentiated consumer demand rather than putting the needs of production first and worrying about customers later. Typically this shift is represented in theories of the demise of uniform Fordist production methods towards the much more flexible post-Fordist methods designed to cater for niche markets (Amin 1994). Aglietta (1987) has seen such a shift as a change in the mode of capitalist regulation that does not dispense with mass consumption but is marked by differentiated patterns of consumption. Either way it seems, the consumer not the producer becomes the central focus. Thirdly, because consumer societies allow the construction of consumerised personal identities, this serves to decentre production-based social conflicts, engaging more social groups in the competitive process of status competition through symbolic exchanges. The concept of the consumer society therefore marks significant changes in the economic, political and cultural spheres as well as in fundamental processes of identity formation.

For many environmentalists such social change intensifies pressures on the natural world. The increasingly central focus on consumption and the ideology of consumerism promote an increasingly rapid turnover of products based on fashionable shifts in the exchange value of commodities and as a result, more waste. Consumer identification with products and brands in ways described in 1950s and 1960s USA by Packard (1964), Galbraith (1958) and Marcuse (1964), and more recently, Klein (2001) makes consumption central to the routines of everyday life. The earlier group of writers tended to distinguish genuine 'needs' from non-necessary 'wants' and 'desires', thus enabling a critical theory of society that pointed out the ultimately irrational character of modern consumer behaviour. This may seem quite straightforward, but determining what counts as a 'need' is at least partially culturally specific and no firm grounds have been generally agreed for making this distinction (Heller and Feher 1988; Dobson [1990] 2001: 79–80). Similarly, for some time the question of a sustainable population level has been a feature of Green politics. In the 1970s and 1980s it was assumed that a prerequisite for reducing high levels of consumption was to slow down population growth and reduce global population levels. However, in more recent years, it has been recognised that it is not just sheer numbers of people that leads to over-exploitation of natural resources, but what consumer practices they engage in which is important. Even if population levels were reduced in developing countries this would be of little relevance globally if the industrialised societies continue to consume resources at current levels. Therefore, as Dobson ([1990] 2001: 98) points out, 'Essential, then, to ecologism's picture of the sustainable society is reduced consumption (in profligate 'advanced' industrial countries, at any rate), and equally essential is the idea that, while this might involve a reduced material standard of living, such sacrifice will be more than made up for by the benefits to be gained.' This perspective amounts to a recasting of ideas about what constitutes 'the good life' and enables Greens to raise issues about the quality of life that might be gained from lower levels of consumption.

Social theorists have argued that the spread of Western forms of consumerism across the world generates ecologically unsustainable practices as products traverse the globe and promote status competition and create inequalities in the developing world. Both Fordist and Post-Fordist models rely on mass consumption, even if the latter does tend towards diversification, and it is mass consumption which, if allowed to spread across the developing world in the same way that it already has in the developed countries, would accelerate biodiversity loss, increase environmental pollution and make global warming much more difficult to reverse. Such Western economic models have produced over-development and need to be reined in rather than exported (Trainer 1985). Rather than promoting Green consumerism, which is after all still a form of consumerism, radical Greens advocate a reduction in consumption, more local production and living simpler lifestyles closer to the land. From this perspective, consumer capitalism represents an intensification of the exploitation of nature not a step back from it, hence it is impossible to believe that consumerism, Green or otherwise, has anything to offer environmental protection.

It may therefore be surprising to see that from within the environmental movement, some have advocated working with rather than against the grain of consumer societies in order to transform them from within. Such arguments can be usefully described as promoting Green consumerism and Green capitalism, both of which see market forces and price mechanisms as effective ways of changing the behaviour of individuals and corporations down a more ecologically sensitive route. Green consumerism attempts to make creative use of the newly found power of consumers and consumer groups to demand ecologically sound products. In this way, consumerism can be used as a tool to transform ecologically damaging production methods and practices. The idea of a Green capitalism generally represents an appeal to businesses to produce in more ecologically sustainable ways. The arguments for them doing so can be couched in environmental terms or may simply appeal to their own self-interest. Companies can be encouraged to 'go Green' because moving in this direction is the right thing to do, regardless of the impact on profits. Such an appeal is likely to fail unless there are other business reasons to make the necessary changes. It may be that the greening of capitalism could be attractive in so far as it is based on waste reduction strategies, which stand to provide benefits for business as well as improving environmental quality. Given the increasing prominence of consumerism both for businesses and for individuals, I will refer to the greening of both business and consumerism as forms of 'Green consumerism'.

First published in the UK, Elkington and Hailes's (1988), *The Green Consumer Guide*, became one of the best selling environmental books of all time with tailored versions appearing in nine other countries including the USA, Canada and Australia within 2 years (McCormick 1991: 107). It seems that many people were interested in how they could consume in environmentally sensitive ways and contribute to solving ecological problems at the same time. However, such a success story shows a reserve of goodwill towards environmentalism rather than evidence that such an approach genuinely could solve ecological problems. The period of the late

1980s followed the Chernobyl nuclear disaster, which significantly raised the profile of the environment as a core concern and in this climate even the British Prime Minister at the time, Margaret Thatcher, attempted in a now famous 1988 speech, to claim Green credentials. Nevertheless, Green consumerism is clearly a much more widespread and long-lasting phenomenon that is now regularly found among large sections of the adult populations in attitude surveys across Europe and North America. People report that they regularly purchase 'environmentally friendly' products as part of lifestyle changes, which also include saving energy, recycling and using less polluting forms of transport when possible (Macnaghten and Urry 1998: Chapter 3).

The connection between Green consumerism and environmental organisations can often be quite close, particularly given the reformist character of most of these organisations. Environmental groups have the potential to use their members' and supporters' consumer power to boycott products or companies and to raise awareness of bad practices or environmentally damaging products. Examples would include the sustained campaign against the McDonalds fast food chain to protest against the company's involvement in converting rain forests in Latin America into beef producing farms: Greenpeace, Lynx and PETA's (People for the Ethical Treatment of Animals) long campaigns against the use of fur in the fashion industry and Friends of the Earth's ultimately successful campaign to raise the issue of aerosols releasing damaging chlorofluorocarbons (CFCs) that cause thinning of the ozone layer (McCormick 1991: Chapter 8). Such examples are not so new however. Consumer pressure and boycotts have been tactics for environmental movements from their very earliest organisations. Yearley (1991: 99–100) points out that in the UK, the RSPB was virtually founded on a consumer boycott by women who signed a pledge not to wear the feathers of birds in their hats in protest against the mass slaughter of seabirds. Similarly, in the late nineteenth century, the Society for Checking the Abuses of Public Advertising (SCAPA) organised a member's boycott of any product advertised on large metal boards by the sides of railway lines, which spoiled the views of nature and the countryside. So, even in the days before Fordist mass manufacture, consumer power was a recognised phenomenon and consumer boycott a legitimate activity, if only sparingly used. What makes contemporary boycotts different are the forms of media available for disseminating the message and their relative immediacy, global spread and visual impact compared with newspapers, pamphlets and placards. What is not clear is just how successful such Green consumerist campaigns are. If we judge their effectiveness on the single issues they address we could draw up a balance sheet of successes and failures though this would not be definitive, as boycotts do not necessarily eliminate the issue forever. Anti-fur campaigners may have been successful in the short term, but given the vicissitudes of the fashion industry it is hardly surprising to see some designers returning to its use again in recent years. Equally, we could judge Green consumerism on its long-term impact on attitudes towards environmental issues, though it would be virtually impossible to select its influence from that of other environmental campaigns, the spread of postmaterial values or the effects of economic restructuring. Despite these problems, most environmentalists now accept that Green consumerism does at least have the potential to bring more people towards environmental awareness, and in that sense it could be beneficial to the wider movement's aims.

The question of whether a Green capitalism can be anything other than an oxymoron is a more intractable problem that usually finds a normative response one way or the other. For marxists, the concept of Green capitalism is faintly ridiculous, whilst for Elkington and Burke (1987) a new form of Green economic growth is not only possible but is already underway. It is quite clear that many corporations have gone to great lengths to create a new environmental image or 'brand' for themselves as a way of greening their public image. This is a galling prospect for many Greens who now see companies they consider the worst environmental offenders, oil companies for instance, using images of the natural world in their advertising and even in company logos. British Petroleum (BP) recently changed its corporate logo from company initials to a naturalistic flower head with green petals. Others use similar natural imagery in their advertising and provide funding for grassroots conservation projects. In a similar vein, the environmental labelling of products is often simply a cheap marketing ploy that bears little relation to a transformed environmental consciousness. Such cosmetic changes obviously do not constitute a genuinely Green form of capitalism. Robinson (1992: 59) suggests that 'At the centre of the 'greening' of capitalism is a process of image reconstruction. In an increasingly sensitive consumer society and against a political climate where competition is encouraged, public relations for companies is given considerable emphasis'. In short, consumers demand that corporations at least *appear* to be Green but do not necessarily push them actually to be so.

What might constitute a Green capitalism are companies beginning to change the way their organisation operates to become less environmentally harmful and polluting and if this has the effect of lowering costs then it may be that a Green capitalism will become more popular. There are three main ways in which this might occur (Robinson 1992: Chapter 2). First, corporate waste reduction strategies could reduce industry's impact on the environment and save money, thus increasing profits. To some extent companies are already involved in this project in so far as reducing waste to increase profits is a basic goal of capitalist business logic. This being the case, it is not surprising to see companies eager to publicise their Green credentials. Secondly, what is already beginning to take shape is an environmental protection industry geared to the production of solar panels, pollution control and monitoring equipment, recycling and so on. This development shows that there is profit to be made in the greening of capitalism, and it is perfectly possible for environmental protection to generate economic development and growth. Green capitalism need not mean an end to technological fixes, provided such technologies help to reduce environmental pollution rather than increasing it. One problem here of course is to assess whether the environmental protection industry really does lead to less pollution. Recycling and environmental production are after all, still industries that produce their own forms of pollution and waste and are not without consequences for environmental quality. Thirdly, if companies genuinely attempt to satisfy the demands of Green consumers, then they will be dragged along in the wake of a changing culture into a more environmentally benign capitalism. Such Green consumer power relies on an environmentally enlightened population, which is able to tell the difference between 'greenwash', the strictly limited and public relations use of Green labelling, and genuine advances in reducing pollution and waste. The difficulty here is that the ability to make this distinction requires the existence of the same Green awareness which the strategy is supposed to be helping to generate.

Whether Green consumerism and progress towards a Green form of capitalism are capable of bringing about the necessary changes to achieve an ecologically sustainable society is a matter of political debate. But we can at least note that the use of the word 'Green' in these ways is something of a misnomer. Even on the most optimistic reading, such solutions bear little relation to the radical ecological perspective. One of the problems with this assimilation of key terms is that it tends to erode the distinction between reform environmentalism and Green politics, making it appear that all attempts to take account of environmental issues constitutes being 'Green'. Whilst this may be useful for those seeking moderate reforms or increased profits, it needs to be remembered that, as we saw in Chapter 4, there is much more to the Green analysis of society than changes in patterns of consumption. Green consumerism could be a useful way of maintaining pressure on companies for environmental reform and has the benefit of offering people a range of positive ways to feel involved in environmental protection. However, if consuming in relatively more Green ways is all they do, then radical ecologists will continue to see Green consumerism as unsatisfactory.

Global sustainable development

The concept of sustainable development is politically contested, flexible and open to conflicting interpretations. It is also not entirely novel and amongst others '... had been espoused by German and Indian foresters, and by Roosevelt and [Gifford] Pinchot' (McCormick 1992: 149). Nonetheless, some version of it underpins the thinking of many environmentalists, governments and international agencies concerned with how environmental problems can adequately be dealt with. Porritt (1984: 126) provides a clear idea of the meaning of sustainability, suggesting that 'Green economics is all about *sustainability* and *social justice*: finding and sustaining such means of creating wealth as will allow us to meet the genuine needs of all people without damaging our fragile biosphere.' The combination of the idea of *sustainability*, with its focus on maintaining the natural environment, and *development*, with the emphasis on economic and social progress, gives the sustainable development concept a particularly inclusive content, promising to unite environmentalists, governments in the north and the south as well as those working for an end to global poverty. Whilst this is a possible strength of 'sustainability talk' (Irwin 2001) it can also make the public discourse of sustainability appear incoherent and discordant, meaning all things to all people.

The modern origin of the concept lies in the catastrophist environmentalist writings of the early 1970s, though arguments in favour of a 'steady state' rather than a constantly expanding economy go back at least as far as John Stuart Mill's *Principles of Political Economy* (1848). Mill's argument against indefinite economic (and population) growth was based on a concern that if not ecologically catastrophic, these were at least sure to reduce the quality of life. He argued that (Mill (1848) cited in Wall 1994: 121)

> Nor is there much satisfaction in contemplating the world with nothing left to the spontaneous activity of nature; with every rood of land brought into cultivation ... every flowery waste or natural pasture ploughed up, all quadrupeds or birds which are not domesticated for man's use exterminated as his rivals for food, every hedgerow or superfluous tree rooted out, and scarcely a place left where a wild shrub or flower could grow without being eradicated as a weed in the name of improved agriculture.

Mill also believed that a stationary economy and population did not mean an end to human improvement but an opportunity for improvements in the 'art of living'.

In the 1970s, two touchstone texts of the period symbolised the quantitative change in such arguments since Mill's time. In the UK, The Ecologist magazine's *Blueprint for Survival* (1972) and in the USA, Meadows and colleagues' *Limits to Growth* (1972) report provoked heated debates. The *Blueprint for Survival* set the terms of debate as involving the very survival of human life on Earth and formed the basis for the Green Party's first manifesto. The *Limits* team constructed a computer model based on five global trends: accelerating industrialisation, rapid population growth, widespread malnutrition, depletion of non-renewable resources and a deteriorating environment (Meadows *et al.* 1974: 21). By manipulating these variables they were able to create different scenarios designed to test the proposition that there are no limits to economic growth. On a 'business as usual' run in which current trends continued, economic growth was ended due to the exhaustion of non-renewable resources around 2100. In other scenarios, previous problems were 'solved' by assuming changes in each variable, but concluded that despite doubling the amount of resources, reducing pollution levels to pre-1970s levels and introducing new technologies, the model still predicted an end to growth before 2100 (Dobson [1990] 2001: Chapter 3). For Greens, two conclusions can be drawn from this exercise. First, technological innovations cannot stave off the collapse of expanding economies forever and we need to begin to plan to stave off the inevitable. Secondly, and contrary to Condorcet's optimism, nature *has* set limits to what human societies can achieve. Because the report used computer modelling and scientific testing rather than simply being another normative critique of industrialism, it had wider appeal and helped to popularise sustainability ideas, though for some social scientists its lack of social and political awareness gave its conclusions a purely technical and deterministic feel (Irwin 2001: 36).

The 1970s catastrophist environmentalism took its lead from the ideas of Malthus and others, regarding the need to establish a steady state society, demanding an end to economic growth as the way to achieve ecologically sustainable societies. Since the 1980s however, partly in response to critics in developing countries who saw these ideas as relegating them to a future of poverty and famine, sustainability has been tied to ongoing economic and social development in an attempt to forge a platform capable of uniting countries in both the north and the south as well as business, governments and environmentalists. No small task. We can say therefore that ideas of sustainable development offer a typically 'modernist' solution to the most pressing problems of our time. This is so, because its advocates see global economic and social problems as challenges to be solved rather than as insurmountable facts. Sustainability discourse also relies heavily on an image of the rational actor being persuaded by environmental education and enlightenment to participate in the project. And although disputes have arisen over what sustainable development really means both in theory and practice, as the burgeoning literature on this subject and governmental action plans demonstrate, it cannot now be ignored.

The influence of the *Limits* report was evident at the United Nations Conference on the Human Environment in Stockholm (1972), whose General Secretary had commissioned an unofficial report on 'the relationship between man and his natural habitat' in 1971, later published by Barbara Ward and Rene Dubos as *Only One Earth* (1977). However, it was the International Union for the Conservation of Nature and Natural Resources (IUCN) which proposed 'sustainable development' in 1980 as a principal goal of the World Conservation Strategy (WCS) (Baker *et al.* 1997: 2). The conservationist origin of the concept is important as some argue that at root, sustainable development remains primarily concerned with the industrialised world's issue of environmental protection rather than the developing world's central concern with material poverty. Jacobs (1999: 35) argues for instance that 'There can be little doubt that protecting the environment is the dominant motivation for and idea within, sustainable development.' The seminal report, *Our Common Future* (1987), (known as the Bruntland Report, after its President, Gro Harlam Bruntland) produced by the United Nations Commission on Environment and Development (UNCED), expanded the concept with its definition of sustainable development as '... development which meets the needs of the present without compromising the ability of future generations to meet their own needs' (cited in Macnaghten and Urry 1998: 213). This definition brings together the global conservation of resources and economic development in the developing world and as such appeals to northern environmentalists and activists in the World Development Movement alike, though it is premised on the questionable idea that we could know today what the needs of future generations might be, even when there is still dispute over what constitute genuine 'needs' in the present. The report also linked sustainable development to the elimination of gross inequalities between the north and the south and issues of global resource distribution, thus raising questions about international power relations (Baker *et al.* 1997).

By the time of the 1992 UN 'Earth Summit' in Rio de Janeiro, the concept of sustainable development had become the common currency for debates around environmental and economic justice. The 1992 Summit launched 'Agenda 21', a programme for the implementation of sustainable development initiatives in over 170 countries, and created a Commission for Sustainable Development designed to monitor such implementation. Also, with 'Local Agenda 21', it becomes clear that achieving sustainable development will of course require action by governments, businesses and non-governmental organisations (NGOs), but it will also require the participation of individual citizens as 'stakeholders', who should be empowered to get involved at the community level. In 2002, the World Summit on Sustainable Development held in Johannesburg reaffirmed the concept as the focus for global attempts at environmental protection and tackling poverty, including new targets on access to sanitation and safe drinking water. However, aware of criticism from environmentalists and Greens that Earth Summits have not produced enough concrete reforms, the UN announced that it is foregoing planning any more until governments take more action. Instead, a more rigorous monitoring and 'naming and shaming' policy has been adopted, which is intended to put international pressure on national governments.

It is clear that sustainable development has now become the dominant discursive frame for discussing environmental and development issues. Irwin (2001: 46) argues that sustainable development 'brings together democratic principles, faith in science and technology, a view of the future, an assertion of the moral responsibility of those alive today, and a sense that we are part of a global family', making the concept one that 'we can all feel good about'. There is a striking parallel here with the World Health Organisation's (WHO) strategy for global public health, launched in the 1980s through a 'New Public Health' (NPH) policy. This also aimed to involve a wide range of social actors and to provide information on health matters including lifestyle choices, 'empowering' individuals responsible for their own and the wider public health. However, the NPH has attracted much criticism from sociologists influenced by the ideas of Michel Foucault, as a moralising discourse that, rather than genuinely empowering people, puts pressure on people to participate and conform to new norms of health behaviour (Armstrong 1993). It remains to be seen whether such criticisms will also be applicable to post-1992 ideas of sustainability (Buckingham-Hatfield and Percy 1999), though, as we will see in the next chapter, post-structuralists have already arrived at similar conclusions in relation to Green politics.

In contrast to Green consumerism, sustainable development focuses less on market mechanisms and more on state involvement and international co-operation in environmental protection. In addition, sustainable development brings the World Development

Movement into contact with northern environmentalists, insisting that if global environmental problems are to be solved then tackling some of the gross economic inequalities in the world economic system must be an equal priority. The ideas at the core of the concept also raise issues of time in human affairs (Adam 1996), by looking at both intra- and inter-generational equity (Dobson 1999). In doing so, the discourse and practice of sustainability also promotes taking the long view as well as working on short- to medium-term solutions to particular problems. In these ways, sustainable development has the potential to offer something for radicals who can push for the implementation of its widest goals, and for moderates who can work towards concrete reforms in the here and now.

Modernising ecologically

At the same time that sustainable development was emerging as an all-encompassing perspective and political programme in the early 1980s, a group of academics in Germany, the Netherlands and UK began to produce a new theoretical perspective they termed 'ecological modernisation'. The concept is generally credited to Joseph Huber's work in the early 1980s, which Sonnenfeld (2000: 236) describes as 'industrial restructuring with a green twist'. However, ecological modernisation can also be seen as a constructive response to earlier 'cornucopian' critics of radical ecology, such as Simon and Kahn (1984), who argued that successive technological developments that overcame previous limitations effectively negated arguments that there were clearly defined limits to economic growth (Dobson [1990] 2001: 207). The roots of ecological modernisation may also be found in the ideas of writers such as Lovins (1977) and Dickson (1974) who proposed solutions to environmental problems through 'soft energy paths' (solar power, synthetic fuels and so on) and 'alternative technology' (new approaches to the design of machines and tools). Such ideas point towards the creative scaling down of industrial societies' interventions in the natural world.

The main interests of the early group of ecological modernisation theorists were in the role of technological innovations in production systems, a critique of bureaucratic nation states and the positive use of market mechanisms, and the attempt to utilise a systems-theoretical and evolutionary approach (Mol and Sonnenfeld 2000: 4–5). An initial omission however, which has continued to afflict the approach, was the relative neglect of social and political struggles around environmental issues. Ecological modernisation theorists intervened in the debates around how best to tackle environmental degradation in the wake of the *Limits to Growth* thesis and the emergence of a radical Green analysis of industrialism. Whilst Green radicals promoted de-industrialisation in a general critique of commercial-industrial culture, ecological modernisation theory forged a path that explored that culture's reform. In a sense ecological modernisation took up a position between the radical Green de-industrialisers on one side and the capitalist apologists on the other. They recognised that social and institutional change was required but rejected de-industrialisation as an unrealistic option.

For some, a new form of ecologically benign modernisation could be built around the gradual separation of material and economic 'flows' through society (Jänicke 1985). The argument here is that it is only by making use of high technologies that it becomes possible to break the link between economic growth and resource depletion. Whilst Greens argued for an end to growth on the grounds that more growth means more environmental degradation and faster depletion of resources, ecological modernisers saw in some European leading edge industries, the possibility to achieve a lower use of natural resources *without* this negatively affecting growth. Some went further to argue that such a strategy actually produces an ecological form of economic growth, a win-win situation rather than a zero-sum game. If so, then this calls the radical Green attack on economic growth *per se* into doubt. If environmental protection can be achieved within an advanced industrial society there is no need for a more radical deep Green analysis or a shift towards an ecocentric orientation (Dobson [1990] 2001). The 'materials flow' position is only one element in the broader ecological modernisation paradigm, though others have proposed the principle of 'decoupling' human society from nature as a genuine alternative to de-industrialisation and living closer to nature (Lewis 1994; Huber 1999).

It is possible to see the development of ecological modernisation theory as moving through a series of phases, each attempting to deal with the substantial critical fire aimed at it and to incorporate some of the significant omissions pointed out by critics (Mol and Sonnenfeld 2000). The first phase outlined above gave way in the late 1980s to a second phase, which brought the concept of culture into the overall picture. Critics had remarked that early ecological modernisation ignored the realm of culture in its push for technological and institutional transformation. Hajer (1996) argues that ecological modernisation is at least in part, a form of 'cultural politics' that takes shape within grassroots mobilisations and sub-politics, within which new identities are formed. In common with Melucci (1988, 1989) and new social movement theorists, Rinkevicius (2000: 198) argues that such movements and processes of identity formation are evidence of the movement towards an ecological consciousness and can be interpreted as '...a part of the dialectics of ecological modernisation or ecological transformation of contemporary societies'. This has brought ecological modernisation theory into closer contact with emerging debates in social theory.

By the mid-1990s a third phase can be discerned which brought three more major areas of debate into the ecological modernisation perspective. First, until this point, ecological modernisation theorists accept that their work had been largely restricted to Western European countries, but now research has begun to expand to the rest of the world, including the developing countries of the south. This posed a significant challenge for the theory, as it had tended to assume a set of social institutions modelled on Western democracies. Frijns *et al.* (2000: 258) for example, note eight such institutions:

- A democratic and open political system;
- A legitimate and interventionist state with an advanced and differentiated socio-environmental infrastructure;
- Widespread environmental consciousness and well-organised environmental NGOs that have the resources to push for radical ecological reform;
- Intermediate or business organisations that are able to represent producers in negotiations on a sectoral or regional basis;
- Experience with and tradition in negotiated policy-making and regulatory negotiations;
- A detailed system of environmental monitoring that generates sufficient, reliable and public environmental data;

- A state-regulated market economy that dominates production and consumption processes, covering all the edges of society and strongly integrated in the global market; and
- Advanced technological development in a highly industrialised society.

Such an institutional framework is clearly not applicable outside a few western industrialised societies and it may strike readers as ethnocentric and rather naïve even to attempt to apply it to developing countries. Its Eurocentrism is acknowledged, though it can be argued that attempts to compare it with the situation in the context of developing countries do at least provide a research focus for comparative studies that may lead to a more discriminating theory.

Secondly, the expansion of ecological modernisation theory to cover both industrialised and developing countries pushed it closer to emerging theories of globalisation, though work in this area is still sparse (Mol 2001). Thirdly, it became clear that sociological work on consumerism and theories of the consumer society marked another major omission. Not just production, but consumption needs to be 'ecologised' and this realisation opened up a whole new field of study that is currently being explored. Again, there is a rich field to be investigated here in relation to changing consumption patterns, domestic technologies and sustainable lifestyles (Cowan 1983; Spaargaren 1997; Noorman and Schoot 1998). This is one area where ecological modernisation and sociological theory have much in common, despite the latter's relatively detached position by comparison with the normative position of some ecological modernisers. Bourdieu's (1984) theoretical perspective on the social process of distinction-making and its relationship to class cultures is one obvious point of similarity, as is Urry's (1990, 1995) sociology of tourism, the 'tourist gaze' and the consumption of place.

What advocates and supporters of ecological modernisation point out is that many critics have failed to appreciate the gradual evolution of the perspective over time and are still aiming their criticisms at the first phase rather than the much changed and critically aware current one. Nevertheless, as even ecological modernisers themselves accept, the current phase still maintains a central concern with the transformation and not the removal of the institutional structures of industrial capitalist modernity. This makes the perspective inherently reformist and as such it will inevitably be deemed insufficient by those wishing to see an end to capitalism, industrialism, modernity or all three of these. Nonetheless, it is important to recognise that 'business as usual' is not an option for ecological modernisers, though change always means using and working through existing structures rather than destroying them in the quest for ecological solutions.

The five key social and institutional structures identified for change are: science and technology, markets and economic agents, the nation state, social movements and ideologies (Mol and Sonnenfeld 2000). Science and technology can potentially make a huge impact provided that they are used in preventative rather than curative ways. If ecological considerations can be built in at the design stage then it should be possible to move towards ecologically sensitive production methods. As with Green consumerism, ecological modernisers favour market forces as an efficient means of changing the behaviour of corporations and states alongside pressure from reform-oriented social movements. This means that although the radical Green perspective is rejected, ecological modernisers see most environmental organisations as part of their proposed solutions. Similarly they argue that nation states will need to promote decentralised forms of governance and give up on some of their areas of competence to allow pressure from consumers, social movements and markets to be effective.

Although sharing some common ground, both with ideas of sustainable development and Green consumerism, the ecological modernisation perspective is really quite different in important respects. Unlike sustainable development, ecological modernisation has been less concerned with issues of global inequalities and development in the south and tends to put its faith in the actions of businesses, individuals and non-state actors, unlike the relatively top down UN-sponsored versions of sustainable development initiatives. Similarly, although support for business and market forces initially placed ecological modernisation closer to Green capitalism and consumerism, in its more recent phase, ecological modernisers have attempted to distance their perspective from these. It is argued that

> mainstream ecological modernisation theorists interpret capitalism neither as an essential precondition for, nor as the key obstruction

to, stringent or radical environmental reform. They rather focus on redirecting and transforming 'free market capitalism' in such a way that it less and less obstructs, and increasingly contributes to, the preservation of society's sustenance base in a fundamental/ structural way' (Mol and Spaargaren 2000: 23).

This puts them in a relatively agnostic position, which basically says that capitalism will survive if it can facilitate the necessary institutional changes, but if not, then a different, unspecified form of economic system will emerge from the ecological modernisation of society.

Ecological modernisation is really several things. First, it is a social scientific research programme that explores in what ways social institutions *are* being transformed as they strive to become more ecologically sensitive. This research is ongoing and has produced many interesting and thoughtful studies. However, the research has so far proved inconclusive, suggesting some fairly minor changes in practices rather than a genuine commitment to ecological modernisation across a range of social institutions. Such a conclusion may provide support for the view that it really *does* matter whether ecological modernisation is undertaken because of an ecocentric orientation rather than an anthropocentric one (Dobson [1990] 2001: 207–13). The idea that satisfactory ecological outcomes can be achieved without an environmental ethic or a radical Green perspective (Norton 1991) seems unlikely and ignores the historical evidence of the importance of a dialectical relationship between reform and radical versions of environmental politics in the development of contemporary environmental concern (Sutton 2000). Secondly, ecological modernisation is a political programme, which *promotes* a particular way of dealing with environmental issues at the expense of others. This political programme is especially attractive to northern governments as it is much less threatening than radical Green politics. There is much overlap in this area between ecological modernisation and sustainable development, though their different attitude towards the role of nation states marks one key divide, with ecological modernisers wanting less state involvement whilst sustainable development sees the state as an important actor in promoting sustainability. Thirdly, ecological modernisation covers a wide range of initiatives taken by industrial companies, local government and individuals as consumers that are aimed at reducing human impacts on the natural resource base. The assessment of such initiatives forms a large part of the ecological modernisation research agenda and it is probably too early to reach any firm conclusions. Nevertheless, what makes the ecological modernisation perspective attractive is the role it gives for such a wide range of actors to take responsibility for and to contribute towards the emerging ecologically sustainable society. Finally, ecological modernisation is an evolutionary theory of social change. In this guise it suggests that Western industrialised societies have passed through several 'industrial revolutions' and the latest of these is the ecological version. This means that ecological modernisation theory really is what it says on the tin, a specifically ecological version of the much older modernisation theory. This is perhaps why critics have circled over it so quickly, given the now largely discredited, linear social evolution advocated by the latter.

Some of the same criticisms made against early modernisation theory have also been levelled against ecological modernisation. Critics have pointed to its technocentrism (Redclift 2000), lack of understanding of the dynamics of capitalism (Schnaiberg 1980; O'Connor 1996) and a general neglect of issues of power and human agency (Blühdorn, 2000). Hannigan (1995) sees ecological modernisation as containing an unjustified technological optimism, or what O'Riordan (1981) called 'technocentrism', the belief that environmental problems can be solved through technological creativity and innovation, such as adding catalytic converters to motor vehicles as a solution to their polluting emissions. It is clear that ecological modernisation theory is optimistic about what technological innovations might achieve, though this is tempered by the acknowledgement that this will be ineffective without changes to social institutions. Hajer (1995, 1996) distinguishes two broad forms of ecological modernisation. One, a techno-corporatist form that tends to stop at the level of social institutions, the other a reflexive version that takes ecological modernisation closer to current debates in social theory. It certainly is the case that in recent years these two have moved closer together with ecological modernisers making use of both Beck's and Giddens's theoretical perspectives (Spaargaren and Van Vliet 2000), whilst some sociologists have argued that social theory needs to analyse the way that different types of technology are developed (Irwin 2001: Chapter 6). Hannigan's criticism remains pertinent though, as even in its reflexive version, ecological modernisation, unlike Beck's risk thesis, maintains a central role for science, scientific expertise and technological innovation, which is in part the feature that gives ecological modernisation its originality and differentiates it from the other modernist perspectives outlined above.

Conclusion

One positive aspect of the modernistic solutions advocated in this chapter is that they offer clearly defined ways for individuals, businesses, governments and other agencies to get involved in that oft-repeated, yet scarcely well-defined project of 'saving the planet'. It is somewhat ironic that although Green activists propose 'treading softly on the earth' in their critique of managerial and arrogant anthropocentrism, the very idea of 'saving the planet' puts all previous modern projects in the shade. At the heart of the project of saving the planet is the attempt to prevent human societies from over-exploiting the natural world or the 'resource base', but without ending economic growth or reducing the quality of life in the industrialised north, at the same time eliminating poverty in the developing world and allowing developing countries to generate higher standards of material prosperity. Needless to say, this is quite a task, but one that is entirely consistent with the modern mentality (Bauman 1992).

In the debates around postmodernism in the 1980s, the German social philosopher and critical theorist Habermas (1983) took up a position in defence of modernity and against its postmodern critics, who saw the 'modern project' of the rational restructuring of social life as exhausted. Habermas argued that on the contrary, modernity is very much an 'unfinished project' and rather than lining up to bury it, critical social theorists should be prepared to work out new ways to carry it forward. Similarly, Wellmer (1991: vii) points out that despite the postmodernists' attempts to demonstrate the self-defeating nature of rational modernity, their arguments, being essentially rationally and logically structured themselves, only succeeded in expanding modernity, thus demonstrating that 'modernity is for us, an unsurpassable horizon in a cognitive, aesthetic and moral-political sense', because '. . . the critique of modernity has been part of the modern spirit since its very inception'. Szerszynski (1996) arrived at a similar conclusion in relation to attempts to dispense with the dualisms stemming from the Western philosophical discourse of modernity (Habermas 1990). These attempts all founder because paradoxically they wind up producing new sets of dualisms to replace those they dissolve. There seems to be no easy way out of modernity or modernist ways of thinking about society–nature relations.

The three approaches to environment–society relations outlined in this chapter take injunctions such as those of Habermas and Wellmer seriously, viewing the emergence of the radical ecological critique and Green politics as a challenge to be addressed, not as evidence of the failure of modernity. Green politics and environmental issues have reminded us that the project of modernity is an unfinished social *and* ecological project that demands finding new ways of regulating the interchange between society and nature, and the challenge of this project looks set to exercise us all for some time to come. However, we cannot leave the matter there and Chapter 8 looks at the alternative postmodern and poststructuralist perspectives, which see the solutions advocated here as improbable or dangerous and perhaps both. Though there has been much less research in this area, there is now enough to suggest that postmodern and poststructural analyses may well increase in the coming years.

8 Postmodernity, Poststructuralism and Ecological Diversity

If modernist solutions to environmental problems are diverse, at least they share the central assumption that environmental problems *can* in principle be solved. Sustainable development *is* possible even if it is a long-term project, modernisation *can* be ecological as well as highly technological, capitalism *can* be turned in a Green direction if consumers demand Green products and services and boycott polluting ones, thus making Green production profitable. The optimism embedded within these projects of renewal rests on something akin to a faith in human ingenuity and creativity, a form of modern humanism. For most of the twentieth century, this optimistic modernism kept most fears of the consequences of industrialisation in check, holding out the promise of technical fixes and solutions in the future. However, in the wake of the counter-cultural protests of the 1960s and 1970s and the emergence of a so-called 'new environmentalism' in their wake (Conley 1997), many of the foundational assumptions of modernity as a social formation rooted in Enlightenment ideals came seriously to be questioned.

In the 1980s these questions were discussed under the increasingly popular umbrella term 'postmodern' (Lyotard 1984) and its correlates postmodernism (Jameson 1984; Huyssen 1988; Lash 1990), postmodernity (Bauman 1992, 1993, 1997) and postmodernisation (Crook *et al.* 1992). In the 1990s, as we saw in Chapter 6, a second source of questioning came from risk theorists and their arguments portraying a 'reflexive' form of modernisation and heightened awareness of risk. However, a significant third source of critical questions came from the philosophical perspective of poststructuralism. Associated particularly with Jacques Derrida and Michel Foucault, this perspective opened up modern modes of thought to a deconstruction that attempted to lay bare the strategies of power underlying modern humanism. Taken together, post-modernism and poststructuralism constitute a serious challenge to the Enlightenment ideal of building a rationally ordered society. On these grounds, they might be expected to have close affinities with radical ecological politics, which takes a similarly critical position in relation to the 'project of modernity'. However, although on the surface this does appear to be the case, at a deeper level there seem to be some insurmountable difficulties preventing a genuine meeting of minds amongst poststructuralists or postmodernists and radical ecology activists and theorists. This chapter then explores what, if anything, postmodernism and poststructuralism have to offer in the study of environmental issues.

Poststructuralism and Postmodernism

Poststructuralist philosophical perspectives rose to prominence as an extension and critique of the previous intellectual trend of structuralism, itself represented by the linguistic analysis of Ferdinand de Saussure, the anthropological structuralism of Claude Lévi Strauss and the development of semiotics by Roland Barthes. Taken together, the ideas of these three approaches are often referred to as intro-ducing a 'linguistic turn' into the social sciences (Ritzer 1996: 459). The common theme here is that the study of language is not restricted to analysing human verbal and written communication, but must involve the study of whole forms of life and ways of living. Saussure distinguished the language system (*langue*) from what is actually spoken (*parole*), arguing that only the former is properly amenable to scientific investigation, particularly the way that the system constrains and shapes the creative acts of speakers. Barthes argued that such an approach also applied to the study of 'sign systems' of all kinds, including all of those cultural practices that make up the life of society. Fashions, design, popular culture and home furnishings could all be analysed using a basically structuralist method that sought out the ways in which objects are systematically related to each other in the production of meanings. However, arguably the most influential body of work was produced by Lévi-Strauss. Lévi-Strauss used structuralist methods in his anthropological studies of kinship systems, social relationships and myths, which he saw as types of communication systems, which were therefore open to the same form of linguistic analysis. What marks Lévi-Strauss out as distinct is his argument that the structures of communicative systems are ultimately explained with reference to the structuring processes of the human mind itself. Such processes, he thought, are based in the mind's own logical structure, which therefore sets constraints on human activity.

Conley (1997: 5) suggests that poststructuralism 'refers to a current of thought that grows from the socio-political and environmental awareness of what structuralism had established'. Whilst Lévi-Strauss tried to demonstrate the mental structuring of language and therefore of social life, pointing out constraints on what human societies can achieve, poststructuralists such as Derrida and Foucault focus instead on 'writing' and 'discourse' rather than language. For Derrida, social institutions can be understood in this way as 'nothing but writing' (Ritzer 1996: 460–1), and if so then social life is, potentially at least, radically open to the creative constructions of ordinary people. This move from language to writing allows poststructuralists to investigate unstable and shifting discursive practices and to deconstruct their apparent 'naturalness'. In the work of Foucault, there is a shift of emphasis towards the analysis of power and the way it acts on and trains human bodies. Foucault's ideas have contributed to research in a variety of academic fields as well as influencing social movement activists (Darier 1999b: 5), though environmental issues and environmentalism have only very recently been analysed in broadly poststructuralist ways. This delay can be partly accounted for by noting that poststructuralism, like postmodernism, is typically suspicious of essentialism and rejects arguments that make recourse to an unchangeable state of nature. This suspicion does not sit easily with radical ecological ideas that the 'needs' of nature must come first.

The concept of postmodernity filtered into sociological research in the mid-1980s, the tone set by Jean Francois Lyotard's *The Postmodern Condition* (1984) which argued that modern 'metanarratives' of progress in history, scientific advancement and progressive social change were in long-term demise. Lyotard argued that many people were beginning to question and reject these, turning instead to local knowledges and localities as the authentic sources of knowledge and life. Although the neo-marxist assessments of Jameson (1984) and Harvey (1989) aimed to explain the emergence of this postmodern culture by locating it within the context of shifting forms of capitalist development (a modernist materialist explanation), others have suggested that postmodernism represents a form of post-1968 theorising amongst disappointed former marxists and radicals. Such a disillusioned postmodern perspective is marked out by a refusal to accept materialist explanations such as those of Jameson and Harvey, preferring instead to question the nature of material reality itself. Widely recognised as the most controversial postmodern thinker is the French social philosopher Jean Baudrillard. In a series of provocative essays and books, Baudrillard has laid out his postmodern view of social life that emphasises simulations, the collapse of boundaries between reality and its representations and the emergence of hyperreality (Baudrillard 1983), questioning whether social reality itself is amenable to sociological investigation (Gane 1991). Closer to mainstream sociological theory is Bauman (1992), whose work is much closer to mainstream sociology. Bauman adopts what might be called a 'sociology of postmodernity' rather than taking a postmodern approach to the study of society. The former uses tried and tested sociological concepts and theories to understand the new social formation of postmodernity, whilst the latter suggests that such a formation requires new concepts and theories if sociologists are to grasp its character. Bauman's ideas have been influential in shaping the debate on modernity and postmodernity as particular types of society with their own distinctive structural characteristics and typical mentalities. For Bauman, the postmodern mentality seeks and is good at deconstruction but finds it very hard, perhaps impossible, to engage in reconstruction. To do so risks constructing yet another form of domination. Postmoderns clear the ground, but are incapable of, or do not wish to be involved in building anything new upon it. Such a deconstructive perspective is close to that of poststructuralist theorists.

From these diverse strands a number of recurrent themes can be identified that allow us to bring poststructuralism and postmodernism into contact with environmentalism and Green politics. First, there is a focus on diversity, plurality and, in Lyotard at least, an 'aversion to the universal' (Honneth 1985). In some accounts, diversity is simply a description of the current state of the culture of the advanced industrial societies, but in many others, diversity carries clear normative implications. Not only is increasing diversity and plurality a fact of life, but it should be encouraged as part of a progressive political movement. The so-called 'affirmative postmodernism' allows previously silent voices to be heard and is bound up with disabled people's movements, lesbian and gay movements and others, all of which have used broadly postmodern arguments to support their political campaigns for the acknowledgement of the right to difference. Perhaps the ultimate silent voice is of course that of the natural world itself. Secondly, postmodern thought lays great store in the idea of irreducible difference. This means that forms of solidarity and unity cannot be built on the modern assimilationist principle of integrating minority cultures with majority ones. If there is to be social unity and solidarity then it must be through a new 'unity of diversity' or perhaps, a unity through an acknowledgement of difference. One recent example of this can be found in the field of social welfare movements where Williams (1992, 1999) argues for a 'politics of differentiated universalism', which brings together identity politics and redistributive claims. Such a politics demands a respect for difference as well as an active form of citizenship. Finally, poststructuralism in particular has been characterised as having an 'anti-humanist' tenor. This does not mean that human beings and their interests are not seen as important, but that 'Man', the key figure of modernist thought, is decentred in favour of a perspective that analyses codes of meaning and unstable discourses rather than the actions of heroic individuals or collective social movements. Although Foucault argued that forms of resistance do always accompany power relations, there is little doubt that poststructuralist analysis does not provide much room for active and constructive social agency in intentionally shaping social life. Instead, poststructuralists are alive to the potential for 'radical' movements to produce and impose their own norms of behaviour on society in support of their own worldview. This makes poststructuralists intensely suspicious of social movements that others generally see as 'progressive'.

As outlined above, there are clearly some parallels, or at least affinities, between postmodernism and poststructuralism centred on the ideas of difference, plurality and diversity. However, perhaps the one major fault line between postmodernists and poststructuralists concerns the thorny problem of power in society. This issue was crystallised in Baudrillard's provocative, 'Forget Foucault' (1987). Baudrillard argues that Foucault's version of poststructuralism is fixated on issues of power and its real effects, showing how all social relations involve relations of power. Baudrillard argues that this kind of analysis remains trapped in the very system it aims to critique, and tells us nothing about the 'simulacrum of power' or the appearance of power. In short, Foucault remains trapped in 'the real' and does not analyse 'the hyperreal' which has now replaced it. Notwithstanding this difference, it does make sense to connect poststructuralism and postmodernism as providing theoretical positions that begin from a fundamental critique of modernist modes of thought and attempt to move beyond them. If this assessment is correct then it might be possible to connect these with the Green critique of modern industrialised societies, which also tries to move beyond a simple optimistic modernism.

Green politics as postmodern politics

Green politics, at least in its contemporary manifestations, can be interpreted as a postmodern phenomenon and social movement. Gare (1995: 87) argues that 'Postmodern environmentalists, that is, the "deep ecologists" and associated movements (ecosophy, deep green and eco-feminism), are those who reject Euro-, anthropo- and andro-centrism, and the grand narratives of progress formulated in these terms.' The critique of 'grand narratives' here clearly draws on Lyotard's postmodern reading of contemporary cultural trends. This association of radical ecology and postmodernism is a strong one in so far as the radical ecological critique, if not all of its solutions, goes to the heart of modernity, demanding a genuinely alternative or postmodern society, a society that dispenses with certain fundamental structures and deep-seated attitudes of modernity. Because of this, 'one might reasonably assume that the future of the Earth would be a central concern of postmodernism and that postmodernists would be drawn to environmentalism' (Coates 1998: 185). If we think of some of the central themes of radical ecology this possibility becomes clear.

Greens take a critical stance on modern science and its reduction of nature to a set of passive resources to be exploited more and more efficiently. The implication of science in the exploitation of nature pulls away a major supporting structure from all of the modernist solutions to environmental degradation that rely on scientific analysis and technological fixes. Environmentalists do of course use scientific evidence to support their arguments for reform and to lend weight to their campaigns. This strategy has been extremely successful and has produced some significant environmental reforms. However, radical ecologists critical of the reliance on mechanistic science see more hope in the 'new physics' of quantum mechanics and chaos theory (Capra 1975, 1983; Zukav 1980; Prigogine and Stengers 1984), which are more amenable to an 'ecological' reading that emphasises indeterminacy, uncertainty and the existence of multiple realities. For radical ecologists this (ironically) provides a 'new' scientific legitimacy for their own arguments in favour of promoting diversity, as a 'new age' takes shape. The ecocentric critique of modern science thus challenges one form of scientific knowledge and method, but pins some hope on internal transformations within leading-edge scientific disciplines such as theoretical physics.

Similarly, the modern mentality that emphasises order and predictability is confronted by radical ecological arguments that see instability, unpredictability and creative disorder as producing their own constantly changing 'orders'. If modernist thought constitutes an attempt to hold on to hard-won knowledge and universal scientific laws of nature, radical ecology asks us to try 'letting go' of belief in such certainties. The association with post-modern and poststructuralist thinkers is evident here. Bauman's (1992) memorable image of the benign figure who approaches beneath the protective cloak of modernity, but carrying with them the hidden dagger to plunge into their unsuspecting victim, would be a reasonably accurate representation of the radical ecological concern that the quest for order and control, in the end, always turns nasty. Scott's (1998) study of the many large-scale, state-directed projects, which have been launched with great enthusiasm but eventually ignominiously failed, also lends empirical support to the critics of what he calls 'high modernism'. The backlash of unintended consequences from such attempts to exert control over nature chimes with postmodernism, poststructuralism, radical ecology and, to some extent, also with Ulrich Beck's concept of reflexive modernisation. In a similar vein, Michel Foucault resisted proposing any new system to replace those he sought to deconstruct in order to avoid creating yet another form of domination, whilst radical ecologists ask us simply to accept that there are some things that cannot be controlled and that we should engage in a radical 'letting go' of the mental attitude to control and dominate. Such a view is clearly incompatible with the modernist solutions we explored in the previous chapter.

Linked to the suspicion of the modern mentality is a basic principle of many Green solutions that in terms of social organisation, 'small is beautiful' (Schumacher 1973) as a way of providing a sustainable alternative to the ever-increasing scale of modern life. This principle can also be found in both the social ecology of Murray Bookchin (1980, 1982, 1986, 1987), and Roszak's (1973, 1981) assault on 'the bigness of things'. Bookchin's social ecology advocates a 'return' to decentralised communities as a solution to problems of scale and in order to generate emotionally close human associations, which also re-connect societies with nature. Roszak (1981: 33) speaks for many when he says that, 'The same inordinate scale of industrial enterprise that must grind people into statistical grist for the market place and the work force simultaneously shatters the biosphere in a thousand unforeseen ways.' In his view, the needs of the individual and the planet are coming to be seen as essentially similar, requiring de-industrialisation and a reduction in the scale of human living. Such a commonality promises to produce genuine sustainability and a shift to more environmentally benign ways of living.

Finally, some Greens take the diversity of life within ecosystems as a model for social organisation. Ecological diversity is seen to promote a lively and creative ecosystem that is able to accommodate external change and interference more easily, whilst the reduction of diversity paradoxically makes ecosystems more unstable, less able to manage change and more prone to collapse. Giblet's (1996) critical postmodern study of the damaging modern attitudes and practices in relation to wetlands, such as the draining of swamps and marshes for urban and housing development, is an example of the way that a postmodern reading may be compatible with ecological ideas in attacking the 'masculinist', dominating attitude of modern societies towards nature. Transposed onto social life, such a reading means that social diversity should be encouraged and alternative lifestyles accepted in order to promote the maximum creativity. The connection between all of these Green arguments and postmodern thinking is evident. Taken together, these features of Green thought seem to make it a particularly postmodern mode of thinking and as such, postmodernists and radical ecologists should be able to find many areas of constructive engagement. Nevertheless, despite such potential areas of agreement, there have in fact been very few postmodern approaches to environmental issues. It is also clear that postmodernists tend to take a sceptical view of the concrete claims of environmentalists about the deteriorating state of the natural environment (Cheney 1989; Zimmerman 1994), and are even more critical of sustainable development and ecological modernisation as possible solutions.

Conversely, it is also clear that environmentalists and radical ecologists have, in the main, been highly critical of postmodern culture and postmodernist modes of thought. Myerson (2001) sees the recognition of large-scale ecological damage as confirmation of the view that the ecological problematic effectively 're-legitimises' scientific research. In doing so it takes us, in Beck's (1992) phrase, '*towards* a new modernity' rather than marking a postmodern break *away from* the main constitutive elements of modernity. For many Greens, postmodernist deconstructive philosophy of the kind promoted by Baudrillard constitutes 'not a radical break but a continuation of some of the most destructive and deeply rooted strains in Western philosophy and culture' (Spretnak 1993: 4). Postmodern ideas of the 'death of the author', the ending of belief in metanarratives, a suspicion of essences and claims to have uncovered timeless truths simply extend the modernist critique of taken-for-granted assumptions and traditions. Spretnak argues instead, as does Gare (1995), that there is another version, an 'ecological postmodernism', that accepts the standard postmodern criticisms of modernity and modernism, but sees in these the possibility for spiritual renewal and a 're-enchantment of the world' (Berman 1981). In this view, postmodernism is seen as a kind of ground-clearing exercise which leaves the way open for a reconsideration of the 'wisdom [religious] traditions' as ways of recovering meaning. Spretnak even suggests that ecological postmodernism might itself *become* a wisdom tradition. Of course, it may be objected that reinterpretations of 'postmodernism' such as this seem so far removed from the postmodernism of Lyotard and Baudrillard that they stretch the meaning of 'postmodern' beyond anything originally intended. Nevertheless, it may be better to see postmodernism as an essentially contested term with two divergent meanings. One is a deconstructive approach to social life that mistrusts all attempts at creative reconstruction and the other an affirmative postmodernism that accepts the postmodern critique but continues to search for ways of creative problem solving. Radical ecology clearly falls into the latter category.

Poststructuralist perspectives on environmentalism

Poststructuralism is not a unified field of inquiry, though there are some common poststructuralist themes relating to governmentality, power/knowledge and the creation of individual selves. Therefore it makes more sense to focus on these central themes and what they might add to our understanding of environmentalism and environmental issues rather than discussing poststructuralism. Because most of the work in this area has looked to Foucault rather than other poststructuralist thinkers, those working within a broadly based Foucauldian perspective predominate here. Foucauldian scholars have identified three stages or periods of his thought: The early 'archaeological' period, which was concerned with systems of thought and their changing categories of thinking; the middle 'genealogical' period, which explored power/knowledge and the discursive construction of human beings; and the final period, which was concerned with subjectivity and exploring the possibility of the conscious 'creation of the self' (Darier 1999b). The early archaeological period is often seen as closest to structuralism and ultimately the least successful, the genealogical period and its examination of the imbrication of power and knowledge have attracted the most attention and stimulated most research, whilst the final phase which seeks to explore the possibility of an 'aesthetics of existence' is still to be systematically explored. With these important qualifications in mind, it is possible to identify a specifically post-structuralist body of work on the environment and Green politics.

In relation to Green thinking, one possible area of common ground between poststructuralism and radical ecology could lie in the apparent anti-humanism of both. Poststructuralism has been characterised as anti-humanist for several reasons. Derrida's ideas have been seen as decentring the author or the human subject from the core of inquiry. In his analysis of texts, Derrida connects authors and readers by pointing out that readers, in a very literal sense, 'write' their own text through their own experience. Texts do not simply convey the meanings imputed by their authors, but are interpreted in many ways by readers. Hence, rather than seeking out the 'real' meaning of texts, Derrida suggests that this is a fruitless exercise as such a clear meaning is absent. Texts are indeterminate, open and changeable, their meaning altering at different times. This argument has been widely interpreted as suggesting 'the death of the author'. In the poststructuralism of Foucault, 'texts' are interpreted very widely indeed to take in social narratives, discourses and even discursive practices. In this way, discourses actively construct people's selves, though this is never a completely deterministic process and always provokes resistance. It is not as though some groups of people 'have' power, which they then 'use' like a weapon to assault or control others. Power is more like a liquid that flows throughout the social body, oiling the wheels of social life. Power is productive as well as constraining. All ideas of an escape from power relations into a realm of pure freedom are therefore misguided. Foucault (1975) is clear that power is not simply a repressive force but also has to be seen as productive, enabling the functioning of social institutions and organisations. Similarly, power and knowledge, for instance in the form of the natural and social sciences, are inextricably linked, thus power is also productive of knowledge. Foucault's work has been described as anti-humanist because it removes the active creative individual from the centre of the production of social change. In a much cited passage, he sums up this idea, suggesting that the human sciences today based on the figure of 'Man' could disappear once this 'Man' as the centre of scientific inquiry is decentred, 'like a face drawn in the sand at the edge of the sea'. This does not make Foucault anti-humanist in the sense of hating human beings however, a charge that *has* been levelled at some of the more extreme statements of radical ecologists. Rather, poststructuralist anti-humanism means that one way of 'being human' and studying humans based on the conception of 'Man' as a universal figure and the basis for the modern human sciences is rejected as a contingent product of particular historical circumstances.

As we saw in Chapter 4, ecocentric theorists have relentlessly attacked the anthropocentric, or 'human-centred' thinking of modern western societies and in this sense there is a parallel between the ecocentric analysis and poststructuralism. By locating human beings and their interests above those of non-human nature, anthropo-centrism effectively legitimises the environmental damage produced by continual economic growth in the pursuit of human happiness. The advocacy of ecocentrism as an alternative mode of thought has also been portrayed in some sense as anti-humanist, as it seeks to reverse this valuation, insisting on decentring human societies. As Eckersley (1997) points out however, ecocentrism may not be belligerently anti-human but may simply insist that human interests must not take precedence over those of the rest of nature. None-theless, some radical ecocentrics have gone much further than this. Snyder (1980: 49) states that 'My political position is to be a spokesman for wild nature. I take that as my primary constituency', whilst Earth First! Founder member, Dave Foreman (1989: 14), says that 'John Muir once said that if it ever came to a war between the races, he would side with the bears. That day has arrived...'. Such arguments can and probably should be seen as provocations aimed at redressing the anthropocentric bias of mainstream society and social theory, rather than representing a systematic misanthropic perspective. Nonetheless, they do raise questions about a certain ambiguity in ecocentric thinking relating to the status of human beings. Are they part of nature or not? If they are, then according to ecocentric theory, they deserve as much consideration as all other animals and rather than 'siding with the bears', ecocentrics should find ways of preventing the war in the first place. If they are not, then what kinds of creature are they? A further problem is that there is a danger here of simply reproducing the human–nature dualism, albeit with the relative valuations simply reversed, so that nature's interests (whatever they are taken to be) now take precedence. This is a problem for ecocentric theory in so far as it claims to be moving beyond such dualisms towards more holistic modes of thought.

From the standpoint of ecocentrism, Foucault's poststructuralist anti-humanism remains strangely but firmly anthropocentric. This is because his theoretical perspective focuses on human structures, human power relations and human sciences, leaving no role for nature or natural forces to impinge on social life. As Levy (1999) rightly points out, if there is room for ecology in Foucault's work it is a strangely 'unnatural ecology'. Poststructuralists, after Foucault, remain highly suspicious of essentialism and all arguments that make recourse to some universal or unchallengeable state of nature. This means that all ecological arguments concerning living within nature's laws, respecting the natural limits to economic growth or realising people's authentic ecological selves are to a greater or lesser extent, guilty of falling for the 'naturalistic fallacy', the reading of rules for social life and morality from the restraints imposed by nature. These arguments presume a nature that speaks unambiguously to society when, according to poststructuralists, that 'nature' has been constructed from within religious discourses or the natural sciences. In short, most ecological thought including the whole field of 'environmental ethics' is relatively unreflexive concerning its own assumptions and fundamental premises. These assumptions need to be uncovered and brought out into the open if we are to avoid the imposition of a new set of rules of moral behaviour based on a spurious idea of what nature is and how its 'laws' operate.

For poststructuralist theorists, this new set of rules amounts to the imposition of a form of 'Green governmentality' that uses ecological arguments and scientific findings to intensify and spread the discursive practices that Foucault described as 'biopower' (Rutherford 1994, 1996). Foucault argues that with the emergence of statistical analysis, social surveys and new disciplines such as epidemiology in the eighteenth and early nineteenth centuries, a new and more comprehensive knowledge of national populations became possible, which allowed states to pursue a more effective and comprehensive monitoring and surveillance and to institute a new form of 'normalising' discipline. He describes this as a form of 'biopower', which brings together health, the environment, human populations and the lifestyles of individuals. Through such disciplinary surveillance, people monitor their own behaviour and effectively become self-policing. This is an ideal type of discipline which is actively maintained by 'willing' subjects. As an example, poststructuralists working in the field of health and illness have argued that the so-called 'New Public Health' (NPH), which increasingly lays responsibility on individuals for maintaining their own health, constitutes a different discursive construction of the self. Rather than simply empowering people against medical experts, the NPH regime serves to increase monitoring and surveillance, both of the self and others (Armstrong 1993; Petersen 1997). In this way, it contributes to governmentality which '...explicitly deals with issues of (state) "security", techniques of the control of the population, and new forms of knowledge (*savoirs*)' (Darier 1999b: 21).

Building on Foucault's concerns with governmentality and biopower, some contemporary poststructuralists argue that environmentalism at the international, national and local levels constitutes an extension of biopower to all forms of life. The solutions proffered by those working from a modernist mentality, which we examined in the previous chapter, from a poststructuralist position, are deeply suspect. Sustainable development, ecological modernisation and Green consumerism should not be taken at face value as attempts to solve ecological problems and prevent environmental degradation. Rather, they also have to be seen as discourses that help to construct particular environmental identities and produce new assumptions about the necessary relationship between non-human nature and human societies. This makes poststructuralists intensely suspicious of the supposedly radical and progressive character of environmentalism and Green politics, which, rather than being an obviously radical social movement aiming to democratically transform societies and 'save the planet' in the process, may yet turn out to be advancing another, ever more intensive form of governmentality, this time under the sign of 'nature'. This is the position of Timothy Luke (1983, 1988, 1999; Luke and White 1985), a Foucauldian critical theorist of both environmentalism and radical ecology. Luke argues that 'enviro-discipline', the moral injunction to live within ecological limits and give priority to 'life' or 'the earth' over the interests of groups of human beings, could easily lead to legitimising misanthropy and allowing some communities to die off in order to protect the larger 'Gaian' whole (Neuhaus 1971). This idea has some substance in the 1970s' catastrophist environmental writing on population growth and the need to reduce human numbers, as well as in the images of earth as a spaceship or a lifeboat with limited carrying capacity. The promotion of a 'lifeboat ethic' of exactly the kind that Luke describes is clear in such accounts. They suggest that some human populations, usually in the developing world, should be allowed to die off 'naturally', thereby reducing total population levels and the human impact on the global ecosystem. Although this criticism has validity in relation to some early 1970s catastrophist environmentalism, it misses its target in relation to contemporary environmentalism and radical ecology. The issue of sheer numbers of human population has become much less significant as environmentalists and Greens have become more interested in the high consumption societies of the industrialised north rather than the developing south. In practice, this has brought them much closer to the political left than the right.

A second Foucauldian argument concerns the possibility of developing a Green form of governmentality. Luke (1999: 149) argues that

> Environments are spaces under police supervision, expert management or technocratic control; hence, by taking environmentalistic agendas into the heart of state policy, one finds the ultimate meaning of the police state fulfilled. If the police, as they bind and observe space, are empowered to watch over religion, morals, health, supplies, roads, town buildings, public safety, liberal arts, factories, labour supplies and the poor, then why not add ecology – or the interactions of organisms and their surroundings to the police zones of the state?

From this perspective, the environmental discourse takes discipline and monitoring to new heights, extending state influence across geographical space and into relations with non-human nature. Of course, for some, this is a positive thing if it prevents ecological damage, in spite of the possible expansion of surveillance it demands. Max Nicholson's influential book *The New Environmental Age* (1987) was after all sub-titled, *A Guide for the New Masters of the World*. In it, Nicholson (ibid.: 324) argued that '...the computer age will compel ecology, in spite of the ecologists, to assume a central role, because ecology and its applications in conservation, land use and other ways are fundamental to the management of the earth with computer aid'. Luke's argument would see planetary management of this kind as an extension of biopower and a new Green form of governmentality.

The main problem with Luke's account here, and with other poststructuralist arguments, is that they seem to portray a system of almost total domination, a 'police state'. It should be remembered though, that Foucault himself saw all such regimes as provoking resistance rather than simply passivity. Similarly, if there really are no ways to create a realm of total freedom beyond all disciplinary regimes, then it is tautologous to point out that all social change creates new regimes as if this were a radical new insight. What is surely required are some comparisons of alternative disciplinary regimes in order to assess their relative merits and demerits. Would a 'Green governmentality' be an improvement on previous forms or not? Poststructuralists seem, so far, not to want to systematically engage with this question.

A final poststructuralist theme lies in Foucault's attempt to find ways towards an 'aesthetics of existence' through which people may be able to construct for themselves a way of living or a construction of the self that is outside social determination. For Foucault, this is about as close to individual freedom as human beings can get. Darier (1999b) argues that such a project, which obviously constitutes a continuous process of work on the self, may lead to a 'Green aesthetics of existence'. Such a Green project of self formation could come close to the ideas of those theorists of ecological selves that we explored in Chapter 5. However, there is a quite fundamental difference. Many ecocentric theorists seek to re-connect people with nature, arguing that they are after all natural beings. Such a starting point is at odds with the poststructuralist notion that people *create* their self and that therefore there is no 'deep' self to be discovered. This means that creating a poststructuralist version of radical ecology may be just as difficult as either of the options described above.

Conclusion: what happened to nature?

Postmodernism and radical ecology share a normatively positive attitude towards diversity, plurality and difference. Postmodernists take social diversity as progressive and life affirming, but also as something that has to be striven for as a political goal. Allowing diverse voices to be heard is also a radical democratic strategy that promotes equality and social inclusion. In this way, the characterisation of postmodernism as inevitably nihilistic, unconstructive and politically conservative turns out to be merely one interpretation of the political import of the postmodern turn and not necessarily a reliable guide to all of its political consequences. Similarly, critics of poststructuralism as anti-humanist and lacking a sense of constructive engagement fail to take into account Foucault's later project of an 'aesthetics of the self' that allows for, in fact demands, active self-constructive activity rather than apolitical passivity.

The promotion of social diversity has its parallels in the radical ecological interpretation of the beneficial nature of ecological biodiversity. For some ecocentrics, what works in nature also works in society and encouraging diversity in social life is part of an ecological politics. This parallel between postmodernism, poststructuralism and radical ecology would seem to support Darier's (1999b) argument that radical ecology would be best served through the attempt to encourage a 'Green aesthetics of existence', rather than struggling to find our ecological selves in closer relations with nature.

Despite the apparent affinities between poststructuralist theory and Green politics, there are good reasons to believe that their disagreements are much more striking and fundamental. These disagreements can be boiled down to a dispute over non-human nature and its knowability. For Greens, the widespread and serious damage to nature and therefore the need to do something about it, marks the central reason for their political practice. However, if nature is only contingently knowable, then this dilutes the urgency of this message. Further, ideas of tuning in to a natural, if buried, ecological self rely on an intuitive connectedness to nature that can potentially be re-discovered. But for poststructuralists, there is simply no natural or 'deep' ecological self to be uncovered, selves are created in the social process or ideally, through a reflexive process of self-creation. Again, poststructuralism does not accept that nature forms any kind of grounding for self-realisation nor does it confer political legitimacy. Finally, Green campaigning activities to defend nature assume knowledge of what is best for, or is in the interests of nature as a whole. For poststructuralists, this is a highly dubious claim. Not only is knowledge of nature contingent rather than universal, but the interventions on behalf of nature are not neutral but involve the construction of new forms of Green governmentality that may produce a more intensive form of disciplinary monitoring than previously.

These arguments against naturalism and essentialism mean that ultimately there can be no genuine accommodation between ecocentrism and poststructuralism or postmodernism. It is therefore doubtful whether environmentalism and Green politics has much to gain from poststructuralist theory. For environmentalists who see an urgent need for change, it is not enough simply to hope that an aesthetics of existence 'might' bring about change in a

Green direction. Environmentalists do not want to take such risks, but instead seek to achieve planned changes. It is also unclear exactly why an aesthetics of existence would be Green unless this makes some recourse to a nature that *can* be known. As Gare (1995: 108) says,

> Unless they pave the way for some alternative way of achieving a comprehensive understanding of the world, poststructuralist cultural critiques will merely dissolve the opposition to mainstream culture, leaving no alternative to the forms of thinking which have engendered the rise of Western civilization, its conquests and its domination of the world, and the outcome of all this, the destruction of the environment.

In short, philosophical arguments which suggest that 'anything goes' usually mean that 'everything stays the same'. Encouraging the pursuit of an aesthetics of existence may well generate continuous activity and self-reflexivity, but in itself, this does not make it Green. Levy (1999: 208–9) gets to the heart of the problem when he argues that 'Despite the deconstructive critiques that can be levelled at this notion [the romantic concept of nature], despite its lack of ultimate philosophical justification, environmentalists abandon this – perhaps their most powerful weapon – at the peril of the small gains they have made.' If this assessment is broadly correct, then it is unlikely that poststructuralism will provide enough solid ground for Green politics and will not make major inroads into Green political activism. Environmentalism and Green politics are motivated by feelings of connectedness to nature and a desire to prevent further ecological deterioration and this makes them above all modern, not postmodern. As Karl Mannheim and Klaus Eder have made clear, the Romantic critique of modern industrialism always was and still is bound up with *modernity*. It is not a distinctively post-industrial or postmodern phenomenon.

For sociologists of the environment, poststructuralist analyses of environmentalism and Green politics remind us that such movements, however well intentioned, cannot escape from relations of power. More than this, in order to achieve their goals, such movements have to generate their own forms of governmentality and discipline, thus provoking new types of resistance and criticism. Although a useful reminder, this does not really seem to add much that is not already part of the sociological tradition, for example in Simmel's (1955) ideas on conflictual relationships, in the dynamic of established-outsider relations (Elias and Scotson 1965) and the unintended consequences of intentional actions (Merton 1957), or in various cyclical theories of social movements and collective action (Brand 1990; Tarrow 1998). Indeed the postmodern affirmation of diversity and plurality over uniformity and homogeneity not only takes a normative position, but seems to take contemporary cultural trends as political absolutes, failing to see that such trends are part of longer-term social processes and are not settled states of social life. Hence, it is not so much that poststructuralist and post-modern perspectives have nothing useful to say, but simply that the useful things they do say have mostly been said before, and usually in sociologically more interesting and productive ways.

9 Environment, Self and Society

It is evident that sociological studies of environmental ideas, movements and issues have an extremely broad scope, now constituting a sociological specialism in its own right. This specialism can be alternatively described as 'environmental sociology' or the 'sociology of the environment' and the tension between these two approaches has been one of the main themes running throughout this book. It should be equally clear that some of the central problems in social theory and in society itself are being debated and tackled within this field, which brings together academics and political activists, social and natural scientific findings, theories of the social and of nature, together with all of those interested in what human society's 'proper' relationship to the natural environment could or should be. In short, far from being the marginalised 'outsider' that it once was, the study of society–environment relations is, albeit slowly, emerging as perhaps one of the most significant sociological specialisms.

However, studying society–environment relations does seem to push sociologists towards interdisciplinary collaboration in order to make use of research from the varied disciplines which have an interest in them, including the natural sciences. The practicalities of interdisciplinary working remain a difficult problem however, particularly when the collaboration is across the natural and social sciences with their very different starting points, research methods and disciplinary traditions. Their different approaches mean that genuinely interdisciplinary studies will not be easily achieved. It also needs to be noted that there is a hierarchy of scientific disciplines, which places the natural sciences in relatively more powerful positions than the social sciences (Elias 1982). This relative difference in power chances may partly account for the defensive strategies of sociologists, as they seek to become scientifically established, as well as the attempts by sociobiologists to explain social phenomena using biological concepts and theories, which justifies the relatively powerful position of biologists. Recognition of these wider issues also throws the dispute between social constructionists and critical realists into a new light and shows how, what may seem to be a small local dispute, is framed by longstanding concerns about the scientific status of sociology and the relative autonomy of its object of study, that is, society or the social level of reality. It is therefore not surprising that most sociological approaches to environmental issues are still closer to social constructionism than realism. In the early twenty-first century though, the environmental question appears more pressing than previously and if social life really cannot be studied in isolation from the natural world, then the question of how sociologists should approach environmental issues remains.

Sociology and the 'ecological turn'

As we have already seen, some sociologists are busy reassessing the classical traditions, testing their ability adequately to deal with environmental problems, whilst others have devised new ways of theorising society–environment relations that move away from the classics. What both groups agree on however is that business as usual will not suffice if sociology is to successfully incorporate environmental concerns. In general the 'ecological turn' should be seen as a challenge to the discipline (and others), forcing it to find new ways of bringing together the different elements that would make for a more environmentally sensitive sociology. Such a project would need to encompass three areas.

First, although sociologists have had things to say about the study of society–nature relations, these have been found to be largely inadequate today or have been relatively neglected. Dickens (1992) notes that early sociological theories which combined biology and sociology ultimately failed to inspire research programmes. For example, neither the nineteenth-century social Darwinism of Herbert Spencer, nor the combination of social change and nature–society relations in Ferdinand Tönnies's work have been carried forward in sociology. Arguably, in the case of Spencer, this is because of his tendency to reduce social complexity to basic biological processes, such as importing the idea of 'natural selection' from evolutionary theory directly into the study of society. In the case of Tönnies however, it may well be that despite offering quite a promising starting point for analysing nature–society relations, his ideas fell into neglect in the drive to establish sociology as a distinct scientific discipline. Because sociology developed initially during a period of rapid industrialisation and strong economic growth, many, though not all, of its theories took for granted that nature simply forms the backdrop for human activity but does not shape it. This is becoming an unsatisfactory position today when many sociologists are aware of the deleterious consequences that treating natural environments simply as 'resources' can bring. What is now required are ways of bringing nature back into sociological theories and exploring the way that societies develop over time by exerting a measure of control over the impact of natural processes, yet without seeing this control as complete domination.

Secondly, sociological theories of the formation of the self and the construction of self identities are particularly well placed to investigate political projects aiming at encouraging an environmental identity or an 'ecological self'. Sociological theories insist on the efficacy of the social level of interactions though, as we saw in Chapter 5, there are no compelling reasons to believe that this makes them strictly 'constructionist'. The excessive naturalism or essentialism of many radical ecological theories of ecological selves and the excessive constructionism of poststructuralist theories of the self, seems to cry out for a sociological perspective that drives between these extreme alternatives. Such an intervention could produce a more balanced approach that would allow theories of selves to be connected to sociological theories of society. In this way it could be possible to forge new connections between existing sociological specialisms. In addition, studying the self and social identities could help to bridge the gap between nature and society by showing how changing types of self experience feed into support for environmentalism and identification with natural environments and things.

Thirdly, sociologists are experts in the analysis of social processes, social relations and social structures and have much to say about how environmental problems have been generated. From the classical theoretical traditions of Marx, Weber and Durkheim to the more recent social theories of Giddens, Beck, Eder and others, sociological theory and research methods have much to offer students of environmental issues. There seems to be fairly wide agreement that the serious environmental problems with which we are familiar today have been largely socially generated, connected as they are to the spread of capitalism, industrialisation and continuing technological development, all of which are central to sociological theories of modernity and social change. The study of environmental problems would be much the poorer, not to say seriously flawed, without sociological theories of society. This need not mean that environmental problems should be seen as in some way not 'real', but does mean that in order to fully explain them it is necessary to connect natural scientific knowledge to sociological theories of society.

In order to arrive at a deeper understanding of environmental issues, how they are generated, how they might be dealt with and why people are increasingly drawn to environmental movements, what is required are ways of exploring the relationships between the natural environment, people's self identities and the organisation of social life. There are probably several ways of bringing together these elements within a single theoretical framework, but the final sections discuss one potentially valuable framework which is based on the ideas of Norbert Elias.

Nature, self and society – 'the triad of basic controls'

Elias's work has been significant in the formation of at least two recent sociological specialisms, namely the sociology of the body (Shilling 1997) and the sociology of human emotions (Williams 2001). These are closely connected to the study of environmental issues because in both fields, sociologists are asked to take account of the biological constitution of human life as well as its social structuring. Elias's work lends itself to this task, perhaps more than that of many others, as his sociology takes seriously evolutionary theory developed within the biological sciences. This means that his theories of social life contain from the outset, a recognition that human beings are social *and* natural beings and that the social and biological are so inextricably intertwined in humans as to be inseparable. For sociologists of the body and emotions this has proved to be an extremely useful starting point for empirical research and it is not surprising that there now exists a body of

'Eliasian' work in both of these fields. What is perhaps more surprising is that Elias's ideas have not been used by environmental sociologists or those trying to develop a 'sociology of the environment'. Given that there is no body of literature from which to draw examples, what follows is an initial attempt to show how Elias's approach may be useful for sociologists in taking a significant step beyond the entrenched division between social constructionism and realism.

Elias argues that human societies exert some measure of control over nature or the *natural environment*, over social organisation or *social relationships* and of people's control of their own *individual selves* in the form of 'self-controls'. Mennell (1992: 169) explains these in relation to society as:

1. The extent of its [society's] capacity for exerting control (Elias uses the term 'control-chances') over non-human forces and events – the 'forces of nature' as they are often called.
2. The extent of its capacity for control over interpersonal relationships and events, or 'social forces'.
3. The extent to which each of the members of a society has control over him or herself as an individual.

These three forms of control cannot be assumed simply to increase together, with more control over nature, more control over social relations and more self-controls going hand in hand. Rather, it is how these controls vary that is the subject of sociological research and which provides a useful way of approaching environmental issues. We can explore this further by looking at Elias's understanding of modern societies and the role of scientific knowledge within them.

The extent of society's control chances over natural forces and objects, what we can call the natural environment, involves knowledge about natural processes, types of social organisation and the technological means to intervene in society's interchange with nature. In this way Elias, along with critical realists, assumes that natural processes have a reality outside human categorisation and that the way in which humans know of these processes allows them to exert some measure of control over their impact on society. A simple example here would be natural scientific explanations of the hydrological cycle and associated geological processes, which have allowed modern industrial societies to exert some measure of control over such natural processes through technological means. The latter would include the building of flood defences (based on the knowledge of where best to do so), the construction of reservoirs to collect water supplies and meteorological forecasting through technological devices, which now include human-made satellites orbiting the Earth. Such technological interventions would be unlikely to succeed without the scientific knowledge of natural processes on which their construction depends. Nonetheless, this does not mean that modern societies 'dominate' or 'subjugate' nature, but rather that a measure of control is achieved over the *interchange* between natural processes and the organisation of social life. In this respect, the language of much catastrophist environmentalism and Green politics is misleading, at least to the extent that it makes use of images and ideas of total ecological collapse brought about by the human domination and destruction of nature. This way of discussing society–nature relations gives human interventions an omnipotent power they simply do not possess and has led to exhortations for humans to 'save the planet'. Framed in this way, the language of 'ecological crisis' reproduces that of the early Enlightenment period, in so far as it assumes that not only are human beings powerful enough to destroy the planet, but that they have the power to save it too. Given the Green critique of modernity and Enlightenment rationality, this is a little surprising.

Nevertheless, as societies come to control their relations with natural processes more, people come to fear those natural processes less and experience them as less dangerous. Modern scientific, industrialised societies have exerted a considerable degree of control over the impact of natural forces on society compared with pre-industrial societies and this has allowed for a reduction in levels of fear in relation to nature. Scientific explanations for previously frightening natural events and forces give people a framework of meaning or 'means of orientation' that allows them to see that such events and forces are natural processes which have their own impetus, relatively unrelated to social relationships and beyond the power of the individual. This has made it possible, for instance, for people not only to understand why an event such as a solar eclipse occurs, but also to want to travel large distances to see one and even to be told by scientists within the margin of a few seconds exactly when the eclipse will occur. In such a social context, natural processes are more predictable and hold far fewer real fears for people than in previous times.

However, the Green case against modern societies is that it is precisely the application of scientific knowledge to economic production that has led, eventually, to changes in the global climate, a thinning of atmospheric ozone and other large-scale environmental problems. Rather than bringing safety and security against the vagaries of nature, science is helping to produce new fears in relation to natural processes and demonstrating the reasons why. Similarly, the recent actions to destroy genetically modified (GM) crops shows that new fears are emerging about the extent of human interventions in nature and their potential consequences. Such an ecological awareness shows just how influential the environmental and Green movements have been in alerting people to ecological problems and their causes. Hence, although the natural sciences are able to predict and forecast, often with a high level of accuracy, this does not necessarily mean that people's fears about natural forces have been eliminated for good. And despite the significant gains of a scientific approach to natural processes, which should not be underestimated, there is no simple and parallel gain in relation to the understanding and control of social relations and social organisation.

The control chances over natural environments are dependent on particular social relationships and forms of social organisation, particularly the specialised division of labour, which now extends across larger areas of humanity, binding people together and generating rules and norms of behaviour. This is not a simple process to unravel however. Modern societies are 'complex societies' (Melucci 1989) in terms of their social organisation and extended division of labour and it is this complex organisation that enables the production and use of technologies which enable a heightened control over society's interchange with nature. Paradoxically though, it is this very complexity of social life that leads people to believe that society and social development cannot be understood and controlled to the same extent as nature. The inability of social scientists to accurately predict social development or to 'solve' social problems such as crime is sometimes cited as evidence of this. People's fears about social life, random violence, becoming a victim of crime, of social risks in general, may well militate against more reality-congruent knowledge of society. When people are unable to control their fears and are emotionally involved in social life, this prevents the achievement of the necessary level of detachment, which might allow for a more sober understanding of social processes.

Current research into processes of globalisation shows that relations of human interdependence now spread across larger areas of the planet, bringing with them global means of communication and large-scale co-operation. As we saw in Chapter 6, McNeill (1979) points out that one consequence of greater co-operation amongst larger numbers of people is paying the price of higher level 'vulnerabilities', in what Giddens (1990, 1991, 1999) describes as the 'abstract systems' of modern life. Giddens uses this term to describe those elements that form the infrastructure of the modern world such as the food production, energy generation and air traffic systems. Because of their increasing scale of operation, a breakdown in one part of the system can potentially affect the whole, thus making the entire system more vulnerable and thus requiring tighter control and regulation. Awareness of such vulnerabilities can produce new worries and fears amongst large numbers of people.

A recent example would be the much-vaunted 'Millenium Bug', the inability of modern computerised systems to cope with the change of dates at the end of the twentieth and start of the twenty-first century. This hidden 'bug' was said to threaten the total collapse of all systems which relied on computer networks – banking, administration, air traffic control and so on – as computer systems around the world moved from the year 2000 into the new century. The collapse did not happen of course, perhaps partly because the alarming forecasts convinced government and corporations to check and upgrade their own computerised systems, but the example shows how high-level system vulnerability can generate fears of international and even global catastrophe.

In the terms of Elias's argument, such systems are not just technological networks but are also forms of complex *social* organisation involving many people in a variety of geographical locations. As levels of fear in relation to natural forces diminish, generating the conditions for a less emotionally involved relationship to nature and hence higher levels of control, the complex social relations required to achieve this level of control may well appear to be moving beyond human understanding. In short, 'The growth of the web of social interdependence tends to outstrip people's understanding of it' (Mennell 1992: 170). Thus it may well be that social forces acting 'behind the backs' of everyone concerned produce fears which convince people that social life is beyond understanding, thereby preventing the achievement of a more realistic knowledge.

Emotional involvement in the political battles for control in society tend to filter into social science research and this makes it more difficult to establish the relative detachment required to bring about a more realistic understanding of social processes. Arguably this is one reason why sociology continues to fight the same battles over epistemology, methodology and the ontological status of its object of study into the twenty-first century. People's emotional commitments and involvements in social life, including particular forms of moral and political beliefs, militate against a more detached and less value-committed perspective that would allow for collective solutions to social problems. Sociologists, being humans themselves, are not immune to such involvements. Elias (1987b: 107) argues that it is much more difficult for people to accept that '...voluntary actions take place within a network of human interdependencies which, since it results from the unplanned interweaving of the unplanned needs of many unplanned people, is not the result of the action or the plan of any of them'. Hence, the higher level of control over nature does not automatically lead to correspondingly high levels of control over social relationships. But what this way of analysing society–nature relations brings into view is the way that human knowledge, social relations and control over natural forces are intimately related.

The control of individual people over their own 'self' makes up the third form of control in Elias's 'triad of basic controls'. In his work on civilising processes and the transformation of behaviour and codes of manners over long periods of time, Elias provides a good starting point for thinking about the effectivity of self-controls. In *The Civilizing Process* (2000 [1939]), Elias brings together historical evidence on changes in codes of manners in the European royal courts, as newly emerging courtiers vied for prestige and influence with the monarch. Elias's work shows that as courtly codes of conduct impose a tighter and more even control of emotions and violent outbursts, a more individualised personality type develops amongst people who are effectively the first 'moderns' (Korte 2001: 29). The cultivated and refined manners of courtiers produced a specific pattern, which the rising bourgeois classes aimed to mimic, and which gradually spread to other social groups too. This new code demanded a more even, more balanced and more tightly regulated form of self-control that appears to others as a more detached and calculating personality type. Smith (2001: 26) says that 'The strong self-control of civilized human beings enables them to be relatively "detached" in their responses to what they observe about them. They can look at the world in a "cold" and systematic way, so to speak, keeping their emotions under control.' The new pattern of self-control, so often remarked upon by sociologists and psychologists as typical of the modern personality, came to be accepted as 'second nature' to people, even as its relative novelty was remarked upon. Today, socialisation processes routinely shape personalities in this direction. This relative detachment has arguably also become 'institutionalized in the procedures of modern science' (ibid.). Hence there is a close connection between social organisation, individual self-controls and scientific detachment, and thus the society–environment relationship. Nevertheless, although people may 'keep their emotions under control' more so than they did in the past, thus maintaining a relatively peaceable form of social life,

> With respect to social relations, . . . fantasy and emotion-laden explanations of events frequently gain the upper hand, or are even mixed together with explanations imbued with respectability by laying claim to the status of 'science', such as the explanations of social problems offered by National Socialists in terms derived from biology (Fletcher 1997: 58–9).

It is therefore perfectly possible to imagine a society which exerts a good measure of control over *natural* forces, but which still remains in the grip of an emotionally involved understanding of *social* forces. Racist stereotyping is just one particularly extreme example of this. However, the focus on changing forms of self-controls contributes to our understanding of the way that all of those engaged in the systematic process of mass murder were able to approach their tasks in relatively detached and calculating ways (Bauman 1997).

Conclusion

Social constructionist and realist approaches to environmental issues tend to concentrate on certain aspects often at the expense of others. Whilst constructionists do not deny that environmental problems *may* be real, they tend not to become involved in assessments of the natural scientific evidence. Conversely, realists tend to accept the reality of environmental problems but have less to say about the claims-making process which so exercises constructionists. The great benefit of Elias's perspective is that it allows us to discuss technological interventions in natural processes, social attitudes towards natural forces, changing social relationships and complex social organisation, human emotions and self-controls within one theoretical framework. This could be extremely valuable for sociologists of the environment and environmental sociologists because it avoids taking sides in the polarised debate between realists and social constructionists and yet remains firmly within the sociological tradition of enquiry. As a starting point for a research programme it could also offer advantages over the currently polarised alternatives, though of course, it is not the only theoretical perspective that might offer these advantages. Given the recent attempts to move beyond constructionism and realism, perhaps we can expect more sociologists to become interested in developing broader theoretical perspectives in the future.

Bringing together the environment, the self and society points towards opening up the study of environmental issues rather than corralling them within a new specialism. The problem with specialisms, as Bauman (1989: ix) points out in relation to the study of the Holocaust, is that 'their [Holocaust specialists] impressively productive and crucially important work seldom finds its way back to the mainstream of scholarly discipline and cultural life in general – much like most other specialized interests in our world of specialists and specialization'. In relation to environmental issues, a more inclusive perspective would pull environmental issues closer to mainstream sociology, enabling connections to be made between nature (including human nature), environment and society in ways which do not reduce any of these simply to social constructions, with the implication that they are somehow less 'real', but also avoids positing a simple cause-and-effect relationship between increasing environmental damage and heightened environmental awareness. Instead, we have a framework which is resolutely sociological, takes a long-term view and yet gives adequate weight to the significance of real environmental dilemmas. Rather than leaving the study of environmental issues to the natural and environmental sciences, approaches of this kind offer a potentially promising future for the study of environmental issues as an integral part of a sociology fit for the twenty-first century.

Bibliography

Adam, B. (1996) 'Re-vision: The Centrality of Time for an Ecological Social Science Perspective' in S. Lash, B. Szerszynski and B. Wynne (eds), *Risk, Environment and Modernity: Towards a New Ecology*, London: Sage: 84–103.

Aglietta, M. (1987) *A Theory of Capitalist Regulation: The US Experience*, London: Verso.

Albrow, M. (1992) 'Globalization' in T. Bottomore and W. Outhwaite (eds), *The Blackwell Dictionary of Twentieth Century Social Thought*, Oxford: Basil Blackwell: 248–9.

Allen, D.E. (1978) *The Naturalist in Britain: A Social History*, Harmondsworth: Penguin Books Ltd.

Amin, A. (ed.) (1994) *Post-Fordism: A Reader*, Oxford: Blackwell.

Armstrong, D. (1993) 'From Clinical Gaze to the Regime of Total Health' in A. Beattie *et al.* (eds), *Health and Well-Being: A Reader*, London: Macmillan: 55–67.

Atkinson, A. (1991) *Principles of Political Ecology*, London: Bellhaven Press.

Bagguley, P. (1992) 'Social Change, the Middle Class and the Emergence of New Social Movements: A Critical Analysis', *The Sociological Review*, 40(1), February: 26–48.

Bahro, R. (1982) *Socialism and Survival*, London: Heretic Books.

Bahro, R. (1984) *From Red to Green: Interviews with New Left Review*, London: Verso.

Bahro, R. (1986) *Building the Green Movement*, London: GMP.

Baker, S., Kousis, M., Richardson, D. and Young, S. (eds) (1997) *The Politics of Sustainable Development: Theory, Policy and Practice within the European Union*, London: Routledge.

Baudrillard, J. (1983) *Simulations*, New York: Semiotext(e).

Baudrillard, J. (1987) *Forget Foucault*, New York: Semiotext(e).

Bauman, Z. (1982) *Memories of Class*, London: Routledge and Kegan Paul.

Bauman, Z. (1987) *Legislators and Interpreters: On Modernity, Postmodernity and Intellectuals*, Cambridge: Polity Press.

Bauman, Z. (1989) *Modernity and the Holocaust*, Cambridge: Polity Press.

Bauman, Z. (1992) *Intimations of Postmodernity*, London: Routledge.

Bauman, Z. (1993) *Postmodern Ethics*, Cambridge: Polity Press.

Bauman, Z. (1997) *Postmodernity and its Discontents*, Cambridge: Polity Press.

Bauman, Z. (1998) *Work, Consumerism and the New Poor*, Buckingham: Open University Press.

Beck, U. (1992) *Risk Society: Towards a New Modernity*, London: Sage Publications.

Beck, U. (1994) 'The Reinvention of Politics: Towards a Theory of Reflexive Modernization' in U. Beck, A. Giddens and S. Lash (eds) *Reflexive Modernization: Politics, Tradition and Aesthetics in the Modern Social Order*, Cambridge: Polity Press: 1–55.

Beck, U. (1999) *World Risk Society*, Cambridge: Polity Press.

Beck, U. (2002 [1995]) *Ecological Politics in an Age of Risk*, Cambridge: Polity Press.

Beck, U., Giddens, A. and Lash, S. (1994) *Reflexive Modernization: Politics, Tradition and Aesthetics in the Modern Social Order*, Cambridge: Polity Press.

Beinart, W. and Coates, P. (1995) *Environment and History: The Taming of Nature in the USA and South Africa*, London: Routledge.

Bell, D. (1974) *The Coming of Post-Industrial Society: A Venture in Social Forecasting*, Harmondsworth: Penguin Books.

Bell, M.M. (1998) *An Invitation to Environmental Sociology*, Thousand Oaks, California: Pine Forge Press.

Bennie, L.G., Franklin, M.N. and Rüdig, W. (1995) 'Green Dimensions: The Ideology of the British Greens' in W. Rüdig (ed.), *Green Politics Three*, Edinburgh: Edinburgh University Press: 27–39.

Benton, T. (1988) 'Humanism = Speciesism: Marx on Humans and Animals', *Radical Philosophy*, Autumn: 4–18.

Benton, T. (1991) 'Biology and Social Science – Why the Return of the Repressed Should be Given a Cautious Welcome', *Sociology*, 25: 1–29.

Benton, T. (1994) *Natural Relations: Ecology, Animal Rights and Social Justice*, London: Verso.

Benton, T. (ed.) (1996a) *The Greening of Marxism*, New York: Guilford Press.

Benton, T. (1996b) 'Marxism and Natural Limits: An Ecological Critique and Reconstruction', in T. Benton (ed.), *The Greening of Marxism*, New York: Guilford Press: 157–83.

Berman, M. (1981) *The Re-enchantment of the World*, Ithaca: Cornell University Press.

Bhaskar, R. (1978) *A Realist Theory of Science*, 2nd Edition, Brighton: Harvester.

Bhaskar, R. (1989) *The Possibility of Naturalism*, 2nd Edition, Hemel Hempstead: Harvester.

Bloch, J.P. (1998) 'Alternative Spirituality and Environmentalism', *Review of Religious Research*, 40(1), September: 55–73.

Blocker, T.J. and Eckberg, D.L. (1997) 'Gender and Environmentalism: Results from the 1993 General Social Survey', *Social Science Quarterly*, 78(4), December: 841–58.

Blühdorn, I. (2000) 'Ecological Modernisation and Post-Ecologist Politics' in G. Spaargaren, A.P.J. Mol and F. Buttel (eds), *Environment and Global Modernity*, London: Sage: 209–28.

Bodeman, Y.M. (1985/86) 'The Green Party and the New Nationalism in the Federal Republic of Germany', *The Socialist Register*: 137–57.

Boggs, C. (1986a) 'The Green Alternative and the Struggle for a Post-Marxist Discourse', *Theory and Society*, 15(6): 869–900.

Boggs, C. (1986b) *Social Movements and Political Power: Emerging Forms of Radicalism in the West*, Philadelphia: Temple University Press.

Bookchin, M. (1980) *Towards an Ecological Society*, Montreal: Black Rose Books.

Bookchin, M. (1982) *The Ecology of Freedom: The Emergence and Dissolution of Hierarchy*, Palo Alto: Cheshire Books.

Bookchin, M. (1986) *The Modern Crisis*, Philadelphia: New Society Publishers.

Bookchin, M. (1987) 'Social Ecology Versus Deep Ecology: A Challenge for the Ecology Movement', *Green Perspectives: Newsletter of the Green Program Project*, Summer, 4 & 5: 1–23.

Borgstrom, G. (1969) *Too Many*, New York: Macmillan Press.

Bottomore, T.B. and Rubel, M. (eds) (1990) *Karl Marx: Selected Writings in Sociology and Social Philosophy*, London: Penguin.

Bourdieu, P. (1984) *Distinction: A Social Critique of the Judgement of Taste*, London: Routledge and Kegan Paul.

Lord Brabazon (1881) 'Health and Physique of our City Populations', *The Nineteenth Century*, 10: 80–9.

Bramwell, A. (1989) *Ecology in the Twentieth Century: A History*, London: Yale University Press.

Brand, K.-W. (1990) 'Cyclical Aspects of New Social Movements' in R.J. Dalton and M. Kuechler (eds), *Challenging the Political Order: New Social and Political Movements in Western Democracies*, Cambridge: Polity Press: 23–42.

Braun, B. and Castree, N. (eds) (1998), *Remaking Reality: Nature at the Millennium*, London: Routledge.

Briggs, A. (1984) *A Social History of England*, London: Book Club Associates by arrangement with Weidenfeld and Nicolson.

Briggs, A. (ed.) (1986) *William Morris: News From Nowhere and Selected Writings and Designs*, Harmondsworth: Penguin Books.

Brulle, R.J. (2000) *Agency, Democracy and Nature: The U.S. Environmental Movement from a Critical Theory Perspective*, Massachusetts: MIT Press.

Buckingham-Hatfield, S. and Percy, S. (eds) (1999) *Constructing Local Environmental Agendas: People, Places and Participation*, London: Routledge.

Bunyard, P., Morgan-Grenville, F. and Goldsmith, E. (eds) (1988) *Gaia: The Thesis, the Mechanisms and the Implications*, Wadebridge Ecological Centre: Camelford.

Burke, T. (1982) 'Friends of the Earth and the Conservation of Resources' in P. Willets (ed.), *Pressure Groups in the Global System*, London: Frances Pinter: 105–24.

Burkitt, I. (1998) *Social Selves: Theories of the Social Formation of Personality*, London: Sage Publications Ltd.

Burningham, K. and Cooper, G. (1999) 'Being Constructive: Social Constructionism and the Environment', *Sociology*, 33(2), May: 297–316.

Buttel, F.H. and Taylor, P. (1994) 'Environmental Sociology and Global Environmental Change: A Critical Assessment' in M. Redclift and T. Benton (eds), *Social Theory and the Global Environment*, London: Routledge: 228–55.

Calhoun, C. (1993) 'Postmodernism as Pseudohistory', *Theory, Culture and Society*, 10(1), February: 75–96.

Calhoun, C. (1995a) *Critical Social Theory: Culture, History and the Challenge of Difference*, Oxford: Blackwell.

Calhoun, C. (1995b) ' "New Social Movements" of the Early Nineteenth Century' in M. Traugott (ed.), *Repertoires and Cycles of Collective Action*, Durham, NC: Duke University Press: 173–215.

Callenbach, E. (1978) *Ecotopia: A Novel About Ecology, People and Politics in 1999*, London: Pluto Press.

Campbell, C. (1987) *The Romantic Ethic and the Spirit of Modern Consumerism*, Oxford: Blackwell.

Capra, F. (1975) *The Tao of Physics*, London: Fontana.

Capra, F. (1983) *The Turning Point: Science, Society and the Rising Culture*, London: Fontana.

Carpenter, E. (1917) *Civilization: Its Cause and Cure, and Other Essays*, London: George Allen and Unwin Ltd.

Carson, R. (1962) *Silent Spring*, Boston, Massachusetts: Houghton Mifflin.

Castells, M. (1996) *The Information Age*, Vol. 1, Oxford: Blackwell.

Catton, W.R., Jr (1978) 'Environmental Sociology: A New Paradigm', *The American Sociologist*, 13: 41–9.

Catton, W.R., Jr (1998) 'Darwin, Durkheim and Mutualism', in Freese, L. (ed.), *Advances in Human Ecology*, Greenwich, Conn.: JAI Press, 7: 89–138.

Catton, W.R., Jr (2002) 'Has the Durkheim Legacy Mislead Sociology?' in R.E. Dunlap, F.H. Buttel, P. Dickens and A. Gijswijt (eds), *Sociological Theory and the Environment: Classical Foundations, Contemporary Insights*, Oxford: Rowman & Littlefield: 90–115.

Chandler, W.M. and Siaroff, A. (1986) 'Postindustrial Politics in Germany and the Origins of the Greens', *Comparative Politics*, 18(3), April: 303–25.

Cheney, J. (1989) 'The Neo-Stoicism of Radical Environmentalism', *Environmental Ethics*, 11: 293–325.

Chisholm, A. (1972) *Philosophers of the Earth: Conversations with Ecologists*, London: Sidgwick and Jackson.

Christiansen, T., Jorgensen, K.E. and Wiener, A. (eds) (2001) *The Social Construction of Europe*, London: Sage Publications.

Clapp, B.W. (1994) *An Environmental History of Britain Since the Industrial Revolution*, London: Longman Group UK Ltd.

Clayre, A. (ed.) (1979) *Nature and Industrialization: An Anthology*, Oxford: Oxford University Press.

Coates, P. (1998) *Nature: Western Attitudes Since Ancient Times*, Cambridge: Polity Press.

Cohen, J.L. (1985) 'Strategy or Identity: New Theoretical Paradigms and Contemporary Social Movements', *Social Research*, 52(4): 663–716.

Collingwood, R.G. (1945) *The Idea of Nature*, Oxford: Oxford University Press.

Conford, P. (ed.) (1988) *The Organic Tradition: An Anthology of Writings on Organic Farming 1900–1950*, Bideford, Devon: Green Books.

Conley, V.A. (1997) *Ecopolitics: The Environment in Poststructuralist Thought*, London: Routledge.

Conwentz, H.W. (1909) *The Care of Natural Monuments*, Cambridge: Cambridge University Press.

Cooley, C.H. (1922) *Human Nature and the Social Order* (Revised Edition), New York: Charles Scribner's Sons.

Cornish, V. (1937) *The Preservation of Our Scenery*, Cambridge: Cambridge University Press.

Cotgrove, S. (1982) *Catastrophe or Cornucopia: The Environment, Politics and the Future*, Chichester: John Wiley and Sons.

Cotgrove, S. and Duff, A. (1980) 'Environmentalism, Middle Class Radicalism and Politics', *The Sociological Review*, 28(1): 333–51.

Cotgrove, S. and Duff, A. (1981) 'Environmentalism, Values and Social Change', *The British Journal of Sociology*, 32(1): 92–110.

Cowan, R.S. (1983) *More Work for Mother: The Ironies of Household Technology from the Open Hearth to the Microwave*, New York: Basic Books.

Cramer, J., Eyerman, R. and Jamison, A. (1987) 'The Knowledge Interests of the Environmental Movement and its Potential for Influencing the Development of Science' in S. Blume, J. Bunders, L. Leydesdorff, R. Whitley (eds), *The Social Direction of the Public Sciences: Sociology of the Sciences: A Yearbook, Volume XI*, Dordrecht: Reidel: 89–115.

Crook, S., Pakulski, J. and Waters, M. (1992) *Postmodernization*, London: Sage.

Dalton, R.J. and Kuechler, M. (eds) (1990) *Challenging the Political Order: New Social and Political Movements in Western Democracies*, Cambridge: Polity Press.

Daly, M. (1978) *Gyn/Ecology: The Metaethics of Radical Feminism*, Boston, MA: Beacon Press.

D'Anieri, P., Ernst, C. and Kier, E. (1990) 'New Social Movements in Historical Perspective', *Comparative Politics*, 22(4): 445–56.

Darier, E. (ed.) (1999a) *Discourses of the Environment*, Oxford: Blackwell Publishers.

Darier, E. (ed.) (1999b) 'Foucault and the Environment: An Introduction' in E. Darier (ed.), *Discourses of the Environment*, Oxford: Blackwell Publishers: 1–33.

Demeritt, D. (1998) 'Science, Social Constructivism and Nature' in B. Braun and N. Castree (eds), *Remaking Reality: Nature at the Millenium*, London: Routledge: 173–93.

Devall, B. (1990) *Simple in Means, Rich in Ends: Practising Deep Ecology*, London: Green Print.

Devall, B. and Sessions, G. (1985) *Deep Ecology: Living as if Nature Mattered*, Salt Lake City: Peregrine Smith.

De Vries, G. (2002) 'Transformations in Vulnerability', Paper presented to the Figurational Sociology Study Group, *International Sociological Association, World Congress of Sociology*, Brisbane, 7–13 July.

Diamond, I. and Orenstein, G.F. (eds) (1990) *Reweaving the World: The Emergence of Ecofeminism*, San Francisco: Sierra Club Books.

Diani, M. (1992) 'The Concept of Social Movement', *The Sociological Review*, 40(1): 1–19.

Dickens, P. (1992) *Society and Nature: Towards a Green Social Theory*, Hemel Hempstead: Harvester Wheatsheaf.

Dickens, P. (1996) *Reconstructing Nature: Alienation, Emancipation and the Division of Labour*, London: Routledge.

Dickens, P. (2002) 'A Green Marxism? Labor Processes, Alienation, and the Division of Labour' in R. Dunlap, F.H. Buttel, P. Dickens and A. Gijswijt (eds), *Sociological Theory and the Environment: Classical Foundations, Contemporary Insights*, Oxford: Rowman & Littlefield: 51–72.

Dickson, D. (1974) *Alternative Technology and the Politics of Technical Change*, London: Fontana.

Dobson, A. (ed.) (1991) *The Green Reader*, London: André Deutsch Ltd.

Dobson, A. (ed.) (1999) *Fairness and Futurity: Essays on Environmental Sustainability and Social Justice*, Oxford: Oxford University Press.

Dobson, A. ([[1990] 2001) *Green Political Thought: An Introduction*, 3rd Edition, London: Unwin Hyman Ltd.

Dobson, A and Lucardie, P. (eds) (1995) *The Politics of Nature: Explorations in Green Political Theory*, London: Routledge.

Doughty, R.W. (1975) *Feather Fashions and Bird Preservation: A Study in Nature Protection*, Berkeley: University of California Press.

Douglas, M. (1984) *Purity and Danger*, London: Routledge.

Douglas, M. (1994) *Risk and Blame*, London: Routledge.

Douglas, M.A. and Wildavsky, A. (1982) *Risk and Culture: An Essay on the Selection of Technological and Environmental Dangers*, Berkeley, CA: University of California Press.

Doyle, T. (2000) *Green Power: The Environment Movement in Australia*, Sydney: University of New South Wales Press Ltd.

Drinkwater, C. (1995) *Ecology and Postmodernity*, Unpublished PhD Thesis, Leeds: University of Leeds.

Dryzek, J. (1987) *Rational Ecology: Environment and Political Economy*, Oxford: Blackwell.

Dunlap, R. (1980) 'Paradigmatic Change in Social Science: From Human Exemptionalism to an Ecological Paradigm', *American Behavioural Scientist*, 24(1): 5–13.

Dunlap, R.E. (2002) 'Paradigms, Theories, and Environmental Sociology'. in R.E. Dunlap, F.H. Buttel, P. Dickens and A Gijswijt (eds), *Sociological Theory and the Environment: Classical Foundations, Contemporary Insights*, Oxford: Rowman & Littlefield Publishers Inc.: 329–50.

Dunlap, R.E., Buttel, F.H., Dickens, P. and Gijswijt, A. (eds) (2002) *Sociological Theory and the Environment: Classical Foundations, Contemporary Insights*, Oxford: Rowman & Littlefield Publishers Inc.

Durkheim, É. (1973 [1914]) 'The Dualism of Human Nature and its Social Conditions' in R. Bellah (ed.), *Émile Durkheim on Morality and Society*, Chicago: University of Chicago Press: 149–63.

Dwyer, J.C and Hodge, I.D. (1996) *Countryside in Trust: Land Management by Conservation Recreation and Amenity Organisations*, Chichester: John Wiley and Sons.

Dyos, H.J and Wolff, M. (eds) (1973) *The Victorian City: Images and Realities*, London: Routledge and Kegan Paul.

Eckersley, R. (1989) 'Green Politics and the New Class: Selfishness or Virtue?', *Political Studies*, xxxvii(2): 205–23.

Eckersley, R. (1990) 'Habermas and Green Political Thought: Two Roads Diverging', *Theory and Society*, 19(6), December: 739–76.

Eckersley, R. (1997) *Environmentalism and Political Theory: Toward an Ecocentric Approach*, London: University College London Press.

Eder, K. (1982) 'A New Social Movement?', *Telos*, 52, Summer: 5–20.

Eder, K. (1985) 'The "New Social Movements", Moral Crusades, Political Pressure Groups, or Social Movements?', *Social Research*, 52: 869–90.

Eder, K. (1990) 'The Rise of Counter-Culture Movements Against Modernity: Nature as a New Field of Class Struggle', *Theory, Culture and Society*, 7(4), November: 21–48.

Eder, K. (1993) *The New Politics of Class: Social Movements and Cultural Dynamics in Advanced Societies*, London: Sage Publications.

Eder, K. (1996) *The Social Construction of Nature: A Sociology of Ecological Enlightenment*, London: Sage.

Ehrenfield, D. (1981) *The Arrogance of Humanism*, New York: Oxford University Press.

Ehrlich, P. (1968) *The Population Bomb*, New York: Ballantine Books.

Ehrlich, P.R and Ehrlich, A.H. (1970) *Population Resources, Environment*, San Francisco: W.H. Freeman and Co.

Elias, N. (1982) 'Scientific Establishments' in N. Elias, H. Martins and R. Whitley (eds), *Scientific Establishments and Hierarchies*. *Sociology of the Sciences Volume IV*, Dortrecht, Netherlands: D. Reidel: 3–69.

Elias, N. (1987a) 'The Retreat of Sociologists into the Present', *Theory, Culture and Society*, 4(2–3): 223–48.

Elias, N. (1987b) *Involvement and Detachment*, Oxford: Basil Blackwell Ltd.

Elias, N. (1991) *The Society of Individuals* (edited by M. Schröter, trans. Edmund Jephcott), Oxford: Blackwell Publishers.

Elias, N. (2000 [1939]) *The Civilizing Process: Sociogenetic and Psychogenetic Investigations*, Oxford: Blackwell Publishers.

Elias, N. and Scotson, J. (1965) *The Established and the Outsiders: A Sociological Enquiry into Community Problems*, London: Frank Cass & Co. Ltd.

Elkington, J. and Burke, T. (1987) *The Green Capitalists: Industry's Search for Environmental Excellence*, London: Gollancz Ltd.

Elkington, J. and Hailes, J. (1988) *The Green Consumer Guide*, London: Gollancz.

Enloe, C. (1975) *The Politics of Pollution in a Comparative Perspective*, New York: Davis Mackay.

Enzensberger, H.M. (1974) 'Critique of Political Ecology', *New Left Review*, 84: 3–31.

European Opinion Research Group (2002) *The Attitudes of Europeans Towards the Environment, Eurobarometer 58.0*, EORG.

Evans, D. (1992) *A History of Nature Conservation in Britain*, London: Routledge.

Evans, R. (1893) *The Age of Disfigurement*, London: Remington.

Evernden, N. (1992) *The Social Creation of Nature*, Baltimore: John Hopkins University Press.

Eyerman, R. and Jamison, A. (1991) *Social Movements: A Cognitive Approach*, Cambridge: Polity Press in association with Basil Blackwell.

Faber, D. (ed.) (1998) *The Struggle for Ecological Democracy: Environmental Justice Movements in the United States*, New York and London: Guilford Press.

Fausto-Sterling, A. (2000) *Sexing the Body: Gender Politics and the Construction of Sexuality*, New York: Basic Books.

Featherstone, M. (ed.) (1990) *Global Culture: Nationalism, Globalization and Modernity*, London: Sage Publications.

Featherstone, M. (1991) *Consumer Culture and Postmodernism*, London: Sage.

Fedden, R. (1974) *The National Trust: Past and Present*, London: Jonathon Cape Ltd.

Fletcher, J. (1997) *Violence and Civilization: An Introduction to the Work of Norbert Elias*, Cambridge: Polity Press.

Fogt, H. (1989) 'The Greens and the New Left: Influences of Left Extremism on Green Party Organization and Policies' in E. Kolinsky (ed.), *The Greens in West Germany: Organization and Policy-Making*, Oxford: Berg Publishing: 89–121.

Foreman, D. and Haywood, B. (eds) (1989) *Ecodefense: A Field Guide to Monkey-wrenching*, Tucson: Ned Ludd Books.

Foster, J.B. (2000) *Marx's Ecology: Materialism and Nature*, New York: Monthly Review Press.

Foucault, M. (1975) *Discipline and Punish*, London: Tavistock.

Fox, W. (1984) 'Deep Ecology: A New Philosophy of Our Time?', *The Ecologist*, 14(5 & 6): 194–200.

Fox, W. (1995) *Towards a Transpersonal Ecology: Developing New Foundations for Environmentalism*, New York: State University of New York Press.

Frankel, B. (1987) *The Post-Industrial Utopians*, Cambridge: Polity Press.

Fraser-Darling, F. (1971) *Wilderness and Plenty*, New York: Ballantine.

Frijns, J., Phung Thuy Phuong and Mol, A.P.J. (2000) 'Ecological Modernisation Theory and Industrialising Economies: The Case of Viet Nam', *Environmental Politics*, 9(1), Spring: 257–92.

Gaard, G. (ed.) (1993) *Ecofeminism: Women, Animals, Nature*, Philadelphia: Temple University Press.

Galbraith, J.K. (1958) *The Affluent Society*, London: Hamish Hamilton.

Galtung, J. (1986) 'The Green Movement: A Socio-Historical Explanation', *International Sociology*, 1(1), March: 75–90.

Gane, M. (1991) *Baudrillard: Critical and Fatal Theory*, London: Routledge.

Gare, A.E. (1995) *Postmodernism and the Environmental Crisis*, London and New York: Routledge.

Gaze, J. (1988) *Figures in a Landscape: A History of the National Trust*, London: Barrie and Jenkins in association with The National Trust.

Gellner, E. (1986) *Nations and Nationalism*, Oxford: Blackwell.

Gershuny, J.I. (1978) *After Industrial Society? The Emerging Self-Service Economy*, London: Macmillan Press.

Giblet, R. (1996) *Postmodern Wetlands: Culture, History, Ecology*, Edinburgh: Edinburgh University Press.

Giddens, A. (1990) *The Consequences of Modernity*, Cambridge: Polity Press.

Giddens, A. (1991) *Modernity and Self Identity: Self and Society in the Late Modern Age*, Cambridge: Polity Press.

Giddens, A. (1994) 'Living in a Post-Traditional Society', in U. Beck, A. Giddens and S. Lash (eds), *Reflexive Modernization: Politics, Tradition and Aesthetics in the Modern Social Order*, Cambridge: Polity Press: 56–109.

Giddens, A. (1999) *Runaway World*, London: Profile Books.

Giddens, A. (2000) *Sociology: Third Editon*, Cambridge: Polity Press.

Gilig, A.W. (1981) 'Planning for Nature Conservation: a Struggle for Survival and Political Responsibility' in R. Kain (ed.), *Planning for Conservation*, New York: St. Martin's Press: 97–116.

Glasier, J.B. (1921) *William Morris and the Early Days of the Socialist Movement*, London: Longmans.

Goldblatt, D. (1996) *Social Theory and the Environment*, Cambridge: Polity Press.

Goldsmith, E. (1988) *The Great U-Turn: De-Industrializing Society*, Hartland, Devon: Green Books.

Goldsmith, E., Allen, R., Allaby, M., Davoll, J. and Lawrence, S. (1972) 'A Blueprint for Survival', *The Ecologist*, 2(1), January: 1–43.

Goodin, R.E. (1992) *Green Political Theory*, Oxford: Polity Press.

Gorz, A. (1980) *Ecology as Politics*, London: Pluto Press.

Gorz, A. (1985) *Paths to Paradise: On the Liberation from Work*, London: Pluto Press.

Gorz, A. (1989) *Critique of Economic Reason*, London: Verso.

Gorz, A. (1994) *Capitalism, Socialism, Ecology*, London: Verso.

Goudsblom, J. (1989) 'Human History and Long-Term Social Processes' in J. Goudsblom, E. Jones and S. Mennell (eds), *Human History and Social Process*, Exeter: University of Exeter Press: 11–26.

Goudsblom, J. (1992) *Fire and Civilization*, London: Allen Lane, The Penguin Press.

Gould, P. (1988) *Early Green Politics: Back to Nature, Back to the Land and Socialism in Great Britain 1880–1900*, Brighton: Harvester Press.

Green Party (1986) *Manifesto for a Sustainable Society*, London: Green Party.

Green Party (1992) *General Election Campaign Manifesto – New Directions: The Path to a Green Britain Now*, London: Green Party.

Gregory, R. (1976) 'The Voluntary Amenity Movement' in M. Macewan (ed.), *Future Landscapes*, London: Chatto and Windus: 119–217.

Griffin, S. (1978) *Woman and Nature: The Roaring Inside Her*, New York: Harper and Row.

Grove, R. (1994) *Green Imperialism*, Cambridge: Cambridge University Press.

Grundmann, R. (1991) 'The Ecological Challenge to Marxism', *New Left Review*, 187, May–June: 103–20.

Guha, R. (2000) *Environmentalism: A Global History*, Harlow and New York: Longman.

Habermas, J. (1981) 'New Social Movements', *Telos*, 49, Fall: 33–7.

Habermas, J. (1983) 'Modernity – An Incomplete Project' in H. Foster (ed.), *The Anti-Aesthetic*, Port Townsend, WA: Bay Press: 3–15.

Habermas, J. (1987) *The Theory of Communicative Action*, Vol. 2, Cambridge: Polity Press.

Habermas, J. (1989) *The Structural Transformation of the Public Sphere*, Cambridge: Polity Press.

Habermas, J. (1990) *The Philosophical Discourse of Modernity, Twelve Lectures*, Cambridge: Polity Press.

Hajer, M.A. (1995) *The Politics of Environmental Discourse: Ecological Modernisation and the Policy Process*, Oxford: Clarendon Press.

Hajer, M.A. (1996) 'Ecological Modernisation as Cultural Politics' in S. Lash, B. Szerszynski and B. Wynne (eds), *Risk, Environment and Modernity: Towards a New Ecology*, London: Sage: 246–68.

Hall, S. and Jacques, M. (eds) (1989) *New Times*, London: Lawrence and Wishart.

Hannigan, J.A. (1995) *Environmental Sociology: A Social Constructionist Perspective*, London: Routledge.

Haralambos, M. and Holborn, M. (1995) *Sociology: Themes and Perspectives*, 4th Edition, London: Collins Educational.

Hardin, G. (1968) 'The Tragedy of the Commons', *Science*, 162: 1243–8.

Hardin, G. (1977) *The Limits to Altruism*, Indianapolis: Indiana University Press.

Hardy, D. (1979) *Alternative Communities in Nineteenth Century England*, London: Longman Press.

Harries-Jones, P. (1995) *A Recursive Vision: Ecological Understanding and Gregory Bateson*, Toronto: University of Toronto Press.

Harvey, D. (1989) *The Condition of Postmodernity: An Enquiry into Cultural Change*, Oxford: Blackwell.

Harvey, D. (1993) 'The Nature of Environment: The Dialectics of Social and Environmental Change', *The Socialist Register*: 1–51.

Havel, V. (1988) 'Anti-Political Politics' in J. Keane (ed.), *Civil Society and the State: New European Perpsectives*, London and New York: Verso Press: 381–98.

Hays, S.P. (1985) 'From Conservation to Environment: Environmental Politics in the United States Since World War II' in K.E. Bailes (ed.), *Environmental History: Critical Issues in Comparative Perspective*, Lanham, Maryland: University Press of America: 198–241.

Hays, S.P. (1987) *Beauty, Health and Permanence: Environmental Politics in the U.S., 1955–85*, Cambridge: Cambridge University Press.

Hayward, T. (1998) *Political Theory and Ecological Values*, Cambridge: Polity Press.

Held, D., Anderson, J., Gieben, B., Hall, S., Harris, L., Lewis, P., Parker, N., and Turok, B. (1994) *States and Societies*, Oxford: Blackwell Publishers in association with the Open University.

Heller, A. and Feher, F. (1988) *The Postmodern Political Condition*, Cambridge: Polity Press.

Hepworth, J. (1999) *The Social Construction of Anorexia Nervosa*, London: Sage Publications.

Hetherington, K. (1993) 'Review of J. Pakulski (1991) *Social Movements: The Politics of Moral Protest*', *The Sociological Review*, 41(4): 766–8.

Heywood, A. (1992) *Political Ideologies: An Introduction*, Basingstoke: Macmillan Press Ltd.

Hill, H. (1980) *Freedom to Roam: The Struggle for Access to Britain's Moors and Mountains*, Ashbourne: Moorland Publishing.

Hill, O. (1888) 'More Air for London', *The Nineteenth Century*, February: 181–8.

Hill, O. (1899) 'The Open Spaces of the Future', *The Nineteenth Century*, 46, July–December: 26–35.

Hollis, P. (ed.) (1974) *Pressure From Without in Early Victorian England*, London: Edward Arnold.

Honneth, A. (1985) 'J.F. Lyotard – An Aversion Against the Universal: A Commentary on Lyotard's "Postmodern Condition"', *Theory, Culture and Society*, 2(3): 147–57.

Horigan, S. (1989) *Nature and Culture in Western Discourses*, London: Routledge.

Huber, P. (1999) *Hard Green: Saving the Environment from the Environmentalists: A Conservative Manifesto*, New York: Basic Books.

Hughes, J. (2000) *Ecology and Historical Materialism*, Cambridge: Cambridge University Press.

Hulsberg, W. (1987) *The West German Greens*, London: Verso Press.

Hunter, J. (1995) *On the Other Side of Sorrow: Nature and People in the Scottish Highlands*, Edinburgh: Mainstream Publishing.

Hunter, R. (1980) *The Greenpeace Chronicle*, London: Picador, Pan Books Ltd.

Huyssen, A. (1988) *After the Great Divide: Modernism, Mass Culture, Postmodernism*, Basingstoke: Macmillan.

Inglehart, R. (1977) *The Silent Revolution: Changing Values and Political Styles Among Western Publics*, Princeton: Princeton University Press.

Inglehart, R. (1990) 'Values, Ideology, and Cognitive Mobilization' in R.J. Dalton and M. Kuechler (eds), *Challenging the Political Order: New Social and Political Movements in Western Democracies*, Oxford: Basil Blackwell: 43–66.

Irvine, S. and Ponton, A. (1988) *A Green Manifesto: Policies for a Green Future*, London: Macdonald Optima.

Irwin, A. (2001) *Sociology and the Environment, A Critical Introduction to Society, Nature and Knowledge*, Cambridge: Polity Press.

Jacobs, M. (1999) 'Sustainable Development as a Contested Concept' in A. Dobson (ed.), *Fairness and Futurity: Essays on Environmental Sustainability and Social Justice*, Oxford: Oxford University Press: 21–45.

Jameson, F. (1984) 'Postmodernism, or the Cultural Logic of Late Capitalism', *New Left Review*, 146, July–August: 53–92.

Jamison, A. (1996) 'The Shaping of the Global Agenda: The Role of Non-Governmental Organisations' in S. Lash, B. Szerszynski and B. Wynne (eds), *Risk, Environment & Modernity: Towards a New Ecology*, London: Sage Publications: 224–45.

Jänicke, M. (1985) *Preventive Environmental Policy as Ecological Modernization and Structural Policy*, Berlin: Berlin Science Center.

Jenkins, P. (1994) *Using Murder: The Social Construction of Serial Homicide*, New York: A. de Gruyter.

Jenkins, R. (1996) *Social Identity*, London and New York: Routledge.

Jones, A. (1987) 'The Violence of Materialism in Advanced Industrial Society: An Eco-Sociological Approach', *The Sociological Review*, 35(1): 19–47.

Joseph, L.E. (1990) *Gaia: The Growth of an Idea*, London: Penguin Books.

Kelsen, H. (1944) *Society and Nature: A Sociological Inquiry*, London: K. Paul, Trench, Trubner.

Kilminster, R. (1991) 'Structuration Theory as a World-View' in C.G.A. Bryant and D. Jary (eds), *Giddens' Theory of Structuration: A Critical Appreciation*, London: Routledge: 74–115.

Kilminster, R. (1997) 'Globalization as an Emergent Concept' in Scott, A. (ed.), *The Limits of Globalization*, London: Routledge: 257–83.

Kilminster, R. (1998) *The Sociological Revolution: From the Enlightenment to the Global Age*, London: Routledge.

King, Y. (1990) 'Healing the Wounds: Feminism, Ecology and the Nature/Culture Dualism' in I. Diamond and G.F. Orenstein (eds), *Reweaving the World: The Emergence of Eco-feminism*, San Francisco: Sierra Club Books: 106–21.

Kitschelt, H.P. (1986) 'Political Opportunity Structures and Political Protest: Anti-Nuclear Movements in Four Democracies', *The British Journal of Political Science*, 16, January: 57–85.

Kitschelt, H.P. (1989) *The Logics of Party Formation: Ecological Politics in Belgium and West Germany*, Ithaca, London: Cornell University Press.

Kitschelt, H.P. (1990) 'New Social Movements and the Decline of Party Organization' in R.J. Dalton and M. Kuechler (eds), *Challenging the Political Order: New Social and Political Movements in Western Democracies*, Cambridge: Polity Press: 179–208.

Kitschelt, H.P. (1991) 'Resource Mobilization Theory: A Critique' in D. Rucht (ed.), *Research on Social Movements: The State of the Art in Western Europe and the USA*, Frankfurt: Frankfurt University Press: 323–47.

Klandermans, P.B. (1990) 'Linking "Old" and "New" Movement Networks in the Netherlands' in R.J. Dalton and M. Kuechler (eds), *Challenging the Political Order: New Social and Political Movements in Western Democracies*, Cambridge: Polity Press: 122–36.

Klandermans, P.B. (1991) 'New Social Movements and Resource Mobilization: The European and the American Approach Revisited' in D. Rucht (ed.), *Research on Social Movements: The State of the Art in Western Europe and the USA*, Frankfurt: Frankfurt University Press: 17–44.

Klein, M. (2001) *No Logo*, London: Flamingo.

Kolinsky, E. (1988) 'The West German Greens: A Women's Party?', *Parliamentary Affairs*, 41(1): 129–48.

Korte, H. (2001) 'Perspectives on a Long Life: Norbert Elias and the Process of Civilization' in T. Salumets (ed.), *Norbert Elias and Human Interdependencies*, Montreal & Kingston: McGill-Queen's University Press: 13–31.

Kropotkin, P. (1899) *Fields, Factories and Workshops Tomorrow*, London: Freedom Press.

Kumar, K. (1995) *From Post-Industrial to Post-Modern Society: New Theories of the Contemporary World*, Oxford: Blackwell Publishers Ltd.

Kvistad, G.O. (1987) 'Between State and Society: Green Political Ideology in the Mid-1980s', *West European Politics*, 10(2): 221–8.

Landes, D.S. (1969) *The Unbound Prometheus: Technological Change and Industrial Development in Western Europe from 1750 to the Present*, London: Cambridge University Press.

Lash, S. (1990) *Sociology of Postmodernism*, London: Routledge.

Lash, S. and Urry, J. (1987) *The End of Organized Capitalism*, Cambridge: Polity Press.

Lash, S. and Wynne, B. (1992) 'Introduction' in U. Beck (ed.), *Risk Society: Towards a New Modernity*, London: Sage Publications: 1–8.

Lash, S., Szerszynski, B. and Wynne, B. (eds) (1996) *Risk, Environment and Modernity: Towards a New Ecology*, London: Sage.

Latour, B. (1992) *We Have Never Been Modern*, London: Harvester Wheatsheaf.

Latour, B. (1999) *Pandora's Hope: Essays on the Reality of Science Studies*, Cambridge, MA and London: Harvard University Press.

Latour, B. and Woolgar, S. (1986) *Laboratory Life: The [Social] Construction of Scientific Facts*, Princeton: Princeton University Press.

Lévi-Strauss, C. (1967) *Structural Anthropology*, Garden City, NY: Anchor.

Levy, N. (1999) 'Foucault's Unnatural Ecology' in E. Darier (ed.), *Discourses of the Environment*, Oxford: Blackwell Publishers: 203–16.

Lewis, M.W. (1994) *Green Delusions: An Environmentalist Critique of Radical Environmentalism*, Durham and London: Duke University Press.

Light, A. (2000) 'What is an Ecological Identity?', *Environmental Politics*, 9(4), Winter: 59–81.

Lively, J. (ed.) (1966) *The Enlightenment*, London: Longmans.

Lomborg, B. (2001) *The Skeptical Environmentalist: Measuring the Real State of the World*, Cambridge: Cambridge University Press.

Lovelock, J.E. (1979) *Gaia: A New Look at Life on Earth*, Oxford: Oxford University Press.

Lovelock, J.E. (1986) 'Gaia: The World as a Living Organism', *New Scientist*, 18 December.

Lovelock, J.E. (1988) *The Ages of Gaia: A Biography of our Living Earth*, New York: Norton.

Lovins, A.B. (1977) *Soft Energy Paths: Towards a Durable Peace*, Harmondsworth: Penguin Books Ltd.

Lowe, P.D. and Goyder, J. (1983) *Environmental Groups in Politics*, London: Allen and Unwin.

Lowenthal, D. (2000) *George Perkins Marsh: Prophet of Conservation*, Seattle and London: Washington University Press.

Luhmann, N. (1989) *Ecological Communication*, Cambridge: Polity Press.

Luke, T. (1983) 'Informationalism and Ecology', *Telos*, 56, Summer: 59–73.

Luke, T. (1988) 'The Dreams of Deep Ecology', *Telos*, 76, Summer: 65–92.

Luke, T. (1999) 'Environmentality as Green Governmentality' in E. Darier (ed.), *Discourses of the Environment*, Oxford: Blackwell Publishers: 121–51.

Luke, T. and White, S.K. (1985) 'Critical Theory, the Informational Revolution and an Ecological Path to Modernity' in J. Forester (ed.), *Critical Theory and Public Life*, Cambridge, MA: MIT Press: 22–53.

Lury, C. (1996) *Consumer Culture*, Cambridge: Polity Press.

Lyotard, J.F. (1984) *The Postmodern Condition: A Report on Knowledge*, Manchester: Manchester University Press.

Macnaghten, P. and Urry, J. (1995) 'Towards a Sociology of Nature', *Sociology*, 29(2): 203–20.

Macnaghten, P. and Urry, J. (1998) *Contested Natures*, London: Sage.

Malthus, T.R. (1970 [1798]) *An Essay on the Principles of Population*, Harmondsworth: Penguin.

Manes, C. (1990) *Green Rage: Radical Environmentalism and the Unmaking of Civilization*, Boston: Little, Brown.

Mannheim, K. (1945) *Ideology and Utopia: An Introduction to the Sociology of Knowledge*, London: Kegan Paul.

Marcuse, H. (1964) *One Dimensional Man: Studies in the Ideology of an Advanced Industrial Society*, London: Sphere.

Marien, M. (1977) 'The Two Visions of Post-Industrial Society', *Futures*, 5, October: 415–31.

Marsh, G.P. (1864) *Man and Nature*, Cambridge, Massachusetts: Harvard University Press.

Marsh, J. (1982) *Back to the Land: The Pastoral Impulse in England from 1880–1914*, London: Quartet Books.

Martell, L. (1994) *Ecology and Society: An Introduction*, Cambridge: Polity Press.

Marx, K. (1961 [1844]) *Economic and Philosophic Manuscripts of 1844* (M. Milligan trans.), Moscow: Foreign Languages Publishing House.

Marx, L. (1964) *The Machine in the Garden: Technology and the Pastoral Ideal in America*, New York: Oxford University Press.

Maslow, A.H. (1954) *Motivation and Personality*, New York: Harper.

Mathews, F. (1994) *The Ecological Self*, London: Routledge.

Mattausch, J. (1989) *A Commitment to Campaign: A Sociological Study of CND*, Manchester: Manchester University Press.

McCarthy, J. (1998) 'Environmentalism, Wise Use and the Nature of Accumulation in the Rural West' in B. Braun and N. Castree (eds), *Remaking Reality: Nature at the Millenium*, London and New York: Routledge: 126–49.

McCormick, J. (1991) *British Politics and the Environment*, London: Earthscan Publishers Ltd.

McCormick, J. (1992) *The Global Environmental Movement: Reclaiming Paradise*, London: Bellhaven Press.

McKibben, B. (1990) *The End of Nature*, London: Viking, Penguin.

McNeill, W.H. (1975) *The Rise of the West: A History of the Human Community*, Chicago and London: The University of Chicago Press.

McNeill, W.H. (1979) *A World History*, Oxford: Oxford University Press.

Mead, G.H. (1934) *Mind, Self and Society, From the Standpoint of a Social Behaviourist*, Chicago: Chicago University Press.

Meadows, D.H., Meadows, D.L., Randers, J. and Behrens III, W. (1974) *The Limits to Growth*, London: Pan Books.

Mellos, K. (1990) *Perspective on Ecology: A Critical Essay*, London: Macmillan Press.

Melucci, A. (1980) 'The New Social Movements: A Theoretical Approach', *Social Science Information*, 19(2): 199–226.

Melucci, A. (1985) 'The Symbolic Challenge of Contemporary Movements', *Social Research*, 52: 789–816.

Melucci, A. (1988) 'Social Movements and the Democratization of Everyday Life' in J. Keane (ed.), *Civil Society and the State*, London: Verso Press: 245–60.

Melucci, A. (1989) *Nomads of the Present: Social Movements and Individual Needs in Contemporary Society*, London: Hutchinson Radius.

Melucci, A. (1995) 'The New Social Movements Revisited: Reflections on a Sociological Misunderstanding' in L. Maheu (ed.), *Social Movements and Social Classes: The Future of Collective Action*, London: Sage Publications in association with the International Sociological Association: 107–19.

Melucci, A. (1996), *Challenging Codes: Collective Action in the Information Age*, Cambridge: Cambridge University Press.

Mennell, S. (1992) *Norbert Elias: An Introduction*, Oxford: Blackwell Publishers.

Merchant, C. (1982) *The Death of Nature: Women, Ecology and the Scientific Revolution*, London: Wildwood House.

Merchant, C. (1989) *Ecological Revolutions: Nature, Gender, and Science in New England*, Chapel Hill and London: University of North Carolina Press.

Merchant, C. (1992) *Radical Ecology: The Search for a Liveable World*, London: Routledge.

Merton, R.K. (1957) *Social Theory and Social Structure*, New York: The Free Press.

Mies, M. and Shiva, V. (1993) *Ecofeminism*, London: Zed Press.

Mill, J.S. (1979) 'Nature' from 'Nature, the Utility of Religion, and Theism' [1850–8] in A. Clayre (ed.), *Nature and Industrialization*, Oxford: University Press: 303–12.

Mill, J.S. (1994) 'The Stationary State' in D. Wall (ed.), *Green History: A Reader in Environmental Literature, Philosophy and Politics*, London and New York: Routledge: 120–1.

Mills, C.W. (1959) *The Sociological Imagination*, New York: Oxford University Press.

Mol, A.P.J. (2001) *Globalization and Environmental Reform: The Ecological Modernization of the Global Economy*, Cambridge, Mass.: The MIT Press.

Mol, A.P.J. and Sonnenfeld, D.A. (2000) 'Ecological Modernisation Around the World: An Introduction', *Environmental Politics*, 9(1): 3–14.

Mol, A.P.J. and Spaargaren, G. (2000) 'Ecological Modernisation Theory in Debate: A Review', *Environmental Politics*, 9(1): 17–49.

Morris, W. (1908) *News from nowhere or an Epoch of Rest, being Some Chapters from a Utopian Romance*, London: Longmans, Green, and Co.

Moscovici, S. (1976) *Society Against Nature: The Emergence of Human Societies*, Hassocks: Harvester Press.

Moscovici, S. (1977) 'The Reenchantment of the World' in N. Birnbaum (ed.), *Beyond the Crisis*, Oxford: Oxford University Press: 133–68.

Müller-Rommel, F. (1982) 'Ecology Parties in Western Europe', *West European Politics*, 5(1), January: 68–74.

Müller-Rommel, F. (1989a) 'The German Greens in the 1980s: Short-term Cyclical Protest or Indicator of Transformation?', *Political Studies*, xxxvii(1), March: 114–22.

Müller-Rommel, F. (1989b) *New Politics in Western Europe: The Rise and Success of Green Parties and Alternative Lists*, Boulder: Westview.

Murphy, R. (1994a) *Rationality and Nature*, Boulder, Colorado: Westview.

Murphy, R. (1994b) 'The Sociological Construction of Science Without Nature', *Sociology*, 28(4): 957–74.

Murphy, R. (1997) *Sociology and Nature: Social Action in Context*, Boulder, Colorado: Westview.

Murphy, R. (2002) 'Ecological Materialism and the Sociology of Max Weber' in R.E. Dunlap, F.H. Buttel, P. Dickens and A. Gijswijt (eds), *Sociological Theory and the Environment: Classical Foundations, Contemporary Insights*, Oxford: Rowman & Littlefield: 73–89.

Musgrove, F. (1974) *Ecstasy and Holiness: Counter Culture and the Open Society*, London: Methuen and Co. Ltd.

Myerson, G. (2001) *Ecology and the End of Postmodernism*, Duxford: ICON Books.

Naess, A. (1973) 'The Shallow and the Deep, Long-Range Ecology Movement, A Summary', *Inquiry*, 16: 95–100.

Naess, A. (1984) 'Intuition, Intrinsic Value and Deep Ecology', *The Ecologist*, 14(56): 201–3.

Naess, A. (1985) 'Identification as a Source of Deep Ecological Attitudes' in M. Tobias (ed.), *Deep Ecology*, San Diego: Avant Books: 258–69.

Naess, A. (1988) 'The Basics of Deep Ecology', *Resurgence*, 126: 4–7.

Naess, A. (1989) *Ecology, Community and Lifestyle*, Cambridge: Cambridge University Press.

Nash, R. (1982) *Wilderness and the American Mind*, New Haven, Conn.: Yale University Press.

Neuhaus, R.J. (1971) *In Defence of People: Ecology and the Seduction of Radicalism*, New York: Macmillan.

Nicholson, M. (1972) *The Environmental Revolution*, Harmondsworth: Penguin.

Nicholson, M. (1987) *The New Environmental Age: A Guide for the New Masters of the World*, Cambridge: Cambridge University Press.

Noorman, K.J. and Schoot, T. (eds) (1998) *Green Households? Domestic Consumers, Environment and Sustainability*, London: Earthscan.

Norton, B. (1991) *Toward Unity Among Environmentalists*, Oxford: Oxford University Press.

Noske, B. (1989) *Humans and Other Animals: Beyond the Boundaries of Anthropology*, London: Pluto Press.

O'Brien, M., Penna, S. and Hay, C. (eds) (1999) *Theorising Modernity, Reflexivity, Environment and Identity in Giddens' Social Theory*, London: Longman.

O'Connor, J. (1996) 'The Second Contradiction of Capitalism' in T. Benton (ed.), *The Greening of Marxism*, New York: Guilford Press.

O'Connor, J. (1998) *Natural Causes: Essays in Ecological Marxism*, New York: Guilford Press.

Offe, C. (1985) 'New Social Movements: Challenging the Boundaries of Institutional Politics', *Social Research*, 52, Winter: 817–68.

Offe, C. (1990) 'Reflections on the Institutional Self-Transformation of Movement Politics: A Tentative Stage Model' in R.J. Dalton and M. Kuechler (eds), *Challenging the Political Order: New Social and Political Movements in Western Democracies*, Cambridge: Polity Press: 233–50.

Offe, C. and Wiesenthal, H. (1980) 'Two Logics of Collective Action' in M. Zeitlin (ed.), *Political Power and Social Theory 1*, Greenwich, Conn.: JAI Press: 67–115.

Olofsson, G. (1987) 'After the Working Class Movement? An Essay on What's "New" and What's "Social" in the New Social Movements', *Acta Sociologica*, 31(1): 15–34.

O'Neil, J. (1994) 'Humanism and Nature', *Radical Philosophy*, 66: 21–9.

Ophuls, W. (1977) *Ecology and the Politics of Scarcity: Prologue to a Theory of the Steady State*, San Francisco, California: W.H. Freeman.

O'Riordan, T. (1981) *Environmentalism*, London: Pion.

Packard, V. (1964) *The Hidden Persuaders*, Harmondsworth: Penguin Books.

Paehlke, R. (1989) *Environmentalism and the Future of Progressive Politics*, New Haven, London: Yale University Press.

Pakulski, J. (1991) *Social Movements: The Politics of Moral Protest*, Cheshire: Longman Press.

Palfrey, C. and Harding, N.H. (1997) *The Social Construction of Dementia: Confused Professionals*, London: Jessica Kingsley.

Papadakis, E. (1984) *The Green Movement in West Germany*, London: Croom Helm.

Papadakis, E. (1988) 'Social Movements, Self-Limiting Radicalism and the Green Party in West Germany', *Sociology*, 22(3), August: 433–54.

Parkin, F. (1968) *Middle Class Radicalism*, Manchester: Manchester University Press.

Parkin, S. (1989) *Green Parties: An International Guide*, London: Heretic Books.

Parsons, H. (ed.) (1977) *Marx and Engels on Ecology*, Westport: Greenwood.

Pearce, F. (1991) *Green Warriors: the People and the Politics Behind the Environmental Revolution*, London: Bodley Head.

Pepper, D. (1984) *The Roots of Modern Environmentalism*, London: Croom Helm.

Pepper, D. (1986) 'Radical Environmentalism and the Labour Movement' in J. Weston (ed.), *Red and Green: The New Politics of the Environment*, London: Pluto Press: 115–39.

Pepper, D. (1991) *Communes and the Green Vision: Counterculture, Lifestyle and the New Age*, London: Green Print.

Pepper, D. (1996) *Modern Environmentalism: An Introduction*, London: Routledge.

Perrow, C. (1984) *Normal Accidents*, New York: Basic Books.

Petersen, A. (1997) 'Risk, Governance and the New Public Health' in A. Petersen and R. Bunton (eds), *Foucault, Health and Medicine*, London: Routledge: 189–206.

Plant, J. (ed.) (1989) *Healing the Wounds*, Philadelphia: New Society Publishers.

Plumwood, V. (1986) 'Ecofeminism: An Overview and Discussion of Positions and Arguments on Women and Philosophy', *Australasian Journal of Philosophy*, 64: 120–38.

Plumwood, V. (1988) 'Women, Humanity and Nature', *Radical Philosophy*, Spring: 16–24.

Plumwood, V. (1993) *Feminism and the Mastery of Nature*, London: Routledge.

Poguntke, T. (1987) 'New Politics and Party Systems: The Emergence of a New Type of Party?', *West European Politics*, 10(1), January: 76–88.

Ponting, C. (1993) *A Green History of the World: The Environment and the Collapse of Great Civilizations*, London: Penguin Books.

Porritt, J. (1984) *Seeing Green: The Politics of Ecology Explained*, Oxford: Basil Blackwell.

Porritt, J. (1988) '"Let the Green Spirit Live": Schumacher Lecture 1987', *Resurgence*, 127.

Porritt, J. and Winner, D. (1988) *The Coming of the Greens*, London: Fontana Paperbacks.

Prigogine, I. and Stengers, I. (1984) *Order Out of Chaos: Man's New Dialogue with Nature*, Boulder, Colorado: Random House.

Princen, T. and Finger, M. (1994) *Environmental NGOs in World Politics: Linking the Local and the Global*, London and New York: Routledge.

Prynn, D. (1976) 'The Clarion Clubs, Rambling and the Holiday Associations in Britain Since the 1880s', *Journal of Contemporary History*, XI: 65–77.

Przeworski, A. (1986) *Capitalism and Social Democracy*, Cambridge: Cambridge University Press.

Purdue, B. (1987) *Town and Country*, Milton Keynes: Open University Press.

Purdue, D.A. (2000) *Anti-genetiX: The Emergence of the Anti-GM Movement*, Aldershot: Ashgate Publishing Ltd.

Ranlett, J. (1983) 'Checking Nature's Desecration: Late Victorian Environmental Organization', *Victorian Studies*, Winter: 197–222.

Redclift, M. (2000) 'Environmental Social Theory for a Globalizing World Economy' in G. Spaargaren, A.P.J. Mol and F. Buttel (eds), *Environment and Global Modernity*, London: Sage: 151–62.

Redclift, M. and Benton, T. (eds) (1994) *Social Theory and the Global Environment*, London: Routledge.

Rinkevicius, L. (2000) 'Ecological Modernisation as Cultural Politics: Transformations of Civic Environmental Activism in Lithuania', *Environmental Politics*, 9(1): 171–202.

Ritzer, G. (1996) *Modern Sociological Theory*, 4th Edition, New York: McGraw-Hill.
Roberts, H. (ed.) (1915) *The Simplification of Life (From the Writings of Edward Carpenter)*, London: Allen and Unwin.
Robertson, R. (1992) *Globalization: Social Theory and Global Culture*, London: Sage.
Robinson, M. (1992) *The Greening of British Party Politics*, Manchester: Manchester University Press.
Rose, M. (1991) *The Postmodern and the Postindustrial: A Critical Analysis*, Cambridge: Cambridge University Press.
Ross, E.B. (2000) *The Malthus Factor: Poverty, Politics and Population in Capitalist Development*, London: Zed Books.
Roszak, T. (1969) *The Making of a Counter Culture: Reflections on the Technocratic Society and its Youthful Opposition*, New York: Anchor Books.
Roszak, T. (1973) *Where the Wasteland Ends: Politics and Transcendence in Post-Industrial Society*, London: Faber and Faber.
Roszak, T. (1981) *Person/Planet: The Creative Disintegration of Industrial Society*, St. Albans: Granada.
Rowbotham, S. and Weeks, J. (1977) *Socialism and the New Life: The Personal and Sexual Politics of Edward Carpenter and Havelock Ellis*, London: Pluto Press.
Rucht, D. (1990) 'The Strategies and Action Repertoires of New Movements' in R.J. Dalton and M. Kuechler (eds), *Challenging the Political Order: New Social and Political Movements in Western Democracies*, Cambridge: Polity Press: 156–75.
Rucht, D. (ed.) (1991) *Research on Social Movements: The State of the Art in Western Europe and the USA*, Frankfurt: Frankfurt University Press.
Rucht, D. (1995) 'Ecological Protest as Calculated Law-Breaking: Greenpeace and Earth First! In Comparative Perspective' in W. Rüdig (ed.), *Green Politics Three*, Edinburgh: Edinburgh University Press: 66–89.
Rüdig, W. (ed.) (1990) *Green Politics One*, Edinburgh: Edinburgh University Press.
Rüdig, W. (ed.) (1995) *Green Politics Three*, Edinburgh: Edinburgh University Press.
Rüdig, W. and Lowe, P. (1986) 'The Withered Greening of British Politics: A Study of the Ecology Party', *Political Studies*, xxxiv: 262–84.
Rüdig, W., Bennie, L.G. and Franklin, M.N. (1991) *Green Party Members: A Profile*, Glasgow: Delta Publications.
Rutherford, P. (1994) 'The Administration of Life: Ecological Discourse as "Intellectual Machinery of Government"', *Australian Journal of Communication*, 21(3): 40–55.
Rutherford, P. (1996) 'Policing Nature: Ecology, Natural Science and Ecology' in C. O'Farrell (ed.), *Foucault: The Legacy*, Brisbane: Queensland University of Technology.
Ryle, M. (1988) *Ecology and Socialism*, London: Century Hutchinson.
Sale, K. (1984) 'Bioregionalism, A New Way to Treat the Land', *The Ecologist*, 14(4): 167–73.
Sale, K. (1985) *Dwellers in the Land: The Bioregional Vision*, San Francisco: Sierra Club Books.
Salleh, A. (1997) *Ecofeminism as Politics: Nature, Marx and the Postmodern*, London and New York: Zed Books.

Sandilands, C. (1994) 'Political Animals: The Paradox of Ecofeminist Politics', *The Trumpeter*, 11: 167–72.

Sandilands, C. (1995) 'From Natural Identity to Radical Democracy', *Environmental Ethics*, 17: 75–91.

Sandilands, C. (1999) *The Good-Natured Feminist: Ecofeminism and the Quest for Democracy*, Minneapolis: University of Minnesota Press.

Sargisson, L. (2001) 'What's Wrong with Ecofeminism?', *Environmental Politics*, 10(1), Spring: 52–64.

Sayer, A. (1992) *Method in Social Science: A Realist Approach*, 2nd Edition, London: Routledge.

Schell, J. (1982) *The Fate of the Earth*, London: Pan Books Ltd.

Schmitt, P.J. (1969) *Back to Nature: The Arcadian Myth in Urban America*, New York: Oxford University Press.

Schnaiberg, A. (1980) *The Environment: From Surplus to Scarcity*, New York: Oxford University Press.

Schumacher, E.F. (1973) *Small is Beautiful: A Study of Economics as if People Mattered*, London: Abacus Books.

Scott, A. (1990) *Ideology and the New Social Movements*, London: Unwin Hyman.

Scott, A. (ed.) (1997) *The Limits of Globalization*, London: Routledge.

Scott, A. (2000) 'Risk Society or Angst Society? Two Views of Risk, Consciousness and Community' in B. Adam, U. Beck and J. van Loon (eds), *The Risk Society and Beyond: Critical Issues for Social Theory*, London: Sage: 33–46.

Scott, J.C. (1998) *Seeing Like a State: How Certain Schemes to Improve the Human Condition Have Failed*, New Haven and London: Yale University Press.

Shaw-Lefevre, G. (1894) *English Commons and Forests: The Story of the Battle During the Last 30 Years for Public Rights Over the Commons and Forests of England and Wales*, London: Cassell.

Sheail, J. (1976) *Nature in Trust: The History of Nature Conservation in Britain*, Glasgow: Blackie and Son Ltd.

Sheail, J. (1981) *Rural Conservation in Inter-War Britain*, Oxford: Oxford University Press.

Shepard, P. (1969) 'Introduction – Ecology and Man – A Viewpoint' in P. Shepard and D. McKinley (eds), *The Subversive Science: Essays Toward and Ecology of Man*, Boston: Houghton Mifflin: 1–10.

Shilling, C. (1997) *The Body and Social Theory*, London: Sage.

Shiva, V. (1988) *Staying Alive: Women, Ecology and Survival in India*, London: Zed Books.

Simmel, G. (1955) *Conflict and the Web of Group-Affiliations*, New York: Free Press.

Simmons, I.G. (1993) *Environmental History: A Concise Introduction*, Oxford: Blackwell.

Simon, J. and Kahn, H. (1984) *The Resourceful Earth: A Response to Global 2000*, Oxford: Blackwell.

Singer, P. (1975) *Animal Liberation: A New Ethics for our Treatment of Animals*, New York: Avon.

Sismondo, S. (1993) 'Some Social Constructions', *Social Studies of Science*, 3: 515–53.

Sklair, L. (1991) *Sociology of the Global System*, Hemel Hempstead: Harvester Wheatsheaf.

Sklair, L. (1994) 'Global Sociology and Environmental Change' in M. Redcliff and T. Benton (eds), *Social Theory and the Global Environment*, London: Routledge: 205–27.

Smith, D. (2001) *Norbert Elias and Modern Social Theory*, London: Sage Publications Ltd.

Smith, M.J. (1998) *Ecologism: Towards Ecological Citizenship*, Buckingham: Open University Press.

Snyder, G. (1980) *The Real Work: Interviews and Talks 1964–1979*, New York: New Directions.

Sonnenfeld, D.A. (2000) 'Contradictions of Ecological Modernisation: Pulp and Paper Manufacturing in South-east Asia', *Environmental Politics*, 9(1): 235–56.

Spaargaren, G. (1997) *The Ecological Modernization of Production and Consumption (Essays in Environmental Sociology)*, Wageningen: WAU.

Spaargaren, G. and Van Vliet, B. (2000) 'Lifestyles, Consumption and the Environment: The Ecological Modernisation of Domestic Consumption', *Environmental Politics*, 10(4): 50–77.

Spaargaren, G., Mol, A.P.J. and Buttel, F. (eds) (2000) *Environment and Global Modernity*, London: Sage.

Spretnak, C. (1986) *The Spiritual Dimension of Green Politics*, Santa Fe, NM: Bear and Co.

Spretnak, C. (1993) *States of Grace: The Recovery of Meaning in the Postmodern Age*, New York: HarperCollins Publishers.

Spretnak, C. and Capra, F., in collaboration with Rüdiger Lutz (1984) *Green Politics: The Global Promise*, London: Hutchinson and Co. Ltd.

Stehr, N. (1994) *Knowledge Societies*, London: Sage.

Steinberg, P.E. (2001) *The Social Construction of the Ocean*, Cambridge: Cambridge University Press.

Steinmetz, G. (1994) 'Regulation Theory, Post-Marxism and the New Social Movements', *Comparative Studies in Society and History*, 36(1): 176–212.

Steward, F. (1985a) 'Growing Greens', *Marxism Today*, November: 17–19.

Steward, F. (1985b) 'Rainbow Warriors', *Marxism Today*, November: 20–2.

Stretton, H. (1976) *Capitalism, Socialism and the Environment*, Cambridge: Cambridge University Press.

Strydom, P. (2002) *Risk, Environment and Society: Ongoing Debates, Current Issues and Future Prospects*, Buckingham: Open University Press.

Sturgeon, N. (1997) *Ecofeminist Natures: Race, Gender, Feminist Theory and Political Action*, New York: Routledge.

Sutton, P.W. (1999) 'Genetics and the Politics of Nature', *Sociological Research Online*, 4(3).

Sutton, P.W. (2000) *Explaining Environmentalism: In Search of a New Social Movement*, Aldershot: Ashgate Publishing.

Szatz, A. (1994) *EcoPopulism: Toxic Waste and the Movement for Environmental Justice*, Minneapolis: University of Minneapolis Press.

Szerszynski, B. (1996) 'On Knowing What to Do: Environmentalism and the Modern Problematic' in S. Lash, B. Szerszynski and B. Wynne (eds), *Risk, Environment and Modernity: Towards a New Ecology*, London: Sage: 104–37.

Tarrow, S. (1991) 'Comparing Social Movement Participation in Western Europe and the United States: Problems, Uses and a Proposal for Synthesis' in

D. Rucht (ed.), *Research on Social Movements: The State of the Art in Western Europe and the USA*, Frankfurt: Frankfurt University Press: 392–420.

Tarrow, S. (1998) *Power in Movement: Social Movements, Collective Action and Politics*, Cambridge: Cambridge University Press.

Taylor, R.K.S. (1985) 'Green Politics and the Peace Movement' in D. Coates, G. Johnston and R. Bush (eds), *A Socialist Anatomy of Britain*, Cambridge: Polity Press: 160–70.

Tester, K. (1991) *Animals and Society: The Humanity of Animal Rights*, London: Routledge.

Thomas, K. (1984) *Man and the Natural World: Changing Attitudes in England 1500–1800*, London: Penguin Books.

Thompson, E.P. (1976) *William Morris: Romantic to Revolutionary*, New York: Pantheon.

Toffler, A. (1981) *The Third Wave*, London: Pan Books.

Toulmin, S. (1972) 'The Historical Background to the Anti-Science Movement' in H. Block (Chair) Ciba Foundation Symposium, *Civilization and Science: in Conflict or Collaboration?*, North Holland: Associated Scientific Publishers, Elsevier, Excerpta Medica: 23–32.

Toulmin, S. (1982) *The Return to Cosmology: Postmodern Science and the Theology of Nature*, Berkeley: University of California Press.

Touraine, A. (1969) *The May Movement: Revolt and Reform: May 1968 – The Student Rebellion and Workers' Strikes – The Birth of a Social Movement*, New York: Random House.

Touraine, A. (1971) *The Post-Industrial Society: Tomorrow's Social History: Classes, Conflict and Culture in the Programmed Society*, New York: Random House Inc.

Touraine, A. (1981) *The Voice and the Eye: An Analysis of Social Movements*, Cambridge: Cambridge University Press.

Touraine, A. (1983) *Anti-Nuclear Protest: The Opposition to Nuclear Energy in France*, Cambridge: Cambridge University Press.

Trainer, T. (1985) *Abandon Affluence!: Sustainable Development and Social Change*, London: Zed Books.

Tsuzuki, C. (1980) *Edward Carpenter 1844–1929: Prophet of Human Fellowship*, Cambridge: Cambridge University Press.

Turner, J.H. (1996) 'The Evolution of Emotions in Humans: Darwinian-Durkheimian Analysis', *Journal for the Theory of Social Behaviour*, 26(1): 1–33.

Turner, J.H. (1999) 'Toward a General Sociological Theory of Emotions', *Journal for the Theory of Social Behaviour*, 29(2): 133–62.

Urry, J. (1990) *The Tourist Gaze*, London: Sage.

Urry, J. (1995) *Consuming Places*, London: Routledge.

Velody, I. and Williams, R. (eds) (1998) *The Politics of Constructionism*, London: Sage.

Walby, S. (1990) *Theorizing Patriarchy*, Oxford: Basil Blackwell.

Walker, K.J. (1989) 'The State in Environmental Management: The Ecological Dimension', *Political Studies*, xxxvii(1), March: 25–38.

Wall, D. (ed.) (1994) *Green History: A Reader in Environmental Literature, Philosophy and Politics*, London and New York: Routledge.

Wall, D. (1999) *Earth First! And the Anti-Roads Movement: Radical Environmentalism and Comparative Social Movements*, London: Routledge.

Wallerstein, I. (1974) *The Modern World-System*, New York: Academic.

Wallerstein, I. (1979) *The Capitalist World-Economy*, Cambridge: Cambridge University Press.

Wallerstein, I. (1983) *Historical Capitalism*, London: Verso Press.

Ward, B. and Dubos, R. (1977) *Only One Earth: The Care and Maintenance of a Small Planet*, Harmondsworth: Penguin Books.

Warren, K.J. (1990) 'The Power and the Promise of Ecological Feminism', *Environmental Ethics*, 12: 125–46.

Waters, M. (1998) *Globalization*, London and New York: Routledge.

Wellmer, A. (1991) *The Persistence of Modernity: Essays on Aesthetics, Ethics and Postmodernism*, Cambridge: Polity Press in association with Basil Blackwell.

West, P.C. (1985) 'Max Weber's Human Ecology of the Historical Sciences' in V. Murvar (ed.), *Theory of Liberty, Legitimacy and Power: New Directions in the Intellectual and Scientific Legacy of Max Weber*, London: Routledge and Kegan Paul.

West German Green Party (1983) *Election Manifesto*, London: Heretic Books.

Westen, D. (1985) *Self and Society: Narcissism, Collectivism and the Development of Morals*, Cambridge: Cambridge University Press.

Weston, J. (ed.) (1986) *Red and Green: The New Politics of the Environment*, London: Pluto Press.

White, Lynn Jr (1967) 'The Historical Roots of Our Ecological Crisis', *Science*, 155, March: 1203–7.

Wiener, M. (1981) *English Culture and the Decline of the Industrial Spirit 1850–1980*, Cambridge: Cambridge University Press.

Williams, F. (1992) 'Somewhere Over the Rainbow: Universality and Diversity in Social Policy' in N. Manning and R. Page (eds), *Social Policy Review 4*, Canterbury: Social Policy Association: 200–19.

Williams, F. (1999) 'Good Enough Principles for Welfare', *Journal of Social Policy*, 28(4): 667–87.

Williams, R. (1973) *The Country and the City*, Oxford: Oxford University Press.

Williams, R. (1987) *Keywords: A Vocabulary of Culture and Society*, London: Fontana Paperbacks.

Williams, S.J. (2001) *Emotion and Social Theory: Corporeal Reflections on the (Ir)Rational*, London: Sage.

Wilson, A. (1992) *The Culture of Nature: North American Landscape from Disney to the Exxon Valdez*, Cambridge, Mass.: Blackwell.

Wolf, F.O. (1986) 'Eco-Socialist Transition on the Threshold of the Twenty-First Century', *New Left Review*, 158: 32–42.

Worcester, R. (1995) 'Vital Statistics: Green Gauge of Britain', *BBC Wildlife*, 13: 70–3.

World Commission on Environment and Development. (1987) *Our Common Future*, Oxford: Oxford University Press.

Worster, D. (1985) *Nature's Economy: A History of Ecological Ideas*, Cambridge: Cambridge University Press.

Worster, D. (ed.) (1989) *The Ends of the Earth: Perspectives on Modern Environmental History*, New York: Cambridge University Press.

Wynne, B. (1996) 'May the Sheep Safely Graze? A Reflexive View of the Expert-Lay Knowledge Divide' in S. Lash, B. Szerszynski and B. Wynne (eds), *Risk, Environment and Modernity: Towards a New Ecology*, London: Sage: 44–83.

Yearley, S. (1991) *The Green Case: A Sociology of Environmental Issues, Arguments and Politics*, London: HarperCollins Academic.

Yearley, S. (1996) *Sociology, Environmentalism, Globalization: Reinventing the Globe*, London: Sage Publications Ltd.

Young, J. (1990) *Post Environmentalism*, London: Bellhaven Press.

Young, S.C. (1993) *The Politics of the Environment*, Manchester: Baseline Book Company.

Zald, M. and Ash, R. (1966) 'Social Movement Organizations: Growth, Decay and Change', *Social Forces*, 44: 327–40.

Zald, M. and McCarthy, J. (1987) *Social Movements in an Organizational Society: Collected Essays*, New Brunswick: Transaction.

Zimmerman, M.E. (1994) *Contesting Earth's Future: Radical Ecology and Postmodernity*, Berkeley: University of California Press.

Zonabend, F. (1993) *The Nuclear Peninsula*, Cambridge: Cambridge University Press.

Zukav, G. (1980) *The Dancing Wu Li Masters: An Overview of the New Physics*, London: Fontana.

Index

208

216   *Index*